FINAL CALLS
TO
ABSENT FRIENDS

T0165849

By Cliff Guilliams

TURNER PUBLISHING COMPANY

By: Cliff Guilliams
Editor: Tim Ethridge

Publishing Consultant: Douglas W. Sikes
Designer: Emily Kay Sikes

First Printing: A.D. 2001
Copyright © MMI Cliff Guilliams
All rights reserved
Publishing Rights: Turner Publishing Company

Library of Congress Catalog No. 2001086856
ISBN : 978-1-56311-651-3
LIMITED EDITION

CONTENTS

Part 3: PLACES

Part 4: OTHER FAVORITES

DEDICATION

This project of reminiscences was conceived in the fall of 1998. It wasn't for profit. It was done as a lasting tribute to the subjects who made vivid impressions on society.

The twofold dedication begins with my father, Charlie, my coach, Archie Owen, my mentor, Don Bernhardt, and a chestnut horse named Rustic Knave who are gone. They taught me the meaning of ordeal, triumph and finality.

Secondly, to my gang, Ellis Park's very much alive "boys and girls of summer." You know who you are and how important you are in the scheme of life.

Additionally, my sincere thanks to Alan Marzelli, David Haydon, Chuck Scaravilli and David O'Neill of *Equibase Co., LLC*, for allowing me the time for this project and others.

And lastly, to Mr. and Mrs. Charles W. Hebel Jr. of Louisville, Ky. They vehemently supported this project, renewing my faith that life and death are only temporary; friendships are forever.

ACKNOWLEDGEMENTS

The columns included in this collection originally appeared in *The Evansville Courier & Press* and *Daily Racing Form.*

Reprinted by permission. All rights reserved.

A special thanks to Hall of Fame trainer D. Wayne Lukas for his authorship of the foreword. He's a great friend, a fair gardener and a hell of a horseman.

Front cover photo by Anne M. Eberhardt, by permission of Alex M. Waldrop Jr., president of Churchill Downs. Rear cover photo by Steve Cato, with permission from Joseph Pelaski, proprietor of Joey's, a popular watering hole near downtown Evansville.

FOREWORD

By D. WAYNE LUKAS

During my 48 years as a thoroughbred trainer, many fine sportswriters have walked into my barn or called on the telephone for an interview.

Many of them cover only the Kentucky Derby, Preakness Stakes and Belmont Stakes. Only a few cover the game on a daily basis. A mere handful do it as well as Cliff Guilliams.

To do do, you must love racing and its populace, possess a keen knowledge of the sport's history, know its rules, its politics, and a host of other behind-the-scene facets.

That all sounds simple to the public because the majority of fans are involved only when the gates clang open, the race is run, a winner is declared official and the payoffs are posted in the span of four or five minutes.

However, that's only the beginning. Because then, with impartial judgment, The Jockey Club's official race charts, which are composed by Equibase Co. LLC, must be promptly completed and the event reported under extremely tight deadlines.

As they say about mailmen, neither snow, rain, flood, etc..., can keep them from their duties. All of that is characteristic of chart callers like Cliff. A person in the media wins or loses on reputation. His integrity is unquestionable.

It is a pleasure to annually stable at Churchill Downs because I know that, barring unforseen circumstances, whether looking for a story angle or simply taking a walk, he'll pay a daily visit to my barn, and those of many other trainers, if only to say "hello."

If a horseman has a solid prospect, or a jockey is winning a large percentage of the races, you can be sure that eventually, Cliff will be on the scene. He's welcome in nearly every quarter, because his comments about horses and people are fair, constructive, and shed positive light on our sport.

Nevertheless, when tough situations arise, he isn't afraid to go out on a limb to support people or causes that he believes in, no matter the outcome or consequences.

While he doesn't always pick the winner of the Kentucky Derby, his career batting average is in the Top 10 because he works at it.

The first time we met was in 1981. I was preparing Partez for the Kentucky Derby. Our first conversation wasn't about horses. It involved Big 10 basketball because at the time, we were Indiana University fans. Loyalties change, time flies, but friendships grow lengthy roots.

Annually, I've always considered the Kentucky Derby to be the best story of the year in a sport blessed with so many. In *Final Calls to Absent Friends*, Cliff has paid tribute to many outstanding people and numerous great horses. Most of them were extremely talented, and some were fortunate enough to win American racing's greatest prize, the Kentucky Derby.

He's remembered them with detail, sensitivity and skill. I know, because a couple of those horses came from my stable. And several of the people were dear friends of mine, too.

I appreciate Cliff Guilliams' honesty, his fairness, his loyalty, his ability and his personal friendship.

So sit back, enjoy reading, remembering and reminiscing.

INTRODUCTION

Forty years have passed since my late father, Charlie, led me into a racetrack. And it's been a quarter of a century since I timidly entered a pressbox, a raw, totally unprepared kid who loved and knew quite a bit about horse racing and football, but not the first thing about journalism.

Don Bernhardt and Bill Fluty, late editors of *The Evansville Courier*, got me started in the right direction. Joe Hirsch, executive columnist for the *Daily Racing Form*, added his refined, dignified mystique and opened many doors.

Occasionally, it's hard for me to believe that I'm not the same, in decent shape, ex-college jock who could work all day and play all night. But I'm not. Oh, on rare evenings, like after picking the Kentucky Derby winner in print, I still feel capable of a kid's antics. But that's only temporary, wishful thinking.

Too much stomach where there used to be chest. Too many wrinkles. Too much hair loss. Too many aches and pains requiring unavailable recovery time.

Living, getting old, retiring and dying is a remarkable process. I used to think I'd live forever. But when people you love retire or die — often prematurely — and horses pass on that you've admired in major races and watched develop in the breeding shed, it's time to reaffirm something that I learned at a young age when talking late at night with my father about his World War II experiences. He'd constantly remind me: "All things end. Be prepared to honor the fallen. Don't be afraid of emotion. It's normal."

At the track, people constantly ask, "Who do you like?" I'll politely tell them. They'll often follow up with, "How much are you betting?" They're floored when I say nothing. I don't bet when I'm working. "Why not?" they inquire. Because I used up all my luck getting here. I've had the best parents, teachers and coaches that money can't buy. No need to push it. My primary job as a chart-caller — first for *Daily Racing Form* and now for *Equibase Co. LLC* — has taken me around the great Commonwealth of Kentucky's racing circuit countless times. I've been fortunate to cover racing as a reporter and columnist for *DRF*.

Besides my association with *Equibase*, I'm serving a second tour of duty for my hometown paper, *The Evansville (Ind.) Courier & Press*. I'm eternally indebted to its executive editor, Paul McAuliffe, and sports editor, Tim Ethridge, an old colleague.

The aforementioned people have put me in postion to cover the greatest racing in North America. What makes it the best? The Kentucky Derby and the week leading up to it is one thing. But the hundreds, probably thousands of individuals — human and equine — that I'm fortunate enough to have been up-close and personal with on a daily basis, at Ellis Park, Churchill Downs, Keeneland, and Turfway Park, have made it more of a career among friends than a job among peers.

These people have come from all walks of life, varying significantly in age, color, creed, size, financial background and ability. The horses? As the saying goes: "A good horse can come from anywhere and is dangerous in any man's hands."

Most of them did something remarkable. All of them were newsmakers and commanded respect. And when they retired or passed away, their departure touched many lives, including mine. Rereading these columns, written within hours or a day after the fact, and selecting the best ones for *Final Calls to Absent Friends* rekindled many memories. A few produced rivers of tears.

In saying farewell in print, I tried not to be maudlin. Sometimes, however, it was unavoidable. If I've been repetitive by saying that more than one person was wonderful, terrific, charming or great, I apologize. But that's what they were to me. Several were close, personal, eternally loyal friends. Some were role models whose values and principles helped shape my stance on life.

I remember my final football game as a senior at Evansville's Bosse High School. In his pregame speech, my coach, Archie Owen, as honest as any man who ever lived, was weeping terribly when he bellowed: "Men, this is the last time that all of us will ever be together..."

At that moment, I understood what life, friends and finality were about.

Cliff Guilliams
Evansville, Ind.
December 2000

PART 1:

HORSES

Final Calls to Absent Friends

BOLD FORBES WAS NOBLE
CHAMPION FOR THE 'LITTLE GUY'

August, 2000

Several years ago, *The Blood-Horse Magazine*, in conjunction with the National Turf Writers Association and a couple of other racing organizations, polled writers and readers for their opinions on the greatest single-race ride by a jockey.

My selection was Angel Cordero Jr.'s effort in the 1976 Belmont Stakes aboard the determined little Bold Forbes.

A natural sprinter who wasn't as big as most stable ponies, Bold Forbes was trained by the late Hall of Famer Laz Barrera. Combining his patience with long, stamina-building gallops, Barrera conditioned Bold Forbes to relax and conserve his speed.

In the 1 1/2-mile Belmont, Bold Forbes cruised to a six-length advantage before going a half-mile. As he neared the stretch, I can hear the late, great race caller, Chic Anderson, say: "With a quarter-mile left it's Bold Forbes by eight (lengths). And now they'll have to catch him."

Rallying from a terrific ways back, the stretch-running McKenzie Bridge tried valiantly, but fell a neck short of the exhausted Bold Forbes.

Five weeks prior to the Belmont, it had been much the same scenario in the 102nd Kentucky Derby. Immediately after the start, Cordero sent Bold Forbes to the lead. He opened a five-lengths advantage in a half-mile, then withstood 2-5 favorite Honest Pleasure through the long, unforgiving stretch to win by a length.

Honest Pleasure was owned by Bert Firestone and represented the "big-money establishment."

By defeating him, Bold Forbes struck a blow for the little guy and anti-establishment fans. He was owned by Esteban Rodriguez Tizol, a Puerto Rican who had purchased him for only $15,200 at 1974's Fasig-Tipton yearling sale in Lexington, Ky.

Cordero, also a native of Puerto Rico, was so moved by winning the Derby that he flew to his homeland and placed the garland of roses on the grave of his father.

As a 2-year-old, Bold Forbes made his first five starts in Puerto Rico, so his Kentucky Derby triumph united the entire island. Cordero believed it fitting that the roses be taken there.

After the Belmont, Cordero began referring to Bold Forbes as his "Puerto Rican Rolls Royce."

Originally, the plan was to devote this space to the probable starters in Satuday's $75,000 Governor's Handicap at Ellis Park, but Bold Forbes' death last week intervened.

At age 27, he was the oldest living Kentucky Derby winner. For the past nine years, he had resided at the Kentucky Horse Park in Lexington, which annually attracts thousands of visitors. He was buried at the park in a place of honor alongside multiple champion Forego.

Bold Forbes spent his entire stallion career (1977 to 1990) at Arthur B. Hancock III's Stone Farm in Paris, Ky. A son of Irish Castle-Comely Nell, Bold Forbes sired 460 named foals from 13 crops. Among his offspring were such good ones as Kentucky Oaks winner Tiffany Lass, Bold Apparel, Air Forbes Won and Barb's Bold.

Bold Forbes succumbed to renal and intestinal failure. One day he was fine. The next he was gone. These things happen to aging horses.

It wasn't entirely the rags-to-riches story that earned Bold Forbes his following, although reaching the top from humble beginnings always increases one's popularity with the racing public.

And it wasn't the money he won, although the $523,035 he earned on an impressive record of 13-1-4 from 18 starts was a tidy sum in those days.

And it wasn't his offspring. Like so many, he failed to reproduce himself.

Bold Forbes wasn't particularly handsome. On looks, he wasn't in the same league with Secretariat, Whirlaway, Unbridled, or even Charismatic.

The quality he was best known for was his racing record. Regardless of the track, the footing, distance or competition, he was a rarity because he tried his guts out every time.

There were no excuses.

Horses like Bold Forbes are the sort that people respect, admire, even love. That type is far and few between.

May he rest in peace.

REMEMBERING THE "BULLET"

September, 2000

There's so much to write about the retirement of two-time champion Silverbulletday to Hill 'n' Dale Farm in Lexington, Ky., that it was necessary to sit back a week, sort out 2 1/2 years worth of memories, and get it straight.

Silverbulletday, you see, isn't merely one of the greatest fillies to race in half a century. She's also owned by a loyal, long-standing friend, Mike Pegram. The former Princeton, Ind., resident and Ellis Park regular likened her to a Rembrandt — a priceless artifact that never can be duplicated.

"And when it became obvious that she wasn't going to be 100 percent for the Nov. 4 Breeders' Cup, it was time to pull the plug," Pegram said. "I hated to do it. But by the same token, I'd never do anything that wasn't in her best interest. When I left home (in the late 1970s), I never dreamed that I'd be playing at the upper end of the racing game.

"Having had the pleasure of owning Silverbulletday and winning the Kentucky Derby with Real Quiet has been like a magic carpet ride. I still get goose bumps watching video tapes of their races. I ask myself; 'Was that really us?'"

A 4-year-old daughter of Silver Deputy-Rokeby Rose, by Tom Rolfe, Silverbulletday made her 23rd and final career start on July 23, finishing third in the $600,000 Grade III Delaware Handicap.

Wear and tear of the racing wars caught up with her. She would've hammered that field in better days and was only a shadow of her former self in the final prideful struggles. Nevertheless, Pegram remained optimistic that she'd bounce back and could make the Aug. 26 running of Ellis' Gardenia Stakes. He deeply wanted to run her in front of his "home folks" at Ellis. But it wasn't to be.

After winning only one of five starts this year, she departed as racing's No. 2 all-time leading money-winning filly behind Serena's Song. Silverbulletday earned $3,093,207 on a record of 15-3-1. Not bad for a $155,000 yearling purchase.

Silverbulletday was a frequent flyer. She ran at Churchill Downs, Keeneland, Del Mar, Fair Grounds, Saratoga, Gulfstream Park, Monmouth Park, Belmont Park. Crisscrossing the country wherever the gauntlet was thrown down, she battled every step of the way against the best competition available.

And, in the process, with her catchy name — for Pegram's favorite beverage, Coors Light — she became "America's horse," bringing significant attention, respect and appreciation for filly and mare racing that often is overshadowed by colts.

We could elaborate how Pegram and Baffert listened to friends and skipped running Silverbulletday against the boys in the 1999 Kentucky Derby. They opted, instead, to win the Derby's sister race, the Kentucky Oaks, which was one of the finest efforts of her career.

Or how they didn't listen and hooked males in the Belmont, which was Silverbulletday's third tough race in five weeks.

Or that they failed to give her any down time last summer after her tremendous nine-length romp in Saratoga's Grade I Alabama Stakes.

Or that she'd been basically going around-the-clock since debuting in the spring of 1998 at Churchill Downs.

But all of those things combined are what put Silverbulletday's name in the minds and hearts of the racing public, making her queen of her generation at age 2 and 3. She danced every set, no matter where she ran or the footing. There were no excuses. Champions, for the record, don't need them.

Her best race?

Some might opt for Keeneland's Ashland Stakes. Others will suggest the Alabama. The 1998 Breeders' Cup Juvenile Fillies is a possiblity. It was a dandy. But I'll settle on the 1999 Kentucky Oaks. Sent off 1-10, she rallied from sixth in the field of seven to win going away by two lengths under Gary Stevens.

When the mutuel prices had been posted, Pegram called on the telephone and jubilantly asked if a table could be secured at Furlongs, our favorite eating and drinking emporium in Louisville, Ky., owned by old friend Tom Walters.

It's virtually impossible to get a table on the night before the Kentucky Derby. So I asked how many seats he needed. "Better make it for 40," he laughed. "I've got all the boys from Princeton with me and they're all hungry and thirsty."

The miracle-working Walters turned over the entire patio, iced down several cases of "Silver Bullets," and had the hors d'oeurves ready for the congratulatory story telling, high-fiving and partying that continued into the wee hours. It was a once-in-a-lifetime experience. And it was beautiful.

It's irrelevant whether Silberbulletday reproduces herself for Pegram in the breeding shed. As he'll tell you, "She doesn't owe me or anybody anything."

And, in the future, there may be fillies who'll surpass Silverbulletday's achievements. But when the final history is written, one thing will remain: None ever tried harder or brought more fun and enjoyment to the lives of so many people.

In that capacity, Silverbulletday was in a league of her own.

For parts of two seasons, she truly was "America's horse."

JOHN HENRY STANDS A CUT ABOVE

April, 1986

LEXINGTON, Ky. — Opening day at Keeneland on Saturday furthered my belief that a public address system never will be required for the track's racing-wise patrons.

Under threatening skies, 18,160 packed the stands. They didn't need a repetitious loud-speaker to remind them that John Henry, the most remarkable horse who ever looked through a bridle, would be paraded through the picturesque paddock and walking ring, make two trips past the stands, then pause briefly in the winner's circle — one of the few he didn't visit during his illustrious career.

Film and camera sales obviously prospered. Seemingly every other fan was armed with a keepsake box, ranging from high-priced models to the simplest of Polaroids.

The ceremony, scheduled between the fourth and fifth races, was culminated when Dorothy and Sam Rubin, who campaigned the great gelding under the banner of Dotsam Stable, received a sterling silver julep cup from Keeneland's chairman of the board, Ted Bassett III.

The Rubins dined in the Directors Room with Kentucky Gov. Martha Layne Collins and Ellis Park owners Roger and Lila Kumar.

Now a pensioner, John Henry is quartered and on year-round display 20 minutes from Keeneland at The Kentucky Horse Park.

The Kumars are optimistic that the Rubins and Collins will agree to bring John Henry to Ellis this August as one of the highlights of Summer Festival Week.

"We will monitor him closely during the next two weeks," said Collins. "We're not going to put him on any sort of appearance circuit or tour. But if he is calm and shows no harmful reaction to the crowd stimulation, the possibility is excellent."

The old warrior was retired last July after developing a deep swelling near the flexor tendon of his right foreleg. It takes considerable time to wind down a horse who has been fighting the exciting strains of the track, and the better the horse, the longer the acclimation period. John Henry was definitely a handful for his groom on Saturday as the gelding whirled and kicked at silly spectators who wandered too close.

Before his arrival, there was some bumping, shoving and word exchanges as onlookers jockeyed for a vantage point to aim their cameras at the three-time Horse of the Year.

A hundred pounds of so heavier than at his fighting trim, the champion walked in as he did on days of actual battle — D-bit tightly clenched, light green shadow roll topping off the bridle, ears at attention, coat sparkling.

By coincidence or fate, it had been nearly eight years to the day that John Henry entered this paddock for his only other Kentucky appearance in a career which spanned 83 races and eight summers.

It was the afternoon of April 11, 1978, for an $8,500 allowance race contested at six furlongs. Under Jim McKnight, the big bay was fourth the entire trip, 9 1/2 lengths back at the finish. He took out $425 in purse money.

Prior to that outing, John Henry had won three minor races at Jefferson and Evangeline Downs in Louisiana.

What followed earned him Saturday's return trip to Keeneland, where once he was sold for $1,100, then $2,200, before the Rubins acquired him for $25,000.

John Henry won 39 races, including 17 Grade I events. He added 15 seconds and nine thirds, amassing $6,597,947 in earnings, a record that should last a while.

He wasn't the swiftest, setting one track record and equalling two more, including his final race, the Meadowlands' Ballantine Scotch Classic on Oct. 13, 1984, when he stepped 11 furlongs in 2:13 under 126 pounds.

He wasn't the supreme carrier of weight, shouldering a maximum of 130 three times.

A plain bay, he certainly wasn't as eye-catching as Secretariat, Sunny's Halo, Affirmed or Seattle Slew.

And he didn't possess the most formidable pedigree.

He was by Ole Bob Bowers out of the Double Jay mare Once Double — a heritage capable of producing more scoffs and snores than stakes winners.

Champions come and go each year, but it's John Henry who remains adored, whose presence is constantly requested by track managers who'd like to boost attendance.

He was an equine hero to the masses. The small horsemen trying to make good could identify with him as well as the millionaire who can buy his way into the winner's circle.

And no horse has remained as competitive for so long against the best. John Henry was like an old runningback, always summoning the energy for one last season or game— not for the cash, but for the fans.

Keeneland patrons rarely are wrong with their observations. Above all, they remembered John Henry for what he was — a racehorse who beat the clock to become a cut above.

COUNTRY CAT BROUGHT
JOY TO HER FANS AND CONNECTIONS

September, 1996

FLORENCE, Ky. — This all began in trainer D. Wayne Lukas' office during late June at Churchill Downs.

The traditional visit concludes the spring meeting. Goodbyes, pleasantries and thank-yous are exchanged for the mutual respect shared during the hectic days of the Triple Crown and everyday life.

The visitor annually produces a stakes book for Ellis Park's summer meeting and asks: "Wayne, can you run a horse in this race? And what about this one?"

Here was Lukas' reply in June: "We'll take care of you on that first one. And Country Cat will be at Ellis for the Gardenia."

The Grade III, $200,000 Gardenia Stakes is for fillies and mares at nine furlongs and is the premier event for the meeting. It's run in late August, and by then the six-day race week has taken its toll on the workers. They're dragging physically and wanting mentally and emotionally.

But this year, Overbrook Farm's Country Cat saved their spirits as they gleefully made their way to the winner's circle after she won the Gardenia — her first graded stakes — by two lengths.

It was one of the best efforts of Country Cat's life. And there were some good ones, too, among her nine victories from 25 trips to the post in a career that produced $564,113 in earnings.

It didn't matter if the track was wet or dry — or if the race was on turf. Country Cat, a 4-year-old bay filly by Storm

Cat from the Affirmed mare, La Affirmed, was a headstrong country girl who tried every time she faced the starter.

All of this shockingly came to mind Saturday when Country Cat broke down terribly in her right front leg when beginning the first turn in Turfway Park's ninth race, the Grade II, $300,000 Turfway Breeders' Cup.

Ridden by Donna Barton, perhaps her biggest fan and admirer, Country Cat refused to go down, as many do when suffering such an injury. Likewise, Barton refused to jump off. She had the filly pulled up in three jumps and dismounted. A tiny, 102-pounder, Barton held on to the reins in an attempt to support her 1,100-pound partner.

Headed by Dr. George Mundy, the Kentucky Racing Commission's outstanding team of veterinarians rushed to the scene. The injury, called "catastrophic" by Mundy, was a compound break above the ankle. There was nothing anyone could do. After advising the filly's connections via two-way radio, veterinarians put Country Cat down behind the screen that blocks the public's view.

Earlier that day, Barton had won the $100,000 Kentucky Cup Juvenile, the third leg of the Kentucky Thoroughbred Development Fund's $1 million bonus series, with the up-and-coming Boston Harbor.

Country Cat's stablemate, Golden Attraction, won the Breeders' Cup race. But Country Cat's demise quelled any celebration that evening.

"Country Cat had just switched to her left lead to start the turn and was going for a position," Barton said. "Her right ankle just snapped. If she had to go, I'm glad I was on her and could take care of her. Someone else might have jumped off and left her or let her bobble and fall. She was my big mare. Even in the end, she took care of me by refusing to go down. She kept me from being hurt by staying up on three legs."

Of all the stake winners and top horses that Barton has ridden to victory, Country Cat is the only one she ever paid special heed in pictures. After winning the Gardenia, Barton ordered an oversized 18-by-20-inch collage of winner's circle photographs.

Taking the high road is expected from William T. Young, master of Overbrook Farm. He remained on that path Sunday. Despite the victory of his Editor's Note in the Super Derby at Louisiana Downs, Young sent an Overbrook van to Turfway, which took the remains of Country Cat home to her birthplace for a proper resting place.

Barton is a positive thinker. She looks on the bright side of even the darkest situation. It was no secret that Country Cat was a typical offspring of Stormo Cat. She was nervous, fidgety and headstrong, but always a hickory tough competitor.

"Maybe she chose her own way out," said Barton. "Knowing Country Cat like I did, it's hard to believe she'd have liked being a broodmare. Just didn't seem like her cup of tea."

Barton also believes the tragedy puts life into a truer perspective.

"Country Cat was not simply a horse," she said. "She meant a great deal to the trainer, the Overbrook family and me personally, mentally and financially. But there's also deep sentiment attached. She was a friend. That has no price and we'll miss her a lot."

So will Ellis Park's "boys of summer."

UNBRIDLED WON
WHEN IT COUNTED MOST

November, 1991

LOUISVILLE, Ky. — In the spring of 1990, trainer Carl Nafzger played a role that could have been written by a high-paid Hollywood script writer, describing in his own words the rally by Unbridled as he swept off the stretch turn to a dramatic 3 1/2-length triumph in the Kentucky Derby.

Nafzger was wired for sound by ABC-TV, and cameras were in place as he gave his running description to Mrs. Frances Genter, Unbridled's 92-year-old owner.

It was one of those once-in-a-lifetime moments — spontaneous, warm, honest. When Nafzger said, "You're going to win it, you're going to win the Kentucky Derby...I love you Mrs. Genter," it seemed that all the troubles in the world went away, at least for awhile.

What would bring a frail lady of Mrs. Genter's age, a credit to the industry for more than 50 years, together in a clubhouse box with a former rodeo cowboy about to turn 50?

The answer is horses.

And maybe the best one either will ever be around is Unbridled, a Florida-bred son of the late Fappiano.

We saw something in this bay colt early in the spring of 1990 and picked him to win the Kentucky Derby. We stuck with him when he lost and took some good-natured heckling when he was defeated in the Blue Grass Stakes at Keeneland, his final prep before the Derby.

It's one thing to pick the winner of the feature race on

the second Saturday in May at Churchill Downs, but when you pick the Derby winner, it's a near immortal feeling, and allows for a year's worth of bragging rights — especially when the horse pays $23.60, as Unbridled did.

On Thursday, we paid our respects to the 1990 3-year-old champion and his Eclipse Award-winning trainer. Unbridled stepped into the Sallee Van at 8:35 a.m., marking the last time he and Nafzger would be together at the racetrack. Unbridled was headed off to Gainesway Farm, beginning a new career as a stallion.

There was no roaring Derby Day crowd to send him off. Only a reporter or two and other trainers and racing men stopping to offer a congratulatory handshake for Nafzger, who did a splendid job in preparing Unbridled for major assignments.

A few tears were shed because this was a special horse who will be missed.

"I'm not sure yet whether this is a victory parade or a funeral procession," Nafzger said as we walked up to the racing secretary's office to retrieve the colt's foal papers.

Accompanied by his wife, Wanda, Nafzger acted like he was getting the papers for any old horse under his care.

But he wasn't. When someone asked for a copy of the papers for a scrapbook, the request was accommodated.

"I'm going to miss having him with me," said Nafzger. "But how many horses do you get like him that run at 2, 3 and 4 and go home sound?

"I wouldn't trade the experience for anything. There is relief along with it, though. It's like Christmas, having a horse like this. You're glad when it comes along and glad when it's over."

Unbridled didn't win many, but he won races that counted. In addition to the Derby, he won the 1990 Breeders' Cup Classic, the Florida Derby and a couple of other stakes. He was second in the Super Derby and Preakness, and third in this year's B.C. Classic.

Through a training career filled with ups and downs, Nafzger has remained the same — just an old cowboy at heart who gave the credit to Unbridled and his help, saying he was just along for the ride.

His tack room remains nothing fancy, just the necessities and a worn card table and light-weight chair. It probably looked the same when he and Wanda began their marriage and started out at the small tracks nearly 25 years ago.

Through the period, Nafzger has been his own man. And his theories on bringing a horse to his peak to run the race of his life were proven correct by Unbridled.

So, for the time being, the story of Unbridled has wound down. It will be up to Nafzger to replace him and up to Unbridled to duplicate himself in the breeding shed.

"You know, I can lose everything I have and end up a wino in the street," said the trainer. "They can take everything from me but one thing, and that's winning the Kentucky Derby. It's something I'll always look back on and work to repeat. And I'll always know how much Unbridled did to get me where I'm at."

From 'Carl who' to 'Carl said.' That's what Unbridled did for his master.

Chances are we'll visit Unbridled again. However, we'll always recall him at his fighting trim, giving that burst of speed to reach the lead entering the stretch. A bright May sun will be shimmering off his sleek, dark coat. Craig Perret will be calling for more in the saddle while adorned in those light blue silks of the Genter Stable. Pandemonium wil break loose and it will be May 5, 1990, all over again.

He wasn't the best. He didn't win the most money or the most races. Still, on that day and several others he was magnificent, showing the ability to rise to the occasion on the big day. All the great ones to that, human and equine alike.

FANS' MEMORIES OF
CIGAR WILL BURN BRIGHT

November, 1996

LOUISVILLE, Ky. — "When he came onto the track, the roar of the crowd was something comparable to thunder.

"It was like being in a cave instead of on the apron of a racetrack. Racing fans hardly ever agree on anything. But they rose as one, and it was as if all their shouts and screams were jumbled into one huge blast of appreciation.

"Cigar came onto the track, all shined up and immaculately groomed. Like a statue of a trained assassin, jockey Jerry Bailey sat expressionless on him in Allen Paulson's red, white and blue colors on his way to battle. It was something to behold. Took the game back 20 or 30 years when the big crowds jammed tracks around the country and people appreciated a truly great and remarkable horse."

That's how one man will always remember Cigar. Although he never ran at Churchill Downs, this aforementioned scene will be played for the final time Saturday beneath these famed Twin Spires.

And, perhaps, it's only fitting because Churchill Downs is billed as "The World's Most Legendary Track." As the years pass, the legend of Cigar will burn ever bright.

On his way to stud at Paulson's Brookside Farm near Versailles, Ky., Cigar, with Bailey attired in those famous silks, will be paraded between races at about 4:40 p.m. (EST).

The time should be familiar to the champion. It was about the hour he normally did his best work when he knocked off Grade I races around the world on his way to becoming the sport's all-time leading money winner at $9.9 million.

Cigar trading cards will be given away free to the first 5,000 fans. If you'd like one, here's a word of advice: Come early.

There is no barometer to measure such an appearance. So, it's impossible to come up with a solid over-and-under attendance number. But Churchill Downs' pressbox corps, headed by Tony Terry, believes that if the weather cooperates, it's not out of the question for 25,000 fans to turn out.

Terry bases his evaluation on the unusually high number of request for media credentials he received compared to a typical Saturday in November.

A 6-year-old son of Palace Music, Cigar will be saddled in the paddock as usual, then paraded on the track. A ceremony with the horse, trainer Bill Mott and Paulson will follow in the winner's circle.

During the day, videotapes of Cigar's races, including the record-equaling 16-race winning streak, will be shown on the in-house monitors.

Is he the greatest horse who's ever lived? Probably not. But he certainly has been one of the most exciting and most remarkable. Every time he ran, you knew that at some point you'd see a burst of speed that became as much of a spectacle as any produced in sports.

Our colleague, Joe Hirsch, executive columnist of *Daily Racing Form*, put it best by saying: "Cigar spoiled us with his brilliance, to the point where we had come to expect perfection. The degree of that perfection can be measured by his public appeal. He was able to attract crowds larger than the norm by 10,000 to 20,000 almost every place he raced, and his schedule was extensive. They rooted for him to win regardless of their wagers."

When Cigar pursued the immortal Citation's record, the American public went along for the ride, and he carried the delight of the masses with him.

Through 16 consecutive victories and 19 overall from 33 career starts against primarily the best competition in the world, Cigar dominated his owner's life and drew crowds wherever he raced.

Cigar could be legitimately compared to Babe Ruth, Muhammad Ali, Joe Montana, Jack Nicklaus and John McEnroe. He wasn't just a star or a champion, but also the most colorful figure in racing.

CHAMPION SERENA'S SONG DEPARTS WITH DIGNITY INTACT

November, 1996

LOUISVILLE, Ky. — During the month leading up to the April, 1, 1995 running of Turfway Park's Grade II, $600,000 Jim Beam Stakes, the telephone line between Turfway's press box and trainer D. Wayne Lukas' barn was hot.

Almost daily, Lukas was sizing up the probable field and exchanging scouting reports. He had nominated about a dozen 3-year-olds, including an extraordinary filly named Serena's Song, who is owned by Bob and Beverly Lewis of Newport Beach, Calif.

Lukas was vacillating about running Serena's Song against the boys in this major nine-furlong prep for the Kentucky Derby. He was walking a tightrope without a net, but decided to go for it.

Sent off heavily favored by a growing legion of fans, Serena's Song gained the lead at the start and controlled the pace. She drew off in the upper stretch and coasted home by 3 1/2 lengths to become the only filly ever to win the Jim Beam.

This and a lot more came to mind earlier this week when the Lewises and Lukas decided to retire Serena's Song.

The 4-year-old bay daughter of Rahy was second here on Nov. 9 in the Grade II Churchill Downs Distaff. She earned $45,040 to become the all-time money-winning distaffer with $3,283,388. She accumulated that sum on a record of 18-11-3 from 38 starts, winning 17 stakes — 11 of them Grade I.

When she was chasing the cash, some top scribes around the country asked the following question, "Who holds the record?" These media types know all about Serena's Song, but they couldn't begin to describe the former record-holder, Dance Smartly.

That alone speaks volumes of the worldwide acclaim Serena's Song manufactured with her gameness, grit, durability, dependability and courage under heavy fire.

"With Serena's Song's magnificent record at 2, 3 and 4, we reached a point where it became an absolute privilege to be associated with her," Bob Lewis said. "Ultimately, it became a responsibility for us to have her in top form in order to benefit our great sport, so we could give something back to the game."

Professionals from all walks of life will tell you that it's one thing to become a champion and another to stay on top.

"Everyone is vulnerable in the big arena," Lewis said. "Look at what happened to (beaten boxing champion) Mike Tyson. It can sometimes be a terrible burden to be a champion because you must maintain that status over an extended period of time when everyone is taking potshots at you.

"We have mixed emotions about retiring her. A part of Beverly and me is glad that it's over. But we'll also miss her courage and the joy she brought to so many people.

"However, if anything would have happened to her while racing, it would have hurt the industry and made it difficult for us to go racing again. This is the best thing for everyone involved. We discussed the future with Wayne, and will make our decision in the next two weeks about where to board her and who to breed her to.

"She's traveled around the country and raced over every type of surface against the best. There's nothing more she has to prove. You'd have to believe that in the future, the weight she'd have to carry in handicaps would have been increased. So it's comforting to her great fan base and ourselves to know she's retired in good health. She'll be in good hands, and has earned the long rest and the opportunity to further the sport and better the breed."

In addition to the Jim Beam, Lewis noted three other races he believed to be essential in the greatness of Serena's Song.

The first was the Breeders' Cup Juvenile Fillies here Nov. 5, 1994.

"All we hoped for was that she'd be competitive with Flanders," Lewis said. That day, Serena's Song pushed her champion stablemate to the brink. She gained the lead in deep stretch between calls before surrendering by a neck.

The second was Pimlico's Black Eyed Susan on May 19, 1995, when the boobirds were out. Serena's Song had made the pace for the first mile in the Kentucky Derby 13 days earlier before being wrapped up and galloping under the wire 16th of 19.

"She's through. All washed up," some chanted. Hardly was the case.

In the Black Eyed Susan, Serena's Song drowned her female rivals by nine lengths.

"The Jim Beam would rank third on my personal list," Lewis said. "And I suppose the fourth was the Haskell."

Facing males again on July 30, 1995, at the more suitable nine-furlong distance, Serena's Song made most of the pace to win by three-quarters of a length.

In a final analysis, Serena's Song was a great horse, as tough as any of her time. Like a top heavyweight fighter of any era, she had a will to win matched only by her skill, and she still was on her feet when the last bell sounded. All the great ones have that in common. They depart with dignity.

THEY WENT OUT IN STYLE

June, 1995

LOUISVILLE, Ky. — This trilogy of sorts involves three subjects under a common banner: "All good things must come to pass."

It began on Oct. 15, 1993 at Keeneland. A then-nondescript field of 2-year-olds went to the post for the third running of the seven-furlong Fort Springs Stakes.

Making his first stakes appearance was William T. Young and David P. Reynolds' Tabasco Cat. Young and Reynolds, in their 70s, had been friends since their school days, and Tabasco Cat ultimately would bind them even closer with heroic victories in the Preakness and Belmont Stakes.

Reynolds owned a mare named Barbicue Sauce, a daughter of Sauce Boat. Young owned the up-and-coming stallion Storm Cat, who stood at his Overbrook Farm in Lexington, Ky. They combined these forces to produce Tabasco Cat.

The Fort Springs was the fiery chestnut colt's fifth career start. Locked in a furious duel through rapid fractions of 22 2/5 seconds for the opening quarter-mile and 45 1/5 for the half, Tabasco Cat looked beaten when he fell back in second by a half-length leaving the eighth - pole. But jockey Pat Day asked for more, and Tabasco Cat called on his soon-to-be famous reservoir. He battled back to win by a neck in the lively time of 1:21 4/5.

Trainer D. Wayne Lukas could have run him in the

Keeneland's Breeders' Futurity 10 days after the Fort Springs. But the trainer saw great promise in Tabasco Cat and opted to take a bit more time and go for bigger game in the Grade I Breeders' Cup Juvenile at Santa Anita. The lightly seasoned Tabasco Cat again showed his grit. Third early, he fell back to sixth in the upper stretch, but came again to be third at 33-1. This confirmed his quality and class against top competition, and Lukas had his colt for the following spring's classics.

Later, on a mid-December morning, Tabasco Cat ran over Jeff Lukas, the trainer's son, and nearly killed him.

All of this and a lot more came to mind last Friday when Young and Reynolds announced through Overbrook Farm that Tabasco Cat's career was over. He was retired after ultrasound examinations revealed a tear in the tendon sheath behind his left knee about the size of a pencil eraser.

The most successful son of Storm Cat, Tabasco Cat will remain at Lukas' barn here until the breeding season concludes in early July, then go home to stand stud at Overbrook. He departs with nearly $2.4 million in earnings from eight victories, two seconds and a third from 15 starts.

"Tabasco Cat gained a lot of notoriety because of Jeff's accident," Lukas said. "But that should never enter into it. Let's not remember the colt because of the accident. He was a special racehorse."

At about 5:15 a.m. here 10 days before the 1994 Kentucky Derby, Lukas, accompanied by a friend or two, breezed Tabasco Cat a mile. It was the colt's final major work before the Derby. And Lukas wanted him to go in 1:38.

Instead, the exercise rider missed the mark and went in a dawdling 1:42 4/5. The colt came home the last quarter-mile in 27 seconds and the trainer snapped: "That won't get it."

It didn't, either. Tabasco Cat was a short horse on Derby Day. Or he might have won the Triple Crown.

"In a way, I'm glad he's coming home," Young said. "He was an awful lot of fun for us. There was great romance surrounding Tabasco Cat because of the situations he created and was placed in. I didn't think much about winning the classics until we did. I must tell you there's nothing quite like it. We're very proud of him and optimistic he'll make a great sire."

History shows that few, if any, in racing had a better record together than jockey Pat Day and his agent, Fred

Aimee, who parted company over the weekend when Aimee retired. During the past 10 years, they've been incredible in races, purses and riding titles won.

Since having joined forces, Day won three of his four Eclipse Awards, the Kentucky Derby, three of his four Preakness Stakes, two Belmont Stakes, seven of his eight Breeders' Cup races and also earned a spot in the Hall of Fame.

Aimee and Day will be remembered for all those achievements, as well as the class, style, grace and poise they displayed, complimenting each other with equal verve during the good times and bad. The sport, especially the media, owes them a round of applause.

In a final venue, Bob Holthus, who trained the gallant gelding Potentiality, said it best: "If there's a horse heaven, he's in it."

Potentiality fractured both sesamoids in his left front hoof in a victorious effort in Thursday's feature. He lasted until Saturday morning and was euthanized after "sinker laminits" overwhelmed him despite the world renowned veterinary care of Dr. Alex Harthill and Dr. Doug Byars of Hagyard-Davidson-McGee.

They'd hoped to get the horse over the complications, and then take him to Dr. Doug Herthel in Los Angeles for the implantaion of a titanium rod in the useless leg, much like the process used in humans.

The 9-year-old Potentiality raced for Dan Jones and H.E. "Tex" Sutton. The Florida-bred son of Relaunch made 46 starts, fashioning a 19-9-5 record and earning $534,441. He was in the midst of a great campaign, winning his sixth race from eight starts.

He wasn't Seattle Slew, Secretariat, Twenty Grand or Citation, but Potentiality, because of his age and front-running style, gave fans great pleasure while earning their respect. He will be remember long and warmly.

MEMORABLE SEASONS OF "SUMMER"

November, 1991

LOUISVILLE, Ky. — All through the spring of 1990, the question was asked over and over of trainer Neil Howard: "Will Summer Squall make it to the Kentucky Derby?"

It was generally followed by another: "Will he be ready?"

Cutting through the gray area, Dogwood Stable's Summer Squall made it to the Kentucky Derby. He was prepared, too, as his runner-up finish to Unbridled attests.

After that, the gallant little Storm Bird colt ran one of the fastest Preakness Stakes on record, winning the 1 3/16th-mile classic by 2 1/4 lengths.

Summer Squall stepped out of here the other day to spend the rest of his life at stud in Versailles, Ky., at Will Farish's Lane's End Farm. The horse didn't report on the highest of notes after checking in ninth in the Breeders' Cup Classic, his 20th career start.

However, in 13 of those races Summer Squall came home first and was second on four other occasions, earning nearly $1.9 million. That figure alone denotes he wasn't facing any patsies.

It also illustrates what a superb job Howard did in training the colt through a career laden with ups and downs.

Pitfalls are part of life. They are magnified in any sport when championships are involved. Horses who bleed in cheap claiming races aren't news. But when a horse is attempting to overcome pulmonary problems while chasing a title, that's another story. That fact that he was a bleeder always haunted Summer Squall.

Howard, one of the most popular horsemen on the Kentucky circuit, profited from the experience of training Summer Squall. The horse, likewise, benefitted from the man's skilled hand, calculated training schedule and methods.

How and why Summer Squall became a popular horse around here goes something like this.

He arrived, ready to run, at Howard's barn at Keeneland as a 2-year-old in the spring of 1989. Howard was advised by Cot Campbell, overseer of the Dogwood operation, that the syndicate thought a great deal of the colt's promise.

Howard went over the horse, blew him out, and Summer Squall won nicely, drawing off by 11 lengths in one of those sprints for babies.

Part of the colt's popularity, too, is based upon the fact that he was usually ridden by Pat Day, many times the leading rider at Keeneland and Churchill Downs and a record setter in his own right. When Day didn't ride, Charles Woods Jr., a Louisville product, did. Day termed the colt the most courageous he'd ever ridden.

Summer Squall spent the spring of his juvenile year at Churchill Downs, winning the Kentucky Breeeders' Cup and Bashford Manor Stakes.   It wasn't until he burst through a sliver of daylight in Saratoga's Grade I Hopeful that he began to earn a national reputation.

That race, too, brought about complications. Sometime during the hectic stretch run, Summer Squall suffered an injury. A hairline fracture of the cannon bone cropped up, and it concluded his season. It took a flock of X-rays before it was discovered, but Howard knew and insisted that no detail be left undone to locate the problem.

The following spring, Summer Squall came out with a second-place finish behind Housebuster in Gulfstream Park's seven-furlong Swale Stakes.

During a morning workout soon after, the colt bled from the lungs. He didn't trickle, either. It was a bucket full.

The possibility of making the Derby was in jeopardy.

But Howard had a backup plan. Get the colt over the mental hazard that often follows bleeding and point him for the Jim Beam Stakes at Turfway Park.

The weather is cooler there. Medication can be used and the race is run over nine furlongs, a suitable distance when pointing toward going 1 1/4 miles on the first Saturday in May.

The plan worked to perfection, and Summer Squall came home under Day's hand ride, winning by nearly two lengths.

At Keeneland, the colt further illustrated his ability over wet footing, leading nearly all the way to win the Blue Grass Stakes over Unbridled.

After his Preakness victory, he was rested until September before winning by nearly four lengths in the Pennsylvania Derby. He bled again in the Grade I Meadowlands Handicap and was put away for the year.

This year, Summer Squall prepped in an allowance race at Keeneland, posting the quickest time of the season at 6 1/2 furlongs. He was runner-up in the Pimlico Special, requiring Fama Way to run in track-record time.

Summer Squall's final win came over his old rival, Unbridled, in Keeneland's Grade II Fayette Handicap going nine furlongs, which probably was his best distance.

"Part of the reason he was so popular with people is that he always gave 100 percent," said Howard. "He had class, pedigree, speed and courage, everything it take to make for a great horse. His greatness was minimized by his bleeding. Hard to say what kind he would have been if he hadn't had that problem."

As private trainer for Farish, odds are that Howard may come up with another good colt in the near future. The pedigree and quality needed to compete in the big arena abound at Lane's End, where Summer Squall was bred and raised before being sold at Keeneland's July Select Sale.

Still, the first horse that takes a man to the big dance is like your first real love. You never forget it. And it's difficult to duplicate.

"I will miss him," Howard said. "He took me to some fine places and to the big time.

"I won't miss the worry, though. Good horses have a way of driving a trainer crazy. You have to be so concerned about everything. No detail is too small when you're running in a big-time event. You know, it's something just to start a horse in the Derby or Breeders' Cup."

The son of a glassblower from the Bronx, Howard never has forgotten his humble upbringing and the way in which he's crawled up the ladder of success — from his days as a hotwalker to a seven-year stint with Mack Miller to beginning on Farish's farm after only modest success as a public trainer on his own.

He took over his current job, replacing Del Carroll, who was killed in a terrible mishap during training hours at Keeneland.

Vital lessons were learned and stored away for future

use. Teamwork, a byword for success, was stressed each time.

Those lessons have endured. And while Howard prepares to close out the season and ship his stable south, there is no older horse in his barn who may run for a championship next season. The 2-year-olds haven't shown they're Derby material, either.

Still, odds say that he'll be back in the spotlight soon.

Finally, about Summer Squall. This job had taken me around the state many times and allowed for contact with hundreds of participants. They have varied widely in size, shape and ability — both equine and human. The thing they had in common is that they were people and creatures of action. What they do for a living commands attention, and when they depart, it touches many.

We'll miss Summer Squall. It's only one opinion, but through his pure athleticism, he'll make a fine sire. Enough said.

CAVEAT TACKLED
ADVERSITY WITH GRACE

March, 1995

FLORENCE, Ky. — About 30 years ago, John Hanes, John Olin and John Gaines put up $200,000 apiece and purchased a colt called Bold Bidder.

The term "pinhooked" wasn't in vogue then, but Randy Sechrest had bought him earlier for around $40,000 from the Phipps family and trainer Bill Winfrey.

The new partners sent Bold Bidder to Woody Stephens to train. After the deal was closed, Sechrest reportedly insisted he had something to tell Stephens about how Bold Bidder should be handled.

Before the conversation, Bold Bidder ran a brilliant mile in 1:32 and change to win the Hawthorne Gold Cup. After that, Sechrest was kindly informed that it wasn't necessary to tell Stephens anything about Bold Bidder, or any horse.

Later, Bold Bidder went to stud at Gainesway Farm in Lexington, Ky. His most famous son was Spectacular Bid, who would've been most any sire's best while earning championship honors, banking nearly $3 million while winning 26 of 30 starts, including the Kentucky Derby, Preakness Stakes, Florida Derby and Blue Grass Stakes at 3 and the Charles Strub, Santa Anita Handicap and Woodward Stakes at 4.

Bold Bidder sired two Kentucky Derby winners. The other was Cannonade, winner of the memorable 100th running.

All of this came flashing back to mind the other day when a brief from Chesapeake City, Md., ran under the headline: "Belmont Stakes winner Caveat dies suddenly."

Caveat, a foal of 1980, was the best son of Cannonade and a grandson of Bold Bidder. And, for the record, one of Caveat's sons, a colt called Ops Smile, is nominated for the April 1 running of the $600,000, Grade II Jim Beam Stakes.

A couple of other sons of Caveat have contested the Jim Beam, including the stretch-running Awad.

Bold Bidder, Cannonade and Caveat had the same lineage and were linked further historically through Stephens, who trained them, along with Cefis, arguably Caveat's best son.

Speaking from his Miami Spring, Fla., winter home, Stephens reflected on the star-crossed and extremely unlucky career of Caveat.

"I got a call the day he died," Stephens said. "It was quite a shock because he wasn't that old. I had a lifetime breeding right to him but sold it most of the time because he stood in Maryland. That was a little inconvenient because my mares are at Claiborne Farm in Lexington, Ky.

"Caveat was my second of five straight Belmont winners. He showed great courage that day and overcame problems most horses couldn't have."

Stephens was referring to an incident in the 1983 Belmont when Caveat, rallying through a narrow opening under Laffit Pincay Jr., was bounced off the inner railing leaving the quarter-mile ground when Slew o' Gold leaned in.

Caveat went on to win decisively, but the skirmish took a heavy toll. Shortly after, Stephens discovered Caveat had pulled a ligament behind his left knee. The trainer gave him considerable time off and tried to return him to the races at Saratoga that summer by swimming him. But the ligament wouldn't hold, and Caveat was retired.

Overall, he carved out a 6-6-4 record from 21 starts and earned $542,190 when money had a lot more value than today.

The Belmont wasn't the only tough luck Caveat suffered. He endured a dreadful trip in the Kentucky Derby when forced 15-wide as the tightly bunched group came to the stretch. He finished third, beaten two lengths and neck for everything.

"Pincay told me he should have won the Derby, too," Stephens said. "Even with everything he accomplished, Caveat was a flat unlucky horse."

Linda Bench, who handles bookings at Northview Stallion Station, disclosed that Caveat had covered only two mares this season before his death. And, that the tragedy is something that only time can improve.

We recall Caveat on an overcast, late April day at Churchill Downs. Stephens was prepping him in the Derby Trial, which was conducted over muddy, slow footing. It was one of the horse's lucky days. He came pounding through the goo to win it close and save the chalk players.

While Caveat overall was unlucky, Stephens' luck may still be holding. As noted, he's sold his breeding rights to Caveat annually. He peddled this spring's season last November with no guarantee involved.

"I haven't heard anything from the people about wanting me to give the money back," he said. "Wonder if I will?"

VIVA CANONERO!

November, 1981

Canonero II died reportedly from a heart attack last Monday in Caracas, Venezuela. It was an ordinary racing day.

But the winner of 1971's Kentucky Derby and Preakness was everything but ordinary.

A decade ago, the gallant and gifted Canonero II wrote a thrilling chapter to the Triple Crown story. The once obscure bay colt became a star in a year when the industry desperately needed one.

In brief, 1971's Derby picture became muddled in March when Hoist the Flag, the winterbook favorite, fractured a sesamoid in training.

Canonero II was among the unknown despite decent bloodlines. By the French stallion Pretendre, Canonero II was produced by Dixieland II and was flawed at birth. His right foreleg bent back at the knee.

While carrying Canonero II, the mare was purchased at Keeneland's mixed sale for a mere $2,700.

As a yearling in 1969, Canonero II was purchased for $1,200 by a Venezuelan bloodstock agent.

At 2, the colt won several times in Venezuela. And, by early spring of his 3-year-old season, he'd already run the Derby distance of 1 1/4 miles. He trained and ran in the high altitude of the Andes Mountains, running on deep, sandy surfaces which proved advantageous later at Churchill Downs.

Getting to Louisville, Ky., for the Derby was another

ordeal. Twice the plane carrying Canonero II was forced to turn back to Venezuela because of inclimate weather. When it finally reached Miami, Canonero II was forced into quarantine for two weeks after his connections failed to produce a valid health certificate and blood work. During the interim, he dehydrated, lost 100 pounds and received little exercise.

Then, instead of being flown to Louisville, the colt covered the final 1,000 miles in a hot, rickety, van.

Consequently, seemingly knowledgeable horsemen viewed the Venezuelan contingent as part of the carnival associated with the Derby. They scoffed at their unorthodox training methods. They looked askance when trainer Jose T. Rodriquez, a longtime Kentucky regular who filled in for trainer Juan Arias (who didn't arrive until two days before the Derby), gave Canonero II long, slow gallops, long walks, and a pedestrian-like work or two.

Canonero II galloped under a 165-pound exercise rider. And if the weight wasn't concern enough, imagine what people thought when the boy did it bareback. How comical Canonero II's Derby bid must have seemed, particularly after he worked a half-mile in a "buggy-horse" 54 seconds.

However, on Friday morning before the Derby, shrouded by total darkness in a clandestine move, Rodriquez sent the colt three furlongs in 34 seconds. This wasn't made public until two years later.

On Derby Day, a then-record crowd of 123,284 crammed into Churchill Downs. Calumet Farm, which hadn't had a Derby starter since the Dancer's Image scandal in 1968, had a formidable entry in Bold N' Able and Eastern Fleet, which was favored.

Canonero II was a member of the mutuel field. In the paddock, the high-strung Arias shook so violently he couldn't cinch the girth on the colt. So Rodriquez did it for him. In the field of 20, Canonero wore saddle cloth No. 15.

Racing 17th on the backstretch under Gustavo Avila, Canonero II circled the field on the stretch turn, took over, and won going away by 3 1/4 lengths to shock the world.

"Fluke" cried many observers. "He was lucky," said others. "Who was the first Canonero?" they asked. "Wait until the Preakness," they chanted.

In the Preakness, Canonero II changed tactics. As the field straightened into the backstretch, Eastern Fleet, again the favorite, was in front. But right with him was Canonero II.

They ran as a team, clicking off suicidal fractions. Surely

one will fade, reasoned the then-record crowd of 47,221. Canonero II didn't, winning by 1 1/2 lengths in track record time of 1:54 for the 1 3/16 miles.

Not since Carry Back in 1961 and Citation in 1948 had a horse so captured the fancy of the American public, which loves an uncompromising underdog. Not since Citation had there been a Triple Crown winner, either.

Boosted by a tremendous turnout from New York's Latin American community, a then-record 81,000-plus jammed Belmont Park to watch Canonero II bid for the Triple Crown. However, the long van rides, extraction of two teeth and a severe case of thrush caught up with the colt.

Arias knew the horse wasn't at his best and didn't want to run him. However, a $3.1 million deal had been struck contingent upon a Belmont victory. So, owner Pedro Baptista took the risk and Canonero II ran.

He raced gamely for a mile, then faded to fourth. He later was sold for $1.5 million, but produced little as a stallion. His stud fee dropped as low as $1,500.

Nonetheless, Canonero II achieved a fame men running for president can't attract. Nor can major league sports superstars, actors and beautiful women. During the six weeks of the Triple Crown, this colt with the crab-like motion was a media celebrity throughout South and North America. He was a champion of the many little people and a special horse — an underdog who refused to yield.

And as to that report of him having suffered a fatal heart attack? I've always wondered about that. While he was racing, at least, there was nothing wrong with Canonero II's heart.

A WAR HERO'S FIGHTING FANTASY

May, 1994

LOUISVILLE, Ky. — There are many unsettling and equally emotional paradoxes which surround aging athletes of the human or equine variety.

Thoroughbred horses get old but not gray. They are tired but don't have problems catching their wind. They slow down when leaving the starting gate, but it's not because of the cumbersome weight gain that 36-year-old running backs or outfielders on the downhill side are prone to suffer.

If old racehorses could think about such issues, most would realize that they become obsolete at age 7 or 8 when those of other breeds are settling into a comfortable routine or possibly even moving toward their prime.

The aging process also can be a melancholy thing for those who own these thoroughbreds.

Sentimental attachment is easy when a man's pride is at stake over an animal's performance. That may sound ridiculous, but many a person will tell you that a particular horse carrying a rider wearing their colors often is like a family member.

It is especially true when a horse is handsome enough to be an equine pin-up and earns lots of money, publicity and fanfare.

When these steeds no longer are promising 3-year-olds or valuable as older performers who can compete at a high purse level, it's time to alter their lifestyles.

To Forego, for example, age meant carrying more weight and a final stop at the Kentucky Horse Center.

John Henry ended up there, too. Before he got too long in the tooth to unfurl those furious charges, advancing age meant only a few select races a year, heavy weight burdens to carry and nagging injuries that took longer and longer to heal.

But to more solid and useful horses than anyone can count, age has meant a punishing reversal in form down through the claiming ranks where the pride of the various owners and trainers these steeds worked for consisted only of cashing a ticket to pay the rent.

Only a few old horses bow out gracefully. Ray Cottrell Sr.'s Fighting Fantasy, a tall, attractive, well-muscled chestnut who sports a white blaze, was one who did.

Now 8, he was sent off to stud last Friday. His address is Carrie Wipf's Jump Over the Moon Farm near Elkhorn, Neb. Farm manager Barney Gottsch said the red horse will stand for $750 this season and $1,000 in 1996.

Arguably, Fighting Fantasy is the best son of the stallion Fighting Fit. Out of the stakes-winning mare Ice Fantasy, the iron-legged Fighting Fantasy made 87 career starts, posted 16 victories, added 15 seconds and 14 thirds while earning $572,820 under the supervison of three different trainers.

His bankroll could have been considerably more had he not been plagued with quarter cracks his entire career.

It's also a fact that the owner holds deep reverence for Kentucky racing, especially the Derby.

In the spring of 1990, Fighting Fantasy won a prep for the Illinois Derby. He would have been one of the top three choices in the Illinois Derby. But Cottrell, a highly decorated war hero and founder and owner of Ray's Ford in Brandenburg, Ky., reasoned that there's only one Derby for a Kentucky businessman — the Kentucky Derby.

In the Run For the Roses, Fighting Fantasy made the early pace. He bore out on the first turn and finished 15th behind Unbridled. Even as recently as last month in a local paper, the owner was buffeted for his decision. He's right, though. There's only one Derby.

Fighting Fantasy made his final start on April 19 at Keeneland. He suffered a minor ankle injury, finished sixth and limped onto the van bound for his Churchill Downs base. That was enough to scare the owner and trainer, Marcia Lee Butler, out of their wits, and they mercifully called it quits on the old boy.

On May 5, Kentucky Oaks day, Fighting Fantasy was test-bred to three mares at Dr. Tom Johnson's place in nearby Prospect, Ky. A recent ultrasound revealed one in foal.

Word was received that Fighting Fantasy took to his new career like an old pro, that he became bored easily, listlessly wishing for a stall at the track and his old friends. Perhaps, but anyone who watched his final struggles knew it was time for him to go.

He has been a fine and dependable competitor. It would have been nice to see him say farewell with one of those front-running victories of his youth.

But, that kind of thing makes even toughened veterans like Cottrell weep. So, on second thought, the old horse left the right way. We wish him good luck.

GRINDSTONE: TRIUMPH
AND TRAGEDY FOR W.T. YOUNG

May, 1996

LOUISVILLE, Ky. — A person's ability to handle triumph and tragedy with equal poise is essential for long-term participation in racing.

As William T. Young, owner of Overbrook Farm in Lexington, Ky., again experienced this week, the good news and bad news often follow each other with overwhelming swiftness.

Last Saturday, Grindstone fulfilled Young's lifelong dream of winning racing's most coveted prize — the Kentucky Derby — by a nose.

Thursday, the colt was retired from racing with a chip in his right knee, the same knee that was operated on last summer for a similar injury.

It's the professional opinion here, and of many chart callers and other members of the racing injudstry, that only sound horses charge through Churchill Downs' grueling stretch in the manner Grindstone did to win.

Rallying under jockey Jerry Bailey from nearly 15 lengths off the pace after racing 15th early in the field of 19, Grindstone made up five lengths through the final quarter-mile, including three lengths in the final furlong, to snatch victory from defeat.

The victory proved Grindstone's class and character.

Informed about Grindstone's knee injury Thursday morning, Young never looked for sympathy. Instead, like the role model he is for some many, Young took it in stride and retired the horse.

He followed the same high road after his victorious champion Flanders suffered an injury when capturing the Breeders' Cup Juvenile Fillies, and the gritty, dual class-winning Tabasco Cat was forced to depart centerstage.

When trainer D. Wayne Lukas was attacked in print by some member of the media following Union City's break-down in the 1993 Preakness, it was Young who stepped forward and told the truth. It was he who requested that Lukas run Union City in the Preakness, deflecting some of the criticism from Lukas with unflappable, soft-spoken integrity.

Since having decided to play the game at the top level, Young's relationship with Lukas has been more akin to a father or brother than client to trainer. Their loyalty to each other is unquestioned. First and foremost, they are friends.

With Grindstone, some owners might have opted for more surgery. That would have meant an absence of nearly a year, and there are no guarantees that Grindstone's ability would not have been compromised.

Young would have none of that. He simply said: "We had our day in the sun. He's retired and will come home to Overbrook and stand stud. Hopefully, he'll make a great sire. Now, we'll just have to work harder and get Editor's Note (Grindstone's stablemate) to get the job done in the Preakness."

This is typical of the 78-year-old Young's outlook on life and racing. He accumulated these humble values when graduating from Henry Clay High School in Lexington, Ky., and with honors from the Unviersity of Kentucky in 1939. Good fortune allowed him to found W.T. Young Foods, which he parlayed into great wealth, and other influential companies in banking, storage and hospitals.

Young has never forgotten his roots and has been one of Kentucky's greatest philanthropists, giving millions to charity. In fact, Young purchased the breeding season to Unbridled that produced Grindstone at a charity auction.

Without a worry or a problem, Young started late in racing, becoming active in the early 1980s. Since the beginning, he's remained a shy, almost reclusive owner. It's not right to say that he's embarrassed by winning, but it's close to being accurate. He prefers to let his horses, their riders and Lukas do the communicating.

Despite a brief career, Grindstone spoke volumes.

RUDD'S REASON RARELY FAILED TO FIRE BEST SHOT

August, 1996

Some horses are bred for the big time. Rare Reason made it purely by chance and because of owner Mason Rudd's love of racing in conjunction with trainer Walter Bindner Jr.'s keen eye when selecting horses.

And even with a willing, understanding owner like Rudd, who always has considered racing a sport, and a patient handler like Bindner, it still nearly didn't happen.

After Rare Reason's first start at 3, Bindner bought the colt from Bob Tiller at Woodbine for $75,000 on behalf of Rudd, a fellow Louisville, Ky., native, who also is a longtime client and friend.

The Kentucky-bred gelding, by Rare Performer, had run a huge race sprinting at Woodbine. Naturally, Bindner figured he'd run Rare Reason on dirt.

However, three or four races later, Bindner was about ready to throw in the towel. Rare Reason had shown little during the afternoons, and the trainer was beside himself, grasping at straws and looking for answers. He was ready to admit to the boss that he'd made a bad buy.

But there was one option left. Bindner breezed Rare Reason on the Churchill Downs turf course, and he moved like a totally different horse. Afterward, he ran like it.

What followed were 24 starts on the turf against some of the best company available in the Midwest, South and East. Rare Reason posted eight victories, five seconds and four thirds while amassing $543,695 of his $576,038 career total.

One of his best races came June 30, when he rallied from seventh to win Churchill's Grade III Firecracker Handicap at a mile. He recorded a 99 Beyer Speed Figure and won by a length.

Other notable efforts were Monmouth's Grade III Red Bank Handicap, and his 3 1/2 length triumph in the Sanford Duncan Stakes at Dueling Grounds.

Going into last weekend, Rare Reason was ranked fifth by the Breeders' Cup points committee. Bindner had his eye on this fall's Breeders' Cup Mile at Woodbine.

Disaster struck last Saturday morning at Churchill Downs. Bindner had taken Rare Reason to the track shortly after 6 a.m. for a five-furlong breeze. The horse broke off at the five-eighths pole and was building speed when leaving the three furlong marker. About then, another horse, Jim Bohanon's Miss Carson, got loose and crashed head-on into Rare Reason.

The filly died soon after from a broken neck. Rare Reason lived a few hours but was partially paralyzed. Dr. Alex Harthill, D.V.M., and others did their best. But Rare Reason died on the way to a clinic.

Rob O'Connor II, who trained Miss Carson, was extremely distraught. He visited Bindner at the barn, offering apologies and condolences. But what can anyone really say about such a catastrophic accident?

Rudd, a heavy equipment magnate, has endured similar blows during the past calendar year, including the death of his friends, Nelson Miller and Bob Watson, and the illness of his wife, Mary.

In an effort to alleviate his pain and berevement, Rudd had thrown his energy and interest wholeheartedly into Rare Reason.

How did Rudd cope with the tragedy? A noble gentleman, he put on a smile, went to the barn and consoled everyone involved with the horse. He thanked them for their time, effort and devotion to Rare Reason and told them not to worry. He told them to be happy and thankful for the achievements and memories gained during the three years he raced.

To lift Bindner out of his depression, Rudd sent him to Woodbine to buy some horses. Speaking from Toronto, Bindner said losing the horse was the same as losing a family member.

"It's very difficult going to the barn," he said. "It'll take months for me to get over this. Some people are in racing because they like the game. Some are in it because they simply like horses. This is a very difficult thing when you like both."

Bindner acknowledged that he felt blessed to have had Rare Reason.

There's no telling how much more Rare Reason might have accomplished. And, because he was a gelding, he would have kept on running for a few more seasons.

To Rudd, Bindner and others, everything about Rare Reason — including his name — stood for class.

LIL E. TEE DOING FINE ON THE FARM

September, 1992

FLORENCE, Ky. — Lynn Whiting is a third-generation horseman who has enjoyed considerable success by sticking to basic philosophies.

His greatest conquest came last spring when W. Cal Partee's storybook horse, Lil E. Tee, won the May 2 Kentucky Derby at Churchill Downs, using an earlier victory in Turfway Park's Jim Beam Stakes as a springboard.

We say storybook because of a star-crossed background beginning with the colt's Pennsylvania birth, lack of immunity and subsequent surgery for colic. His racing possibilities looked bleak in the beginning but he emerged as something special.

To be exact, it began to build on March 28 when Lil E. Tee, benefitting from a ground-saving ride by Pat Day, posted a length victory in the Jim Beam, emulating his sire, At the Threshold, and ultimately giving Turfway's premier race more credibility than all the marketing campaigns could produce in a decade.

Anyway, since winning the Derby by a length, Lil E. Tee has been relatively quiet.

The colt wasn't himself when fifth in the Preakness. A lung infection was discovered to have been the trouble, causing the colt to bleed during the race.

Then, in early June, Lil E. Tee was discovered to have a chip in his left front ankle. X-rays revealed the chip and another on the right side, too. They were a matching set, each about the size of a pencil tip eraser.

A trip to Dr. Alex Harthill and Dr. Gary Priest's Castleview Veterinary Clinic in Versailles, Ky., was made for arthroscopic removal of the chips.

Memory recalls vividly that Whiting didn't ask for condolences then, although some were offered. And he isn't asking for them now, either. He was well aware of the ups and downs this business produces and is looking to the future.

There's no need to labor the point that Lil E. Tee, a winner of $1,177,106 on a record of 5-3-1 in 10 starts, was forced to miss the 3-year-old series during the summer at Arlington.

Appearances in various other derbys in the Midwest were negated, too, and a shot in the historic Travers Stakes at Saratoga was out of the question.

His status was pronounced: "Out indefinitely."

Still, Whiting's longstanding belief kept the ship afloat. "Don't take anything for granted in this business," he said. "Every time you send a horse to the track, every time you wake up, it's a new day. And that horse is only as good as he is today. You've got to look to the future. You can't go back to the past."

Well, the future is nearly here. And following surgery, two blisters on the ankles and considerable pasture time at Warner L. Jones Jr.'s Hermitage Farm in Goshen, Ky., Lil E. Tee is about ready to rejoin Whiting's stable at Churchill.

"He's been on grass for six weeks, put on weight and looks great," said Whiting, who regularly makes the 40-minute journey from Churchill to the farm to monitor the colt. "We plan on bringing him into Churchill on Oct. 7 for light training.

"We'll go to Oaklawn Park after the fall meeting at Churchill. His next will be at Oaklawn Park."

A horse is eligible for the classics but once in a lifetime. Still, there is no resentment on the trainer's part for missing those dances.

You might expect as much. Because this is the same, modest guy who proclaimed his popular Derby victory as "one for all the guys who come to the backstretch every day and never had the opportunity to win it."

And so the saga continues. And soon, the big bay horse, about 16.2 hands tall and 1,200 pounds, with the alert head, handsome shoulders and muscular hindquarters, will return to the barn he made famous.

"They say everything happens for the best. So let's stick

with that," added Whiting. "The time away had to do him a world of good and I hope he'll be a tremendous older horse."

Whiting isn't by himself. A lot of the guys who never made it to the big show, or won the eighth race on the first Saturday in May at Churchill Downs, are solidly in his rooting section.

ABORIGINAL APEX
OVERCAME HUMBLE ROOTS

August, 2000

By all rights, multiple stakes-winning Aboriginal Apex should never have made it to the races.

But he did, winning 10 times in a 42-race career that produced $525,000 in earnings and included victories in the 1997 and 1998 runnings of Ellis Park's $75,000-added Tri-State Handicap. Several others were worth a lot more.

His career ended Friday when trainer Larry Mayo called to say that he and owner Gary Knapp had decided to retire the 7-year-old gelding following his (seventh-place) finish Thursday in the allowance feature.

This story began six years ago when the horse was purchased as a yearling by Knapp, an economist from Lexington, Ky. He planned to use the horse as sort of a guinea pig on his farm, where he was experimenting with a treadmill device that improves horses' fitness without the wear and tear of training.

Knapp needed several horses to perfect the test and purchased three for a modest sum. The one he bought for $1,700 was a non-descript bay by Trapp Mountain, produced by a mare named Dangerous Native.

Incorporating the pedigree, Knapp decided to name him Aboriginal Apex.

The dictionary defines aboriginal as a "primal native." "Apex," of course, means the highest point.

Aboriginal Apex didn't start at 2 and won only one of 10 races on the dirt the following year.

Then Mayo decided to try the horse on the turf. What a

brilliant decision it was. Not only did he win stakes and allowance races here, he also won them at Louisiana Downs, Fair Grounds, and more than held his own at Saratoga and Keeneland and Churchill Downs against some of the finest turf horses in America.

By becoming "a poor man's good thing," many fans became aware of his rags to riches story. And, because few things move hardcore, blue-collar racegoers like a bargain buy that overcomes the odds and defeats high-priced runners, he developed quite a following.

His past performances don't show it, but Aboriginal Apex hasn't been the same horse since being involved in a van accident last April 27 at Keeneland. The axle on the trailer he was riding in was sheared off and the horse was thrown to the floor in the trailer.

"There's nothing wrong with him physically," confirmed Mayo. "But you have no way of telling what kind of trauma he went through. We love this horse and would never embarrass him by dropping him into the claiming ranks and watching him suffer.

"He's been great to us and has put a lot of money in his fans' pockets. I'll miss him. But unless he shows me that he'd like to be my lead pony at the track, he'll spend the rest of his days enjoying the good life on the farm."

SILVER CHARM
WILL BE MISSED GREATLY

October, 1999

LEXINGTON, Ky. — It was 5:34 p.m. (EDT) on May 3, 1997 at Churchill Downs when the Kentucky Derby was run for the 123rd time.

About 10 hours earlier, my professional position and longstanding camaraderie allowed me to conduct an annual tour for friends from Evansville through the Derby barns. The folks enjoyed a rare, upclose look at the contenders while visiting and bidding good luck to trainers and owners attempting to win the world's greatest race.

That morning, though, things were different when chatting with trainer Bob Baffert at Barn 33. Relaxed and full of life, the irreverent Baffert bellowed: "Cliff, have you seen Silver Charm? Bring your friends. Come on in and check him over."

Trainers of Derby horses detest interruptions like this. But Baffert insisted.

Jim Kornblum, a prominent Evansville attorney and Derby regular, had his youngest daughter, Jessica, in tow. About to graduate from DePauw University, she was accompanied by several of her sorority sisters.

They rubbed Silver Charm's noble head and had their pictures taken with him. It didn't dawn on them what a big deal it was until after the battleship gray colt outgamed favored Captain Bodgit through the Derby's final furlong to win by a neck.

Naturally, Jim Kornblum had purchased several hefty mutuel tickets involving Silver Charm for his daughter and her friends. They cashed in, thinking this was how every Derby Day should be. It's a memory that'll last forever.

Several days earlier Dennis Brinkmeyer, also an Evansville lawyer, visited the Louisville track while celebrating his 50th birthday. I asked if he'd like a present that money can't buy.

Silver Charm was scheduled to work for the final time before the race. So I said to Brinkmeyer: "Tomorrow morning, we'll visit the horse who'll win the Derby."

On a perfect spring morning, we accompanied Silver Charm trackside for a five furlong breeze. Afterwards, walking alongside the colt as he returned to the barn, I said: "Happy birthday Dennis! You're with the Derby Winner. And look — he's not blowing enough to put out a match. He'll be there on Saturday. Stick with him."

Then we enjoyed a lovely conversation with the horse's owners, Bob and Beverly Lewis.

These memories and more came to mind recently at Keeneland, where Silver Charm made his final public appearance. He'd been retired to Lane's End Farm near here last spring following his final race, the $800,000 Grade II Stephen Foster at Churchill Downs.

It seemed odd, though. At Keeneland, the rider wasn't attired in those famous green and gold colors of the Lewises. And, after Silver Charm was led through the paddock and walking ring, he stepped into the winner's circle before galloping away. The applause of the 21,000 on-track fans was generous, and probably confused the horse because it was the only time he ever entered a winner's circle without working for it.

Silver Charm started 24 times, posting a 12-7-2 record. One of only six Florida-breds to win the Kentucky Derby, he earned $6,944,369, ranking him third all-time behind Cigar ($9,999,815) and Skip Away ($9,616,360).

It wasn't his rags-to-riches saga that won Silver Charm his fame and following, although making it big from lower ranks often enhances an athlete's popularity. It wasn't the fact that he won all that money. And he wasn't an equine pin-up when compared to Secretariat, Unbridled, Seattle Slew or even Charismatic.

Silver Charm's quality was best expressed by his grit and refusal to lose when it counted most.

Like an aging athlete, numerous contradictions surround horses like Silver Charm. At age 5, he is tired but not short of breath. He's lost that once dashing burst of speed. He's hugely muscled and fleshy. He weighs in at more than 1,300 pounds, or about 10 percent more than his fighting weight. But he's not obese.

These things happen primarily to great horses. When they can't compete at the highest level, they become obsolete at the track and in demand at the breeding shed, sometimes never reproducing themselves.

Any knowledgeable person watching Silver Charm's prideful struggles early this year knew he'd been slipping. And the time he required between races became longer, the comebacks more labored.

For this gallant steed, the adulatory press conferences that Baffert once held outside the barn are over. Silver Charm never again will travel in front of a large, adoring crowd. His presence was so powerful that he once drew 3,500 for a morning workout. And he'll never again compete for six- or seven-figure purses. But when the breeding season begins next spring, his manner with attractive fillies will improve.

Horses like Silver Charm are animals that people can love, admire, respect, enjoy betting on or simply like watching perform. On the *Blood-Horse Magazine*'s list of the 100 greatest horses of this century, he was No. 63.

Personally, I had him several notches higher. Because during the 1990s, Silver Charm gave race-goers as much pleasure as any horse who raced. And by the friends he made, he'll be remembered long and warmly for the breathtaking battles he waged, not the offspring he sires.

He was a pal who brought great joy to a wonderful year of life. With the Breeders' Cup only 13 days away, it's without question that Baffert, the Lewises and Silver Charm's legion of admirers miss him greatly. I certainly do.

ZITO'S FALL MEET
RUINED BY INJURIES TO
STAR STANDARD AND OTHERS

OCTOBER, 1997

LEXINGTON, Ky. — "He put his foot down wrong and the ankle absolutely exploded."

That sentence is how trainer Nick Zito described the injury that William Condren and Joseph Cornacchia's Star Standard suffered to his left front ankle Wednesday when dueling for the lead during Keeneland's eighth race, a seven furlong allowance event in which he was the 6-5 favorite.

Star Standard was making his first start since the Grade I Pimlico Special on May 11, 1996. He'd been training forwardly since recovering from an injury to his left front cannon bone. Wednesday's breakdown was unrelated.

In fact, last Monday, Zito had received a clean bill of health on the horse after ordering a set of X-rays. "He was ready to run during the summer at Saratoga but popped a splint on the opposite leg. It was very minor, so we just backed off for awhile," said the bereaved, ashen-faced Zito. "He was so good in the paddock Wednesday and acted like a 2-year-old. Then he broke in front like a rocket.

"This past week has proved to me what all coaches and military men go through. Coaches always worry about players suffering a career-ending injury and say, 'How good would he have been if he hadn't been injured?' And military leaders know that there are times they must order men to their certain deaths," he added. "Breakdowns produce an awful feeling, one you can never get over. And I don't care how much of a cold-hearted mercenary a guy is. Unless you've got ice water in your veins and no brains, it'll get to you. It's been difficult for me to sleep much because in every instance, somebody is accountable. In this case, it's me. I put the saddle on him, and I feel guilty."

Star Standard is a winner of $1.1 million and arguably Risen Star's best son with a victory in Keeneland's 1995 Lexington Stakes, a second-place finish in the Belmont and Woodward Stakes and a third-place effort in the Jockey Club Gold Cup. The 5-year-old Star Standard benefitted Wednesday from having Hall of Famer Pat Day on his back.

Without Day's "magic hands" pulling him to a halt within 50 yards of the incident, Star Standard would have furthered the injury. Day dismounted and soothingly kept the horse calm and motionless in the moments before the Kentucky Racing Commission's equine trauma team arrived. They were outstanding, too, applying an inflatable cast to the horse and coaxing him into the ambulance.

The big bay horse remains in critical condition at Rood & Riddle equine hospital in Lexington, Ky. Dr. Larry Bramlage performed surgery from 8 a.m. until noon Thursday to piece the ankle back together. The cannon bone, fetlock and phalanx of the pastern were involved.

Bramlage, whom Zito labeled "the Michelangelo of veterinarians," used a bone plate, 22 screws and 36 inches of orthopedic wire in his valiant effort to save the horse.

"I don't care what it takes," said Zito. "I want him to have the best of everything. Room service if they have it. I told them to keep him as long as they wanted to. Keep him a year. Just save him. He won't be out of the woods for several weeks because he must learn to accommodate the injury. But he's been a great patient in the past."

It was the second crisis for the great trainer during Keeneland's fall meeting. He was merely a shell of his usually confident, jubilant self when visiting friends Thursday.

The first bomb dropped on Zito Oct. 17 when the promising Universe, a 3-year-old Seeking the Gold colt, suffered a catastrophic injury on the first turn of the Fayette Stakes and was euthanized on the track.

In each case, Zito jumped the grandstand fence and rushed to his stricken charge. "I can't take this anymore," he confided. "I won't be bringing a horse back to the races after an injury in the future. It's too tough on the help and myself emotinally, mentally and physically, and not my kind of business. Next time we have one injured, someone else is gonig to train him or he's going home.

"It's different when a horse is injured and you can't forsee it happening. But when you're worrying about one that was previously injured, it's just too draining."

This past week marked the first time in 10 years that Zito has had one vanned off. "We had a filly win and go lame, but she made it back to the barn before limping," he recalled. "This has been a terrible, terrible week."

Zito's stable will remain in Kentucky during the Churchill Downs meet. "We'll be stabled in one of the training barns at Keeneland and very objectively ship over to run at Churchill. I want to keep all my horses together and can manage them under one roof by staying at Keeneland."

And as for his 2-year-olds – primarily Laydown – running in Churchill's Iroquois or Jockey Club Stakes: "I'll discuss it with the owner. We may stop on them for the year or run either at Churchill or in the Remsen at Aqueduct.

"Bottom line is, I want something healthy to bring back for the spring classics. Getting there is half the battle, and we want to get back and be a factor in the Triple Crown."

A two-time winner of the Kentucky Derby, Zito, a Brooklyn, N.Y., native, has become one of the Commonwealth's favorite adopted sons and one of racing's greatest ambassadors.

Hopefully, for him, next spring's Triple Crown will bring rays of sunshine and wash away the perils he's encountered this October.

IT WILL BE A SWALE DERBY

MAY, 1984

LOUISVILLE, Ky. — Last fall, when I watched Swale win Keeneland's Breeders' Futurity, I wrote how I thought he could win the Kentucky Derby.

The day of reckoning is upon us. I have only 300 words to tell you why I'm sticking to my guns.

So here goes.

For his entire career, until this most important moment, Swale has been in the shadow of his touted stablemate, Devil's Bag, who was withdrawn from Derby contention Tuesday by trainer Woody Stephens.

Swale was ranked second to Devil's Bag in last year's Eclipse Award balloting for champion 2-year-old honors. He has always been looked on by most as second best. I don't buy that.

Although Swale was upset by He Is A Great Deal in his final Derby prep over a sloppy track in Keeneland's Lexington Stakes, I still maintain he has what it takes to win the great race.

What he needs is a fast track and the same gallant effort he exhibited in the Florida Derby when holding off Dr. Carter the length of the stretch.

Maybe more important than anything is Swale's pedigree. He is by 1977 Triple Crown winner and Horse of the Year Seattle Slew, one of the gamest horses ever to look through a bridle. Currently, he is one of the top sires in the land.

Swale, like "Slew," is almost black. Swale is long of body

with a fine chest and neck. He races much like his sire. Ears pinned, eyes ablaze in spirit. His flowing mane rushes against the wind when in top stride.

Swale isn't as good an athlete as Seattle Slew. But few are.

So for me, this Derby won't be measured by the blinking of numbers on the tote board where the audiences preferences are mirrored.

It will be gauged by Swale and his rider, Laffit Pincay Jr., who will attempt to turn the clock back to a better time on a spring Derby Day in 1977 when an unbeaten runner from humble beginnings named Seattle Slew electrified the racing world. He kept his unbeaten record intact in the process.

Perhaps it's only a fairy tale. Derby legends are based on those. But, rest assured of one criteria, Swale will give you his earnest best. That's all anyone can ask.

KENTUCKY DERBY
WINNER SWALE NEVER WAVERED

MAY, 1984

LOUISVILLE, Ky. — Claiborne Farm's courageous Swale vindicated his trainer, his followers, and most importantly himself with his relatively easy 3 1/4-length win in Saturday's 116th Kentucky Derby.

From birth, the colt had been rapped and forced to play second string. As late as last Friday evening, doubters still existed. A story in a New York paper had Swale lame after he worked a half-mile in 50 seconds Thursday. Knowledgeable horsemen don't drill Derby horses in record time 48 hours before the Kentucky Derby. They save something for the stretch.

And Swale had plenty.

The fallacy of lameness could not have been further from the truth. The uninformed source failed to mention that before that leisurely half-mile, Swale had worked five furlongs in a sharp 59 2/5 seconds. He came back to briskly move seven furlongs in 1:29 2/5. The final quarter of that work was 23 1/5, the last eighth in 1 13/5. That alone made him the horse to beat.

The triumph was the first for the world-famous Claiborne Farm, which has been trying to breed and race a Derby winner for decades. Its best chance previously came in 1969 when Dike finished third after having a rundown bandage come unraveled during the race.

It was the second Derby victory for ailing trainer Woody Stephens, who was hospitalized 10 days prior to the race with pneumonia.

watched the race from Churchill's board of directors room. He dispatched Cannonade to take the roses in 1974. Cannonade, like Swale, was the less heralded of an entry. He was coupled with Judger, who ironically was owned by Claiborne Farm president Seth Hancock. Judger finished eighth.

Stephens said early in the day he wouldn't go to the winner's circle if his charge won. He changed his mind and was there to welcome his star, leading him into the coveted infield winner's circle before the pagoda, where only Derby winners walk. During the picture-taking ceremonies, Swale stood calmly. As if on cue, he placed his head on Stephens' shoulder.

Until Saturday, Swale was supposed to be the understudy to his highly touted stablemate, Devil's Bag.

The 'Bag, syndicated for $36 million, was withdrawn from Derby consideration last Tuesday when it became apparent he couldn't endure the gruelling 1 1/4-mile test.

Magnificently ridden by Laffit Pincay Jr., Swale broke from the No. 15 post position. With Pincay still high in the irons, Swale stalked front-running Althea and Bear Hunt for a half-mile before flying past the latter.

The son of 1977 Triple Crown winner Seattle Slew is out of Tuerta, the last mare the late A.B. "Bull" Hancock saw carry his orange silks to victory in 1972. Swale was obtained in a foal sharing deal with Tayhill Stable, which raced Seattle Slew.

Each year, Claiborne takes one of two foals. Swale became the 11th Derby winner sired by a previous one.

After six furongs, Swale gave Althea a dose of her own medicine. Through the next quarter-mile, he looked her in the eye and raced her into submission.

Favored by the smaller than usual crowd of 126,453, Althea stopped to a walk and beat just one horse in the field of 20. That was Majestic Shore, who broke down.

Swale dispensed with Althea, and took over for keeps leaving the three-eighths pole. Midway of the final turn, Pincay went to the whip twice and Swale accelerated, increasing the margin to three lengths as he straightened into the stretch.

Three-sixteenths of a mile from home, Pincay put his steed next to the inner railing and swatted him twice more left-handed as he spurted ahead by five lengths.

The last 50 yards, when it was obvious that Swale had earned Pincay his first Derby win in 11 attempts, the Hall of Fame reinsman put his whip away and eased the flashy black home. He won with plenty left and wasn't fully extended in the time of 2:02 2/5, very creditable because no one forced the issue. He earned $537,400.

Coax Me Chad, a member of the mutuel field, got through all the way along the rail and gained the place. At The Threshold ran impressively, rallying from 11th for third, a head behind Coax Me Chad.

On the trip back for the presentation, Pincay was saluting the crowd's cheering with a whip-clenched fist thrust to the heavens.

"It's an unbelievable feeling," said Pincay, who at 37 joined Jean Cruguet as the oldest rider of a Derby winner. "It's fantastic. I wish my wife and family could have been here. I was gonna get drunk tonight but I ride tomorrow in California."

Pincay said he was concerned about the break. "He got away good and was going very easily. I could have taken Althea when I wanted her became (Chris) McCarron was trying to get by with a slow pace. Mr. Stephens told me to stay close to her and not let Althea steal it. Swale was as game today as he was in winning the Florida Derby.

"He's a very professional horse. He rated for me and the crowd didn't bother him. He takes care of himself."

After that Florida Derby victory, many hailed Swale as the Derby favorite. A number jumped ship when he was defeated over a sloppy surface in Keeneland's Lexington Stakes, falling by eight lengths to He Is A Great Deal. "I thought for a second he got hurt in that race. But he didn't," said Pincay.

When the media started second-guessing Stephens after the loss, he blasted them, accusing them of trying to train his horses when they knew nothing of the profession.

Saturday, looking pale and thin and still wearing his hospital band, Stephens had his statement ready. "He was always a top horse and was right there with Devil's Bag last year," said Stephens. "He couldn't handle the mud in Lexington and few believed me.

"This year, he's shown more than Devil's Bag except for that one race. We threw it out and were confident. I believe he'll go on to make a great horse."

While Stephens has been away, the task of dealing with the pressure has fallen on trainer Mike Griffin, a top horseman in his own right. He trained Copelan last year but since has become yearling manager at Claiborne.

"Mike has done a great job in keeping this horse on his form. I have a top team and love them all," said Stephens.

Griffin admitted he was nearly overcome with emotion. "It's a great feeling. We got carried wide into the first turn but Pincay was able to overcome it. I've seen him ride a lot of races and this was one of his absolute best."

"When we went into the paddock, Woody said the colt couldn't look any better and that's the way he ran. When he made the lead, I knew he was in. Everything went our way this week. He trained beautifully."

Earlier, it was announced that Swale would skip the Preakness and allow Devil's Bag a shot at the limelight. The Hancocks never have been fond of Maryland racing. They'll decide whether to send Swale to the Preakness this week.

For a brief instant Saturday, as the fluid-striding colt turned down the long stretch by himself, I rekindled a scene from seven years ago when Seattle Slew, carrying Cruguet in the bright yellow and black silks of Karen Taylor, silenced disbelievers.

Called upon when everything was riding, Swale also responded convincingly. Like his sire, he never wavered.

ALCOVY MISSES FALLS CITY 'CAP BUT BOWS OUT A WINNER

NOVEMBER, 1997

LOUISVILLE, Ky. — Churchill Downs will run the Grade III, $250,000 Falls City Handicap for fillies and mares on Thanksgiving Day for the 81st time.

It's a mile and an eighth test on the main track in which a flock of good ones have exhibited their prowess. For example, Fred Hooper's champion Susan's Girl captured the 1975 running under 126 pounds; Old Hat prevailed in 1964 under Don Brumfield and 128; Queen Alexandra tallied under Brumfield and 125 in 1986, to name only a few.

Several times, management has split this popular event into divisions after the entry box overflowed.

Without question, the Falls City Handicap deserves a separate page in this track's storied history. It stirs memories because each running is a story within a story.

Few, though, have had better finishes that the 1994 running. Unofficially, it became the race of that fall's meeting. Riley Mangum's Alcovy appeared beaten at the eighth pole after giving up the lead. But she dug in and came again under jockey Scott Miller to win by a whisker over a stubborn Pennyhill Park.

Alcovy's trainer, William G. "Blackie" Hufman, is a native Louisvillian who grew up outside the back gate here at 4003 S. Second Street. He walked hots as a youth and then hustled to beat the 7:30 a.m. bell at Holy Name Elementary.

Through hard work and perseverance, Huffman made himself into one of the most respected horsemen on these wanted more than 10 or 12 in his stable, and because of his personal touch and attention to fine detail, he handled Alcovy with kid gloves from the first day she looked through a bridle at 2.

In fact, he came to know Alcovy almost as well as he did his wife, Mary Ann, and had Alcovy primed to defend her Falls City title last year.

But Mariah's Storm was a little better, and Alcovy finished second. All of this and much more came to mind Wednesday when Huffman and Mangum decided not to go on with Alcovy.

"She's officially retired," said Huffman. "She hasn't run since finishing third in Ellis' Grade III Gardenia. We don'[t make excuses. She simply wasn't herself and gave a dull effort that day after being in a perfect position to win.

"We were hoping to make the Falls City this year and kept thinking she'd come back around to her old self, because she always had. She didn't this time, so it's time for her to go home. We could have run her in an allowance race, but that wouldn't have proved anything. She's already a multiple graded winner. She'll depart with four good, sound legs under her. Not many leave like that after going through tough races against some of the best in the country."

A career record of 14-3-7 from 29 starts and earnings of $897,590 prove her consistency, toughness and dependability.

It didn't matter if the track was fast, muddy, sloppy, good, cuppy or otherwise. Alcovy never needed to carry her track with her, and she always ran her race.

It was the same when Huffman tried her on the turf. She won a stakes the first time she'd been on the lawn since leaving the side of her dam, Forever Cup.

Alcovy immediately was taken in as a member of the Huffman family. The trainer's son, Pat, or his wife, former jockey Laura Hernan, became the exercise people and were instrumental in the successes.

"Alcovy had a mind of her own and trained herself," said Blackie Hufman. "When she wanted to gallop fast, she did, and had a lot of unscheduled breezes because of it," he said. "When she came to me, she was a big, gangly, rather plain-looking filly. But she showed a lot of quality the first time we breezed her. She was special to us, exactly like part of the family, and we'll miss her."

Further memories of Alcovy start with Huffman hoping

to get the mare over the $1 million mark in career earnings. She would have gone over seven figures long ago. Despite being a Kentucky-bred, she wasn't eligible for the Kentucky Thoroughbred Development Fund because the sire stood in Maryland.

There also was the morning of the 1995 Gardenia Stakes at Ellis when Huffman had to scratch Alcovy after she was found to be lame leaving the stall because of an abcess in a hoof wall.

Mangum, an ink manufacturer from Atlanta, thought about retiring Alcovy last year. But this mare makes her own decisions. Last December, a couple of days before she was scheduled to board a van for Mangum's Georgia farm, she won Turfway's My Charmer Stakes, and she enjoyed a banner 1996, with a 3-1-3 record from eight starts while banking $375,115.

To whom will Alcovy be bred? "Nothing on that for sure," said Huffman. "Riley has a list of six or seven stallions under consideration, and they're all top horses. She's earned the trip. And you can be on one thing: The foals will all be eligible for the KTDF."

As they say, hope springs eternal, even if the first offspring is three years away.

FORTY NINER HAS EARNED HIS NICHE IN RACING HISTORY

NOVEMBER, 1988

LOUISVILLE, Ky. — A sad thing happened following Breeders' Cup Day last Saturday at Churchill Downs.

What? How could a day with $10 million in purses spread over seven outstanding races be sad?

Because little did the crowd on hand in cold, threatening weather, as well as a national television audience realize, but they were bidding farewell from competition to a truly remarkable champion, Claiborne Farm's stout-hearted Forty Niner.

By Mr. Prospector from the Tom Rolfe matron, File, Forty Niner hails from a distinguished Claiborne family, and he did nothing but uphold and enhance the lineage. Forty Niner ran fourth behind Alysheba in the $3 million Breeders' Cup Classic, as he made his 19th and final appearance carrying the famed orange colors. He earned $210,000 for his effort. Only three times did Forty Niner fail to finish in the money, and he departs with an outstanding record of 11-5-0 and earnings of $2,726,000.

Run in the growing darkness, it was impossible on race day to decipher why Forty Niner dropped back to next to last in the field of nine approaching the stretch of the Classic. That was reminiscent of his Kentucky Derby effort in May when he fell back on the second turn, then came on again with a furious stretch run to be second, a neck short of Winning Colors.

Originally, someone mentioned after the Classic that Forty Niner may have stepped in a hole. He didn't. Seth

Hancock, master of Claiborne Farm, analyzed the tapes of the race carefully, and it was determined that Forty Niner hesitated slightly when shadows appeared on the racetrack leaving the turn. Then, as he has done throughout his career, he rallied, this time missing third money by a neck.

Forty Niner, who was shipped back to Belmont Park with trainer Woody Stephens, is being let down gradually to make the transition to the breeding shed at Claiborne where he will stand for $60,000. The compact chestnut retires as a sound horse whose only experience with medication was Butazolidin in the Derby to alleviate some discomfort he'd encountered after being shod improperly two weeks before the race.

"He never so much as had an aspirin other than that," confirmed Stephens by telephone from his home on Long Island, N.Y. "We're proud of that, and he probably didn't need it in the Derby. But you don't take chances in that one."

It should be noted that Forty Niner was the only member of the Classic field who ran "clean." That isn't derogatory of the other participants, merely a fact.

Back to the reason for melancholy concerning Forty Niner's departure.

We won't dwell on the fact that the huge majority of racing stars leave the track early with the public waiting on edge for their next appearances that never come. Forty Niner's case is slightly different. He's a homebred with a bit more emotion and devotion from his contingency than the public may be aware.

To study the colt's career is like inspecting the travels of a Rocky Balboa, or a wild card National Football League team fighting its way to the championship game on the road.

Much controversy surrounded Forty Niner and his merits, which are numerous and sometimes greatly overshadowed, such as the Preakness incident and the jockey strike in New York. Both affected his stature.

Through all of this, however, Forty Niner remained a favorite of those who appreciate true substance in a racehorse.

He had "big" speed, and he could carry it. And speed, it must be conceded, is the most necessary qualification for victory.

However, the word most often used to describe Forty Niner was "game." He had more "gameness" than any horse we can recall in this decade, at least. Forty Niner didn't display his grit once, or twice, he did so throughout his career. His victory margins of a neck, a nose and a nose in his last three wins are proof that his owner and trainer have strong hearts, because the stretch runs in those races — the NYRA Mile, Travers Stakes and Haskell — were breathtaking.

Forty Niner lost some close ones, too — the Derby by a neck, Lexington Stakes by a head, Florida Derby by a neck, and Woodward by a neck. This was a horse that you had to beat, who never yielded an inch, and whose determination, in seasons to come, will be recalled with fond memories.

Horsemen will agree on few things, but one they do agree on is courage being the most respected characteristic of a horse. Class, and Forty Niner had a world of class, makes no difference if a horse isn't a "tryer." There is no adequate substitute for heart, and Forty Niner had plenty of it. He was pure hickory.

Hall of Famer Stephens has trained 11 champions. His praise of Forty Niner, last year's 2-year-old champion, was special. "He wasn't the best horse I've had, but he was the gamest. He fought it out hard in a lot of tight ones. I've had a lot of calls from people who wanted to buy a share in him, but Seth (Hancock) is going to stand him. I've encouraged people to breed to him. Lucille (Mrs. Stephens) and I have six mares, and we're going to breed one to him. Forty Niner will make a great sire," Stephens said.

The master horseman, a sprightly 75, said he has mixed emotions about sending Forty Niner home. The colt goes to Claiborne Nov. 20. "We could have run him again. But realistically, what did he have to prove? Now, he can go home sound, and I can go to the farm when I'm in Kentucky and look out in that paddock and the memories will come to me. We lost Swale and Stephan's Odyssey. I would have worried a whole lot about Forty Niner if he stayed with me and ran next year," Stephens added.

Consistency is the mark of a pro and a champion. To Hancock, that was Forty Niner's prime virtue. "Each time he went to the paddock, we knew he'd give his best. I've always admired that in horses and in people. It's very gratifying when individuals have the ability to reach down and give it their best when sometimes that effort isn't within them."

Hancock added that he holds great faith in Forty Niner's future, and he believes the horse will make an extremely successful sire. "I'd say in five or six years, Forty Niner will be one of the most desirable stallions in the world," he said.

Perhaps there's a final note to the gallant little chestnut's retirement. His sire, Mr. Prospector, has vaulted to the pinnacle of the breeding industry. Like Forty Niner, he made his final start at Churchill Downs in May of 1973. Since then, his achievements in the breeding shed have become legend.

The heir apparent will arrive home at the Paris, Ky., nursery soon. We wish Forty Niner good fortune, and we treasure his memorable duels. Forty Niner earned his chevrons the old fashion way. He fought for them.

BIGGEST WINNER AT ELLIS
CAPS FINE RACING CAREER

SEPTEMBER, 1984

The crowd of 4,123 which reported Friday at Ellis Park didn't know it, but they bade a fond farewell to the old campaigner Don Din.

Owner-trainer Steve Duncan, who along with his father, Morris Duncan, own Green River Stables in Evansville, sent the longtime local favorite from the paddock for the final time in the fifth race.

Through infirmities, the 10-year-old chestnut gelding has lost most of the ability which once allowed him to rocket off the final turn and fly at the leaders on the outside.

Friday, in a race he would've once dominated, he finished ninth in the field of 12, and was never in the hunt.

Despite the dismal finale, Don Din retires as the all-time leader in races won at Ellis Park.

Seventeen times he stepped across the wire first in a career which spanned 93 races. His initial win came in his native country of Argentina against maidens.

The last 16 were earned at Ellis Park, and 13 came while carrying a rider wearing Duncan's green and white silks. The old warrior amassed more than $47,000 in earnings, and he did it the hard way against platers of the $2,500-$3,750 variety.

Steve Duncan claimed him in 1979 at Churchill Downs. Like clockwork, the gelding captured three races each summer at Ellis from 1979 through 1982. He managed a single win in 1983. Leroy Tauzin, now retired, was in the saddle for nine of Don Din's victories.

The trainer admitted feeling a touch of remorse as he sent the red horse to his finale in the four familiar white bandages, white bridle, blinkers and light green shadow roll which were his trademarks.

"I was pretty fond of him for several years and still am," said Duncan. "He's the last one I have left from when I entered the game. He was the best gambling horse I've ever had. It's a funny thing, but he was at his best when he was 8. The last two years have been touch and go. He hasn't changed leads in his last 12 races. I don't know how he won the one last year."

Duncan isn't sure what he'll do with Don Din. He entered him in the paddock sale last Monday hoping to secure a good home.

The horse drew a $350 bid and Duncan bought him back for $400 for fear the 'killers' may get him. A trip to Waterford Park to compete for $1,500 may be upcoming this fall but he won't be back at Ellis.

"I'd like to keep him but it wouldn't be practical. I try not to think about him leaving," Duncan said. "But we have so many young horses at the farm and he's another mouth to feed. I can't afford to pension him. Plus, we can't turn him out with the mares because he fights all the time. I wish he didn't have to go out this way but it happens to all of them who stay around long enough"

A $5 spot will get you $10 that Don Din will wind up leading a life of leisure in a pasture on Green River Road.

AFFIRMED, TRIPLE CROWN WINNER AND GREAT TEACHER

JANUARY, 2001

On Jan. 12, a news release from Jonabell Farm in Lexington, Ky., reported the death at age 26 of Affirmed, the great racehorse and stallion.

Previously, he'd stood stud at Spendthrift Farm and Calumet Farm. Ironically, at Calumet, he was in bird's-eye view of his great rival, Alydar.

Champion 2-year-old colt in 1977, Affirmed also won the following year's Triple Crown to become champion 3-year-old, and was Horse of the Year in 1978 and 1979, adding championship honors at 4 as top older male.

When a great equine or human athlete dies, one simple theme holds true: They left indelible imprints, touched many lives, and cause considerable reminiscing.

Since Affirmed's passing, volumes of copy has been written by people much closer to the horse than me about his memorable battles at 2 and 3 with Alydar.

Fact is, I wasn't in Affirmed's camp. Getting swept up in the emotional return to prominence by Calumet Farm under then and now trainer John Veitch, I went down swinging with Alydar, which we'll get too soon.

Anyway, an era ended when Affirmed died. And few people wrote anything about him without ranting and raving about how former jockey Steve Cauthen, the one-time whiz kid from Walton, Ky., was the rider.

They rarely tell you that Laffit Pincay Jr., the great Panamanian virtuoso, rode Affirmed to nine of the horse's 22 career victories from 29 starts. Pincay rode the brilliant chestnut 10 times, and would've run the table. But in the Aug. 19, 1978 running of the Travers Stakes under Pincay, Affirmed was disqualified from first and placed second behind Alydar for interference leaving the far turn.

During Affirmed's final seven races, six of which were Grade I, Pincay was astride, winning them all.

Cauthen rode Affirmed 16 times, winning 11. It just so happened that his tenure in the saddle included the Kentucky Derby, Preakness and Belmont Stakes. And Cauthen was young, fresh and polite, sporting that "yes sir, no sir" and "aw shucks" approach.

In history, no horse ever meant more in a jockey's career than Affirmed to Cauthen's. National television and Affirmed put Cauthen into America's living rooms. Later, the legendary steed carried him into the Hall of Fame despite modest credentials when compared to guys like Don Brumfield, Pat Day, Pincay, Bill Shoemaker and others.

As I said, great horses touch lives. And while I've never thought of Affirmed in the same light ability wise as Triple Crown winners Seattle Slew and Secretariat, I'll always remember him as a strong, tough, durable and dependable star. The fact that he raced 29 months is proof of that.

As a stallion, he was decent, never duplicating himself. But he sired several champions including Flawlessly, Peteski, Quiet Resolve and Affirmed Success.

More than anything, I'll remember Affirmed as a personal teacher. By losing $500 on Alydar against him in the 1978 Kentucky Derby, Affirmed taught me the greatest two-part turf lesson I've ever learned.

Part A: On Derby Day, be careful at the windows. The Derby is only one race and you don't have to bet everything you have merely because it's the most important race of the year.

Part B: In the Derby, it's best for a horse to be near the pace and avoid traffic, no matter the field size. Ground is extremely difficult to make up in the final quarter-mile.

May 6, 1978, was initiation, or ceremonial day at Hadi Shrine Temple. As an officer in the Oriental Band, I was committed to be at the Shrine, missing the Derby.

But compadre Steve Cato carried $500 of my cash to Churchill Downs with these instructions: "All of it to win on Alydar."

That day, and on most others when they met, Affirmed was the better horse. I'm reminded that he was better each time I enter Cato's kitchen. He and his wife, Pat, wallpapered one of their side rooms with racing memorabilia, programs, newspaper stories, pictures, and alas, pari-mutuel tickets. Ten of them in $50 denominations on Alydar are mine.

PART 2:

PEOPLE

Final Calls to Absent Friends

WOODY STEPHENS:
A GENUINE FRIEND
WHO'S IN A "REAL TIGHT ONE"

MAY, 1990

LOUISVILLE, Ky. — The good 3-year-old filly De la Devil, who carries the colors of Henryk deKwiatkowski, was a respectable fourth last Friday in Churchill Downs' 116th Kentucky Oaks. The program and past performances identified her trainer as Woody Stephens.

One of the master conditioners of all time didn't saddle the filly, though, and wasn't there to watch the race with the confident manner that can soothe the most strained of nerves.

In the 76th year of his life, Stephens is seriously ill in Norton Hospital here, and racing, the sport he has become a very symbol of with great dignity for more than 60 years since leaving a sharecropper's existence, is holding its collective breath and praying that he can outgame his constant opponent, emphysema.

It was lost in the Derby Week shuffle to some that Stephens is ailing. Some may pick up the theme and write how he became a contract rider for the John S. Ward family in his early teens.

Others may say or print of his fame as a trainer, developer of 11 champions, victorious in five straight Belmont Stakes, two Kentucky Derbys, a Preakness and countless graded stakes races of national importance which could fill up pages.

His achievements were with horses like Blue Man, Never Bend, Bald Eagle, Swale, Conquistador Cielo, Caveat, Creme Fraiche, Forty Niner, Devil's Bag, De La Rose, Miss Oceana and Cannonade to name only a few.

We prefer to write about a genuine friend. A man of great patience, consideration and loyalty. A gracious host. A warm companion who bubbles over with the laughter and mischief of a school boy. A man of wisdom and sincerity who has been a dictionary of information and anecdote.

Merely thinking of Woody brings to mind many memories. Mornings on the backstretch at Keeneland and Churchill Downs where he often had his little dog, Muskie, out for a walk. Or trekking up to get Sanka (juice as he says) at the track kitchen.

Perhaps a sitting at the Executive Inn or a trip to Claiborne Farm.

When all, including the state brass, believed in July of 1986 that "Woody Stephens Day" at Ellis Park would be a bust, it was the man who proved them wrong as fans turned out in droves to gain a copy of his autograph and autobiography, "Guess I'm Lucky."

Mornings around the barn were always special, with Woody pointing and patiently touching on areas to look for in the conformation of a top horse. "Look how this horse's legs sit under him. Look at his barrel. When you want a horse that can stay a route of ground, go for this.

"Look at these feet. They're as big as pie pans and this is going to be a good grass horse."

We visited Stephens, on Sunday, 25 blocks from the famed Twin Spires in his hospital room.

No question, Stephens is in a tough one. Chronic problems with the emphysema and a lung infection have taken a dreadful toll on the Kentuckian, who numbers 63 years in the game in one fashion or another.

During those decades, Stephens rose to become perhaps the sport's most celebrated conditioner. The hard work, often refusing to yield when the red light was on, has collared "the master."

Always a tough guy, he spoke quietly and admitted that this time, he's "in a real tight one."

Sheer exhaustion has teamed up with the illness, leaving him weak and peaked. Dr. David Richardson, who has brought Woody through many close scrapes, has advised him to remain bedfast at least through this Sunday before returning to his home on Long Island, N.Y.

Oxygen is being provided to combat his shortness of breath along with antibiotics to overcome the lung infection.

"I didn't feel well in Florida this past winter," said Stephens. "We shipped to Keeneland and I felt worse. The weather was going up and down with some rapid changes between 80 and 40 degrees and it got me. We ran several horses on closing day at Keeneland and it got me down. I came on over here the next day and went into the hospital.

"I've got to think of myself now and not my horses. I don't like it, but it has to be done. I haven't talked to my assistant (Sandy Bruno) in New York in nearly a week. Mary (Strickland) shipped the horses from Kentucky to New York on Monday. I don't have much choice. It has to be this way whether I like it or not."

Often in private conversations, Stephens has informed us of chronic ailments getting worse by inches. He has been battling emphysema for more than 20 years.

This time, it's more severe. His visitors and calls are screened and he's contemplating a major cutback in his operation. He normally carries 36 horses in New York.

He's attempted to cut back for several years, but horses of considerable promise, several which turned out to be stalwarts, have kept him at his task long past retirement age.

One of them is De la Devil, fourth in the Grade I Oaks which Stephens attempted to win for the sixth time.

Woody no more could have made the arduous trek through the large Oaks Day crowd than he could have walked on the sun. "I couldn't have gone to the track if I'd been with a horse in the Derby, he added. "I'm really weak and haven't been hungry since coming into this hospital. If I can lick it this time, I'm going to slow way down and quit pushing myself. I know I'm not getting any younger."

However, the fiery competitor still exists. He tabbed Summer Squall to win the Derby with Unbridled second but didn't have his wife, Lucille, box them in the exacta.

And about the Oaks? "I sure didn't think (Wayne) Lukas had two that could beat De La Devil. But damned if he didn't."

That's Woody Stephens, down but not out.

BLACK TIE TESTIMONIAL
SHOWS WOODY'S BACK IN FORM

NOVEMBER, 1991

LOUISVILLE, Ky. — Last Saturday's $3 million Breeders' Cup Classic wasn't the only Black Tie Affair of the week.

On Tuesday preceeding the race, the Kentucky Lung Association honored Hall of Fame trainer Woody Stephens at a black tie testimonial dinner at the Seelbach Hotel.

It was a good thing, and for much more than the $25,000 raised for this worthwhile charity. For it brought together about 350 people from various walks of life, many of them horseracing novices.

The $125 donation per person was small payment for those non-racing people who were in attendance, because in about 30 minutes, they were taken through Stephens' 63-year career with horses. It's a fascinating trip and a cherished part of racing history.

Chris Lincoln, who hosted the program, did a superb job of piecing together the past and present deeds of Stephens. A video, shown nationally earlier, was included in the program, along with a vast number of tributes from around the country.

These remarks were sent on video tape and included thoughts from Laffit Pincay Jr., Pat Day, Angel Cordero Jr., Bill Shoemaker, Sandy Bruno and *Daily Racing Form*'s Joe Hirsch.

A common theme ran through each of their testimonials: Woody Stephens not only is a great trainer of the thoroughbred horse, but a genuine nice guy.

As Dr. Robert Powell, a member of the American Lung

Association of Kentucky's board of directors, noted in his address to open the program, "Stephens has overcome great adversity in life both with horses and on his own. But nowhere has he displayed more courage than overcoming his illness."

To set the record straight, it's no secret that this writer and Stephens have been friends for many years.

We recall that dreadful spring of 1990 when Stephens outfinished his longtime foe, emphysema, in a stiff drive at nearby Norton Hospital. It was a close call but the subsequent quadruple bypasss surgery appears to have been successful.

Woody never will have 40 horses and a barnful of promising 2-year-olds again, although he probably could if he wanted them. It's just that he realizes he can no longer devote the necessary time.

So at the end of this week, he'll send his string of 10 to Hialeah for the winter, closely followed by himself and his best friend and bride of more than 50 years, Lucille.

We recall the day after Unbridled swept to victory on the stretch turn to win the 1990 Kentucky Derby. Many in the pressbox knew that Stephens had been hospitalized a couple of days earlier. Few, though, knew the severity of the matter.

Chatting with Mrs. Stephens on the telephone to get Woody's updated condition, we sensed that the jury was held in chambers, so to speak.

The conversation went something like this. "Lucille, would it be possible to come see him just for a minute? You know, I'm not looking for a story. It's purely personal."

"I'll ask him," she replied, and did. So, on a cool, dreary, rainy morning after the world's greatest race, we went to Norton Hospital and left doubtful that we'd be crossing paths with this hardboot from Stanton, Ky., again.

He was a mere ghost of himself, but the watch, depicting the five consecutive Belmont Stakes winners he'd saddled, hung on his wrist.

That sad scene and the lengthy discussion we had about life, all flashed back to mind last Tuesday night as Stephens, decked out in a tuxedo with Lucille by his side, weaved through the crowd, shaking hands and thoroughly enjoying himself. It was good, pure, honest and real.

And Stephens showed with one crack that he's enjoying life again.

Although much has been made of a longstanding feud

he's had with Wayne Lukas, it's way overplayed. While good natured barbs have been exchanged, it's more like humorous banter than a shootout at the OK Corral.

Anyway, thinking back to the hospital scene, I remember Stephens assessing the 1990 Kentucky Oaks. His filly, De la Devil, finished fourth. Lukas won the race with Seaside Attraction. In fact, Lukas-trained fillies finished first and third.

From his hospital bed, Woody jabbered; "Even if I didn't win the Oaks, damn if I thought Lukas had two that could beat me."

Well, last Tuesday night, at the tail end of the program, Stephens fielded questions from the audience. One person asked, "What would you have done had you not been a successful trainer?"

Without blinking an eye, Stephens quipped, "Probably would've walked hots for Lukas."

It brought the house down.

Maybe Stephens could have been a comedian if he hadn't been around horses as a kid.

It's only one opinion, but I'm glad he's just a plain old horse trainer. And from the look of the other night, Woody's feeling pretty good about it too.

WOODY STEPHENS:
THOROUGHBRED OF A MAN

AUGUST, 1998

LEXINGTON, Ky. — It's not proper for us mortals to suggest that one of us has lived too long. Yet, for those who knew, loved and revered Hall of Fame trainer Woody Stephens, it's difficult to comprehend that his final days were anything close to the once magnificent life he led that was a beacon in the night to many.

At the end, he was old, terribly ill and merely a shadow of the great figure who at one time could produce more enthusiasm and zest for life in an hour than most will know in 10 years.

Many people loved him and some, believe it or not, feared him, especially those who had to saddle a horse against him in a big race. But everyone involved with racing respected him. As far as I know, nobody ever disliked him during his 84 years of life.

Only the most fortunate of men can appreciate their own success and at the same time enjoy it. Stephens was among that selected few.

Woody entered racing when it was a game for tough, uneducated people who hacked out a living and the stuffed-shirt elitists who had it all. There was no middleman.

Stephens saw the two parties merge and the sport become respectable. He lived to become the very embodiment of the game's integrity and loved every second of a career spanning seven decades.

He had an innocent vanity that traced to his roots as a

Kentucky farmboy who emerged from a sharecropper's existence to become the most sought after trainer in history.

There isn't much that hasn't already been said or written about his record five consecutive Belmont Stakes victories, two Kentucky Derby wins or the 11 champions he trained.

Instead, I choose to remember his greatest attributes: a deep love for people and horses and a reputation for steadfast loyalty to his friends. One of the greatest privileges I'll ever have is being included on that list.

In June of 1986, Danzig Connection won Stephens' fifth Belmont Stakes. Six weeks later, Stephens made his only visit to Ellis Park.

For two hours in 90-degree conditions, a block-long line of Stephens' admirers remained constant as he signed everything from books to $100 bills. He delighted in meeting fellow Kentuckians as an all-time Ellis Park Wednesday record crowd of 4,600 turned out.

During the funeral, Seth Hancock, president of Claiborne Farm, eulogized Stephens by saying: "Horses knew him, they trusted him and they ran their hearts out for him."

That's because Stephens himself was a thoroughbred of a man.

He never lost his temper, never harbored a grudge and was immediately sorry for doing or saying anything out of the ordinary.

Most historic figures have a single great moment when they achieved what no one else has.

Woody Stephens had several such moments, thus making himself indispensable to the current day success of racing.

All his life, Stephens loved to take trips. And, when he wasn't accompanied by Lucille, his lovely wife of 60 years, he enjoyed behing with friends who he affectionately called his boys.

This time, for the final journey, a lot of them went along. For us, it was a friendship that could end only one way. Like it did last Saturday.

Editor's note: Funeral services were held on Wednesday in Lexington, Ky., for Hall of Fame trainer Woody Stephens, who died on Saturday from complications of chronic emphysema. He was 84. Courier & Press Turf Writer Cliff Guilliams was a close friend of Stephens' and wrote this after the services.

JACK PRICE'S LEGENDARY
EXPLOITS WILL LIVE FOREVER

JUNE, 1995

LOUISVILLE, Ky. — When Jack Price died Wednesday in Miami at age 87, the obituary could have bestowed upon him the honorary title of "World's Greatest Kentucky Derby Fan."

The obit briefly told that Price trained Carry Back, the champion 3-year-old male of 1961. And that during the colt's career, from 1960-63, he became racing's fourth millionaire, earning $1,241,165 on a 21-11-11 record from 61 starts.

Modestly bred by Saggy from the non-winning mare, Joppy, Carry Back was conceived in Maryland and foaled in Florida. He won the Cowdin and Remsen at 2 and followed with the Kentucky Derby, Flamingo, Everglades, Florida Derby and Preakness at 3.

His Triple Crown bid was dashed in the Belmont when he finished seventh as the 2-5 favorite.

Nevertheless, it ws quite a feat for a colt whose mating came about only because Price called in an unpaid board bill of $150 and added $150 of his own cash, which made him the owner of the mare. The stallion stood for $750, but Price got a discount fee of $400 by breeding two other mares. The other two foals didn't amount to much.

Carry Back's rags-to-riches accomplishments were achieved through a hard-charging, blue-collar style. Those glorious efforts made him "the People's Choice," words that were inscribed on his tombstone when his ashes were moved from their original Ocala, Fla., resting place to the courtyard outside the Kentucky Derby Museum at Churchill Downs.

Carry Back was named for an accounting term and not for Jack Price being "carried back" after too many cocktails, as many thought. At age 4, the colt won the Metropolitan, Monmouth and Whitney Handicaps.

Price was an astute businessman who made an early bundle in the tool and die business, creating aircraft parts in his native Cleveland, Ohio. He also was a genuine sportsman. And, through trial and error, he made himself a thorough, knowledgeable horseman.

During the 1962 season, Carry Back traveled 3,000 miles over the Atlantic Ocean to run at Longchamp in the Prix de l'Arc Triomphe. He remains the only Kentucky Derby winner to attempt the feat. Price's brave undertaking was undone by a "quite unsatisfactory ride" from an Australian, Scobie Beasley. The colt finished 10th, beaten about six lengths.

Brought back from stud duty at 5, Carry Back won the Trenton Handicap before calling it quits on the track.

Price could have further etched his name in history as one of only three ever to breed, own and train a Kentucky Derby winner. Thomas McDowell in 1902 was the first with Alan-a-Dale. T.P. Hayes followed in 1913 with Donerail. But for clerical purposes, the stretch-running Carry Back ran in the name of Katherine "Kay" Price, Jack's beloved wife of 55 years. She died in February of 1987 after suffering several years from cancer, and he missed her dreadfully.

There were some famous exchanges between Jack and Kay. One happened before the 1961 Derby. A Louisville, Ky., newspaper sensationalized Price's pre-Derby thoughts.

"I got to town very, very early to train the horse," Jack recalled one evening. "Only the local press guys were at the track. They asked me if I was excited about being at the Derby. With tongue in cheeck, I said something like, 'I wasn't a racing bigshot or an oil man and I certainly didn't come from a wealthy family. I was mostly interested in the winner's share of the purse.'"

The story made the wire services and Mrs. Price, still in Florida, read the account which stated: "Jack Price should be tarred and feathered and run out of town." Kay called and told Jack: "You keep your mouth shut or I'll get another trainer."

Carry Back did the talking on Derby Day, rallying from 13 lengths back after a mile to win by three-quarters of a length under John Sellers. At that moment, the Prices realized that they'd caught lightning in a bottle and were living a long, cherished dream.

In the early 1950s, Price sold his business to his brothers. He started training his own horses in 1955. He estimated he ruined "about $200,000 worth of horses" before learning the business. He called his own shots and loved every second of it.

He missed only two Derbys — in 1970, and this year — after his 1961 triumph. He came to hold the grand event in the deepest reverence.

"I'd have been just a statistic if not for Carry Back," Price would say. "The horse changed our entire lives. We had two daughters but came to regard Carry Back as our son."

Price gave his Kentucky Derby trophy and many items of memorabilia to the Derby Museum. And it is with Carry Back, on the grounds of Churchill Downs, that Price recently told friends he'd like to be buried.

One horse made him famous. But it was people like Jim Bolus, Chick Lang, Billy Reed, Joe Hirsch, Jack Wilson, Bill Phillips and many, many others who went out of their way to attain Price's company.

The gifted little man loved people and they loved him. He regularly visited the stable area during Derby week and relished coming to the press box to renew old friendships and make new ones.

Price wasn't supposed to be a statesman or orator and didn't pretend to be. But when he spoke, people listened. He was a wonderful friend, a polished professional, a keen judge of whiskey and a man of simple honesty.

When Carry Back failed in the Belmont, a case of champagne arrived in the pressbox anyway. The attached card read: "You hailed me in victory, now drink to me in defeat. (Signed) Carry Back."

This proves the essential thing about Jack Price: He was one of the most charming men you'll ever meet. We shall miss him, lots.

BOLUS LEAVES LEGACY
OF EXCELLENCE, INTEGRITY

MAY, 1997

LOUISVILLE, Ky. — Springtime in Kentucky will never be the same. And this city isn't what it once was because Jim Bolus, the absolute authority on Kentucky Derby history, isn't here anymore.

Bolus, who collapsed and died suddenly Wednesday night from a heart attack at age 54, was one of the greatest men I've known.

The news came late from his son, Jim Jr. Better known as "Bo," he's a bright young lawyer in Louisville. And, in a loving way several years ago, we'd dubbed his father "The Doctor of Derbyology."

Wednesday, young Bolus said simply into the receiver: "The Doctor of Derbyology is gone. He bit the big one."

Then Bo provided the still unbelievable details.

How could this be? Jim Bolus skipped his trip to the recent Preakness Stakes to begin a family vacation in the Caribbean.

Young Bolus and his wife, Tana, are the proud parents of a strapping toddler named Eli. He was named after Jim Bolus' father and had become the apple of his grandfather's eye.

Jim was alongside this desk last Sunday, flashing that ever-present grin, joking about whether his necktie was suitable while providing a 94-year-old news clip on the 1903 Derby.

He was an enormous talent, a loving family man and a gentleman of the first rank. One of the highest privileges

I've had was knowing, working and counting on him in situations only true friends can relate. I shall cherish the honor all my life.

I don't mourn for Jimmy. He's in a more peaceful place. I mourn for the racing industry and society in general. They are both poorer without him and shall miss him more and more as the days pass.

Besides his family and talent, the greatest thing Bolus possessed was his heart and spirit, which accounted for his all-world kindness. Next to that was his humility. He hated the spotlight and shied from taking bows. He thought grandstanding was classless.

Before he gained fame as a Derby historian, Bolus spent nearly 25 years working on newspapers here. He prepped at the *The Courier-Journal* while earning his degree from the University of Louisville. Upon graduation, he hooked on with *The Louisville Times.* When it, like many afternoon papers, folded, he returned to *The Courier-Journal.*

Bolus was a newsman of the purest sense. He was a digger for truth and a stickler for accuracy, often making a dozen telephone calls to clarify facts in a single sentence. He knew his job was to take the reader behind the scenes.

Before graduating from Louisville Male High School in 1961, he'd been recruited by numerous college football powers but settled on the University of Kentucky. When the UK coach was fired after Bolus' freshman year, he and many of his teammates detested the replacement and left, too. He enrolled at U of L and never played again.

Every fall, though, he'd follow the college teams and backed his choices with his pocketbook.

Bolus had principles as an athlete and in 1987 left *The Courier-Journal* because of the same guidelines. Proceedings there were spinning into a corporate maze. The action sickened Bolus, and he quit. "I'd had enough and wasn't going to ruin my life with that system," he told me. "It was wrong what was going on, and I wasn't going to take it. A man has to do what he believes in."

Racing benefitted most from that decision because Bolus spent the last 10 years of his life religiously researching the sport. "I'm always learning something new," he confirmed last month. "I'll find out something about a Derby from 20 years ago and can't believe it hasn't been written before."

At the suggestion of *Daily Racing Form*'s executive columnist, Joe Hirsch, Bolus in 1974 wrote *Run for the Roses:*

the First 100 years. They teamed in 1994 to complete *Kentucky Derby: Chance of a lifetime.*

Bolus wrote five other books on the Derby. The last one, *Derby Magic,* reached bookstores last month. Light, yet eloquent and full of not-your-everyday Derby stories, *Kentucky Derby Stories, Remembering the Derby, Derby Fever,* and *Derby Dreams* will be read and re-read annually.

Bolus saw his first Derby in 1952 and witnessed every one that followed except 1964, when he worked the sports desk. Through hard work and insurmountable credibility, he made himself into a big man in the racing industry. Yet, you didn't have to be big-time to be his friend.

Upon inspection, though, his close associates included a Hall of Fame roster of guys like Hirsch, Nick Zito, Billy Reed, D. Wayne Lukas, Jimmy Jones, Woody Stephens, Sonny Hine, Ted Bassett, Pat Day, Eddie Arcaro, Wayne Perkey, Don Brumfield, Jack Price, Keene Daingerfield, Bernie Hettel, Bill Greely, Bob Baffert, Seth Hancock, Dan Farley and many, many more.

They didn't always agree on everything. But friendships likes those end one way. Like they did Wednesday night.

BOLUS WOULD HAVE
LOVED SKIP AWAY'S CLASSIC

NOVEMBER, 1997

LOUISVILLE, Ky. — Chapter seven of *Derby Magic*, the last of eight books authored by our late friend, Jim Bolus, is titled: "Diary of a champion, Skip Away."

It's the book's longest and most detailed section, entailing 21 pages of thought, heartfelt emotion, fact and feeling.

Bolus, the world's foremost Kentucky Derby authority, ex-newspaperman and secretary-treasurer of the National Turf Writers Association, died suddenly on May 14 from a heart attack at age 54.

In a sense, the chapter on Skip Away was almost as if Bolus were saying farewell to the gray colt who's captured the hearts of millions.

He began his text on Skip Away this way: "When trainer Hubert 'Sonny' Hine brought Skip Away to Kentucky in the spring of 1996, it was my privilege to follow the colt's progress during his time at Keeneland and Churchill Downs. Checking each day for a month with Sonny was quite a learning experience for me, not only about horses but about life. He and his wife, Carolyn, in whose name Skip Away raced, could write a book about how to enjoy horses and life at the same time.

"In more than 30 years of covering the Kentucky Derby, I've never been closer to a trainer and owner than I was to Sonny and Carolyn in the month leading up to the Derby. If I don't enjoy another such experience the rest of my life, at least I will always have the memory of this lovely

couple who came to Kentucky, enjoyed Southern hospital-
ity, and made such a favorable impression on the people
they met."

The chapter concludes: "Skip Away was tough in the
races down the road. He won the Ohio Derby, Haskell Invi-
tational, Woodbine Million, Jockey Club Gold Cup (defeating the celebrated Cigar) and earned the Eclipse Award as
champion 3-year-old colt. The award couldn't have gone to
two finer people, Carolyn and Sonny Hine. Thanks for the
memories."

During the week leading up to the Nov. 8 Breeders' Cup,
many of Bolus' friends, headed by Carolyn and Sonny Hine,
were thinking and talking about him.

They were still talking about the great journalist after
the B.C. Classic, too. And Bolus would have loved the outcome after the way Skip Away overpowered his opposition
by six lengths in a brilliant performance.

Earlier, during B.C. week, Bolus' wife, Suzanne, and son
Jim Jr. (Bo), were at Hollywood Park to receive the National
Turf Writers' prestigious Joe Palmer Award for meritorious
service to racing and the Walter Haight Award for excellence in turf journalism.

The NTWA membership voted the awards to Bolus post-
humously. It is the only time in the organization's history
for a dual winner.

After agonizing over whether to supplement Skip Away
into the $4 million B.C. Classic for $480,000, the Hines decided to dedicate the race to Sonny's late father, Arthur,
and Bolus.

"My dad gave me a wonderful foundation with horses,"
Hine said. "He saddled his last winner in 1972. I have the
winner's circle picture on my office wall. And I never had a
better friend than Jim Bolus. The chapter he dedicated to
Skip Away was very emotional to my wife and me. He sent
us a book, and we cried when reading it.

"Jim was the kind of person whose presence and understanding touched people. I never knew a kinder soul. But if
anyone ever talked unfavorably about Skip Away, Jim took
it personal and would be ready to come to blows. He loved
the horse as much as we did.

"That's why we ran him in the Classic. Not for the money.
But for our love and a lot of other people's love of the horse.
We don't belong to country clubs, and lead a simple life.
Like after the Classic, we had a club sandwich and went to
bed, same as if we hadn't been there."

Bolus met Hine in 1976 when he was training Cojak for the Kentucky Derby. They immediately became friends. And once, when Hine's health was unsatisfactory, Bolus accepted a trophy for him from the United Thoroughbred Trainer's Association.

Next Friday, the Kentucky Thoroughbred Owners Inc. will honor the Bolus family at its annual awards dinner with the Warner L. Jones Jr. Award as Horseman of the Year. Hine was uncertain whether he could make the trip here but was checking on flight arrangements from Miami.

Whether Carolyn and Sonny make it to Louisville for the KTO dinner isn't the point because in spirit, they'll be here regardless. Remember, they dedicated the Classic to Arthur Hine and Jim Bolus. "It might have been those two who guided Skip Away in the Classic. At least I'd like to think it was," Hine concluded.

JERRY ROMANS: THE "PHANTOM" WHO STOOD OUT

NOVEMBER, 2000

About midway through 1981's Ellis Park meeting, the banner headline over one of the late Don Bernhardt's daily features in *The Evansville Courier* read: "Phantom trainer strikes again at Ellis."

That afternoon, someone asked Bernhardt: "How can you call Jerry Romans a phantom trainer? Together, you two and Ed Flint (former HBPA president) have been battling the Kentucky legislature over tax relief for Ellis. And you've been friends for years. You even knew Jerry when he sat the bench in the early 1960s for Kentucky Wesleyan behind 'King' Kelly Coleman.

"Jerry doesn't wear a mask or sneak around like a phantom. He's a good guy. Works hard at two jobs in order to take care of his kids. In fact, Dale, one of his young sons, is really into racing. Might be a top trainer some day. So what gives?"

Bernhardt, always politically correct, laughingly replied: "You're right on all counts. I used the word 'phantom' because he's going to win Ellis' training title, and he should make a more conscientious effort to be in the winner's circle. Just looks better when the boss is there."

Romans' stable won that title with 23 victories and again in 1982 with 21 wins.

The 'phantom' story further explained that Romans was born, raised and lived in Louisville, Ky. He'd graduated from Shawnee High School and was an outstanding high school basketball player. He'd transferred from Kentucky Wesleyan to the University of Louisville, graduated from there, taught school awhile, and coached roundball at the AAU level.

Durings summers, the majority of Romans' large stable was based at Ellis Park with an assistant and one of his sons.

Bernhardt also reported that the elder Romans dearly loved Ellis Park and Western Kentucky. But, because he held a fulltime job as a supervisor for Durkee Foods in the Derby City, he visited primarily on weekends, bringing down the stable's payroll when one of his better horses, like Field House or Captain's Rose, was running.

In those days, Jerry Romans was a racing secretary's best friend. He dealt primarily in cheap claimers, filling the entries by running them once a week, regardless of weather or track condition.

On Thanksgiving Day, Romans died peacefully at his Louisville residence. He was only 58. These stories and many others came to mind. Like the year his guest at the Derby was basketball analyst Dick Vitale. What an act they put on in the stable area.

And who'll ever forget the 1988 Kentucky Derby day incident when an error was made identitying the Romans-trained Blairwood, who won the first race on the card and paid $71 under the name Briarwood.

That incredible snafu caused Romans to be suspended for 10 months by the Kentucky Racing Commission. Later, he received a $50,000 judgment from that body after a jury agreed he was slandered by its chairman, Lyle G. Robey.

This is America, though. When a guy's knocked down like Jerry was, he can get up, walk down Main Street, and his true friends are still there no matter what.

Romans bounced back. In 1995, after expanding and putting together a package of horses to train and own in a partnership with the late Allen Paulson and Frank L. Jones Jr., Romans enjoyed his best overall year, establishing personal records for wins and purses earned.

He continued to roll until July 25, 1998, the day he suffered a cerebral hemorrhage and stroke from which he never recovered. Cancer struck him the fatal blow.

Romans' parents weren't racetrackers. They were in real estate. So for a guy who didn't see his first race until age 22 and bought his first horse for $500, he accomplished a great deal.

Romans won a training title at Turfway Park to go along with his two from Ellis Park. During Churchill's ultra-tough spring meetings of 1989, 1990, 1992 and 1995, Romans' work for Jones, his primary client and longtime friend, was good enough for Jones to be the track's leading owner.

Jones' titles were due in part to Romans realizing during the mid-1980s that there was no future in a stable full of bottom claimers. So he consistently improved his stock. Overall, he did well enough to saddle 199 winners at Churchill Downs, to rank 15th all-time.

While Jerry Romans never won a training crown at Churchill, son Dale tied for 1999's spring title. At 34, Dale Romans has become one of the top young horsemen making a circuit of Kentucky, Gulfstream Park and Saratoga.

Father and son were tremendously good friends. And Jerry's pride in Dale was something to behold. Jerry was confident that a couple years of seasoning and a decent horse or two were all Dale needed to reach the big-time.

Jerry wasn't always right. But he was about Dale, who gives most of the credit to his old man for making it to the next level.

In the final analysis, "Old" Romans, as we called Jerry in the presence of Dale, was a fun-loving man with a soft chuckle, dry humor and bushy eyebrows who could get the job done with any man's horse. He worked like hell. And he earned his eternal rest.

ANTLEY COULDN'T OUTRIDE DEMONS

DECEMBER, 2000

On Saturday, in Elloree, S.C., Chris Antley's family and friends buried the two-time Kentucky Derby winning jockey.

On Dec. 3, Antley was killed in his Pasadena, Calif. home. The autoposy said the cause of death was "severe trauma to the head."

Officials are investigating the matter as a homicide, looking closely at Timothy W. Tyler Jr., a former house guest. *(Eventually the death was ruled an accidental overdose.)*

There are innumerable stories — heartwarming and disgusting — that can be told about Antley.

Here are several tame ones, which hopefully will furnish you some insight about a guy who never knew fear in the saddle, yet had trouble knowing what was best for himself.

He did most things impulsively, choosing the wrong path as often as he did the correct one. Few people in racing ever have experienced the tremendous elation and miserable, lower-than-dirt lows, that Antley did.

He burst onto the scene at age 17 in 1984 at Pimlico. In his first year, Antley was among the circuit leaders. Headlines called him things like "ace apprentice." And he was.

In 1985, he piloted 469 winners, more than any other rider in North America. One day in 1987, he rode a record nine winners in one day — four at Aqueduct and five at the Meadowlands.

In 1989, he rode at least one winner for 64 consecutive days.

That was a season after he was suspended for the first time for cocaine use. He'd been battling substance abuse and related emotional problems since 1988.

In December of 1988, Antley entered a drug rehab program for the first time, making his problems public. His second drug-related suspension came in September of 1989. Again, he entered rehab.

Back riding in April of 1990, he had a big year, sustained his sobriety and won the 1991 Kentucky Derby aboard Strike the Gold. But, with big money at his disposal and a swaggering reputation as a top race rider, Antley became somewhat snooty, arrogant. And his career spiraled downward during the mid-1990s until he was overweight, both out of shape and out of a job.

In September of 1997, Antley decided to make a comeback. His scales read about 150 pounds. He spent the next 16 months working and running — sometimes 25 miles a day — toward getting his body in shape and career back on track. Weight isn't the only thing he lost. He ditched the chip on his shoulder and replaced it with boyish enthusiasm.

One of the first to recognize Antley's effort was trainer Wayne Lukas. And, after Jerry Bailey opted to ride another horse instead of Charismatic in the 1999 Kentucky Derby, Lukas turned to Antley. Lukas did so because Antley had earlier flown to the Fair Grounds in New Orleans to ride a colt in a non-descript stakes. The horse, Mountain Range, lost. But Lukas told Antley afterwards, "I'll make it up to you."

The day before Charismatic won the Lexington Stakes, his final prep before the Derby, Lukas told Antley: "Watch Charismatic. He's a different horse than when you last saw him. He'll win the Lexington. And he'll get the Derby distance (1 1/4 miles), too."

Before giving Antley the mount, Lukas asked him: "Will you listen to me, move exactly when I tell you to and have total confidence in this horse? If you do, he'll win."

The former bad boy and ex-claiming horse won the roses and became racing's story of the year.

Never will another Derby pass that I won't recall how the kid wept openly after Charismatic won.

Many people might also remember Antley's humane spirit during that year's Belmont Stakes. Going for the first Triple Crown in 31 years, Charismatic broke down in the stretch and was pulled up lame past the wire. Antley hopped off and saved the horse from further injury by cradling his foreleg until the equine ambulance arrived.

Bottom line: Antley, who leaves a mother, father, brother, new wife and unborn child, was a good kid who made more than his share of personal mistakes. Unfortunately, they proved to be fatal.

DEATH OF JACK WILLIAMS LEAVES VOID AT ELLIS PARK

APRIL, 1999

Ellis Park won't be the same track without Jack Williams.

Williams died at age 63 Tuesday at his west Evansville home following a seven-month bout with liver cancer. He was the kind of steadfastly loyal friend who everyone should be lucky enough to have during a lifetime.

Whether he was officiating high school football and basketball games, teaching journalism at Reitz High School or running Ellis Park's mutuel department, Williams was a great talent. He also was a great gentleman.

The only thing greater than his talent was his heart. And his gentle courtesy, world class kindness and humility weren't many lengths behind. It was a privilege knowing him and going around with him as a friend. I'm grateful for the lessons he taught.

In his final days, he was extremely gaunt and terribly ill. Heavily medicated to alleviate excruciating pain, he couldn't recognize family members. Sitting in a stupor and being unaware of goings on wasn't the articulate, high-spirited, fun-loving Williams we knew. So I don't mourn for him, who welcomed peace. I mourn for us.

Williams enjoyed all sports, especially Indiana University basketball when the Hoosiers were winning. He and his wife, Benita, put their two sons through IU. But it's also true that, given his druthers, he'd as soon be watching and wagering on the horses at Ellis Park.

It's a fact that when Williams first visited Ellis during

the 1950s as a Bosse High School student, the facility was a joke among racetracks nationally. The barns were pitiful, the current clubhouse hadn't been built, the grandstand paint was peeling and the horses were — to be both kind and accurate — slow.

However, there were those once famous hot dogs with relish and Sterling draft beer which, along with the mutuel windows, were the necessities of life for patrons during that era.

Williams also found that people there were friendly and the informal aura captivated him. So, in 1960, after graduating from the University of Evansville, he applied at Ellis for summer employment in the mutuel department. In a spiritual sense, he never left.

Race meetings ran only 29 days then. And there was no modern Am-Tote 300 Cash-Sell system, or Inter-Track Wagering or Full-Card Simulcasting. Williams' first job was working the $2 show window. In 1966, he moved up to the $10 line and in 1974 stepped into the mutuel office.

The extra effort he made learning the clerical, calculating and assignment portions of how a mutuel department operates came in handy. In 1982, he was named Ellis' director of mutuels. How good was he? Extremely good. And professional enough to keep the position through four different track owners and five general managers, becoming a major figure not only at Ellis, but the entire Kentucky circuit.

What a shame that he couldn't have worked at least a season with Ellis' new general manager Paul Kuerzi. He's a mutuel man, too, and a grand fellow. They'd have gotten along famously.

But, with his health rapidly declining, Williams worked his last day in October. On March 10, he visited Ellis for the final time, lunched with buddies in the clubhouse and, in a heartwarming scene, said farewell to many friends and former employees who visited his table.

There was a period when Williams made Ellis' morning line. He also did a stint making selections in *The Evansville Press* under the title "Railbird." And from 1989-1990, he and I voiced our choices for each race every day to the world via Ellis' Inter-Track Wagering signal.

One story that must be told happened last Labor Day at Ellis. It involved the longstanding tradition of a pressbox bar. The scribes who fight the daily battle along with a couple of their cronies and several horsemen have a libation or two after the last race each night. They stash their empties in a closet, keeping a running tally while attempting to surpass the previous year's total.

After each meeting concluded, Williams always would pick up the empties, take them home, and along with his neighbor and our longtime compadre, Jerry Canterbury, use them to bottle homemade wine.

Anyway, last Labor Day, the pressbox boys had tied the record for empties and called Williams' office, asking him to visit. He'd been diagnosed as terminal and they sensed that it would be his final day of live racing and the last time they'd be together. They wanted to honor Jack with a farewell cocktail. Additionally, out of deep respect, they wanted him to finish off the record-breaking bottle. It was a touching scene, kind of like a team calling timeout to allow an old running back to enter the game and crash in from the one-yard-line for a touchdown on the last carry of his career.

With that ever-present grin, Williams bravely entered the room. The record-breaking bottle had "one little old taste" left. A new record was reached to a round of applause as Jack mixed a final vodka and tonic and put the empty in the closet.

There are August mornings at Ellis when ground fog is so dense you can't see the tote board from the stands. Sometimes, workouts are canceled. It's eerie, too, because the fog also fills the area beneath the stands. Ruth Adkins ran Ellis Park for nearly 30 years, retiring in 1985. She used to say that on those mornings, God was using the fog to hide a party within the infield that the ghosts of Ellis' old guard were having.

"Only the great boosters, the true friends of Ellis Park are allowed to participate," explained Adkins. "The guests are those who gave of everything of themselves to make the track succeed. Like Mr. Ellis, Miss Anna Fisher, Lester Yeager, Dan Scism, Don Bernhardt, Chic Anderson, my late husband (Clyde Adkins), Ray Gates and Leroy Tauzin to name a few..."

If Adkins' assessments are correct, the select group will welcome a new member.

FOSTER WAS
READY FOR END OF RIDE

SEPTEMBER, 1996

HENDERSON, Ky. — The jockey called this office.

That immediately tells you that Darrell Foster was a veteran in 1992 when the conversation occurred.

You see, jockeys who are young men don't normally waste time calling sportswriters who are male. Seasoned old pros do because they have been in enough tough situations to greatly appreciate friends who don't ask for favors or free drinks.

Foster called me to say that he would finish the 1992 summer meeting at Ellis Park. But there wouldn't be any more. He would ride until Labor Day and hang up his tack. He added that there weren't many races left in his beat-up body, and he was uncertain about what to do with the rest of his life.

Primarily, his fear was like that of special old men who die pitifully, although they've been extremely brave in their youth. These kind know how to win and lose with equal dignity. But there are no guidelines for an athlete when he retires into an afterlife following his sporting career. And, for the record, dignity is something that Darrell Foster always has possessed.

He often illustrated that but never more so than in 1986. Trainer Gerge Baker, also retired, was stabled at Ellis Park with the wonderful mare named Queen Alexandra. A multiple stakes winner of more than $1 million, Queen Alexandra had developed a problem at the starting gate.

Foster and Baker were longtime friends, and the rider vol-

unteered to solve the Queen's mystery. To show his appreciation, Baker gave Foster the mount for the $100,000 Ellis Park
Breeders' Cup and $200,000 Gardenia Stakes.

Up front, Baker told Foster that Don Brumfield would
go back on the mare after the meeting concluded. On
Foster's recommendation, Baker had the assistant starters
begin blindfolding Queen Alexandra before loading her into
the gate. Queen Alexandra won both stakes and still is hailed
as one of the best horses ever to run at Ellis Park.

From 1977 through 1992, Foster won a lot of races here
and other places. So whatever happened to him?

Nothing, really. And he actually never left. The mast-
head on the daily track program reads, "Assistant clerk of
scales: Darrell Foster."

He holds the same position at Churchill Downs and
Dueling Grounds. The job came open because of the overlap with Churchill, and Foster has become a mainstay.

"Riding 16 years took its toll on me," said Foster, 45.
"Near the end, I learned a lot about life and people. You'll
have some that will stick with you, and others won't. It hurt
me emotionally when I lost outfits. But looking back, I was
getting injured all the time and wasn't as good as I used to
be.

"I remember late in my last meeting, I'd only ridden 38
horses. Hell, I rode that many a week in the old days. It was
time to go. But you know, to this day, I still love riding and
always will."

The fact that he ever arrived is a story in itself. Foster
grew up in nearby Philpot, Ky., a whistlestop outside
Owensboro that produced riders such as Foster's cousin,
Willie Lee Johnson, and, brothers Patrick and Joe Johnson,
unrelated to Willie Lee.

Foster's parents were against his becoming a jockey.
They'd seen the wild life Willie Lee led and didn't want that
for their son. But, at age 25, Foster could stand it no longer.
He was working at an auto parts store and helping on the
family farm. He left to be with thoroughbreds.

He'd been breaking and riding ponies for a fellow named
Cy Smith and had ridden at county fairs and in training
races. Ellis Park regulars Charlie Hundley and Shirley Greene
took Foster under their tutelage, and the rest, as they say,
is history.

In addition to Kentucky tracks, Foster rode successfully
at Sportsman's Park, Hawthorne, Tampa Bay Downs and
Oaklawn Park.

Besides mending from injuries, the hardest thing he ever endured was watching horses he'd previously won on do so under another jockey. "That was tough to swallow," he confided. "But I realize now that nothing lasts forever. All things, good and bad, have an end."

Various athletes play tactical games with time. For example, some veterans keep their weights beneath what they were years earlier, others anticipate or prepare better by reviewing countless experiences.

As to Foster, he's never been better mentally, physically or emotionally. And because he worked hard at it, he's successfully made the switch from jockey to official. In this spot, he'll last a long time.

"PAPA" JOE UNFRIED: NICEST TOUGH GUY

AUGUST, 2000

Art Acker was the first to go. Then Archie Owen died. Last Saturday, after a 10-year fight with cancer, death claimed Joe Unfried.

So now it's over. The three men most responsible for making football respectable at Evansville's Bosse High School are gone. They were my coaches. And for me, they were the palace guard. A symbol of invincibility. Fall evenings at Enlow Field never will be the same.

During the 1960s and 1970s, when Owen was winning renown as Bosse's head football coach, the varsity was only one of his responsibilites.

He also coached tennis and wrestling, and taught Sunday School. In those days, his only actual assistant was Unfried. While Owen handled the linemen and tight ends, Unfried tutored the varsity backs and skill players.

Acker handled the junior varsity. He was sweet guy who always gave kids a break.

Most practices started with Owen giving preliminary instructions to the entire squad. Then we'd break into groups for individual drills. An hour or so later, Owen would sarcastically shout across the field something like, "Coach Unfried, would you be kind enough bring those cupcakes over here. It's time for team drills."

Unfried would reply, "Hell, Arch, these kids are hardly warmed up. None of them are even bleeding yet!"

Owen and Unfried played the "good cop/bad cop" act to perfection. Owen wanted everyone to like him, rarely disciplined anyone off the field and smiled as much as possible regardless of how infuriated he was.

It took me several years to realize that he left the dirty work to Unfried. Because if a player was unruly in another teacher's class, Unfried might pay him a personal visit. Or if a guy's ego ballooned, Unfried would humble the loudmouth in seconds.

But that was window dressing. Actually, Unfried was a great bear of a man with an extraordinary heart and soft chuckle who loved his students as much as life. He was a gifted athlete and instructor, but his real strength was coaching the game of life. He understood people and their needs, treating them accordingly.

I can hear him now, bellowing a sermon on hard work, commitment and integrity.

Because of him, I've got an edge. Because I've found that in life, only 15 or 20 percent of the people do things right all the time. And whenever I'm tempted to loaf or cut corners, I see his eyes staring me down as he screams, "Mister, this is the right way to get the job done. Which way are you gonna to do it?"

His death draws such memories to mind. As a coach, educator and administrator, he was so skilled, tough, strong, competitive, durable and loyal. I figured he'd be doing something for charity, running a golf tournament or working part-time until he was at least 90. He was granted only 71 birthdays. But that was ample time for him to brighten the lives of everyone fortunate enough to know him.

I knew him for 32 years. And he was the niceest tough guy, or toughest nice guy, I've ever met.

Through the years, we remained close and talked often, including several times the past few months. The tumor in his throat grew, making it increasingly difficult to speak. The last time I called, I asked Lois, his wife of 49 years, if "Papa Joe" felt like talking. She said that 'he'd love to speak to one of his boys'.

His voice was no more than a harsh whisper. We didn't talk long, maybe 10 minutes. Before saying goodbye, he said, "Do me a favor, tell the guys I'll always love them."

That was his way of saying farewell. Being the man's man that he was, he never whimpered or asked for sympathy. He was optimistic until the end, certain that he'd whip the dreadful disease like he had everything else.

All of our turns will come and go. I'll conclude by saying, Papa Joe, for all the guys whose lives you touched, we love you, too. And may you walk in green pastures.

He fought the good fight. He earned it.

RUTH ADKINS, AFTER 37 YEARS, ENDS RUN AT ELLIS PARK

MAY, 1986

The Ellis era was concluded after 62 years on Sept. 2 when Ruth Adkins, one of only two women ever to manage a thoroughbred racing operation, walked through Ellis Park's south gate for the final time as an official.

It followed a meet during which every attendance and wagering record was established.

Because of a commitment to oversee the finances of Lester E. Yeager, former president of Ellis Park, Adkins won't return in a working capacity after 37 summers.

She became director of operations in 1966. The last 11 years were spent as executive vice-president, treasurer and general manager.

Yeager, 86, represented the heirs of James C. Ellis' estate and sold the facility to Roger and Lila Kumar in April of 1985. Yeager granted Adkins one summer away from his company desk to help the changing of the guard.

Yeager broke an arm in September and has been semi-confined since.

"I fully intended to work in public relations (at the track)," Adkins said. "I wouldn't have minded being associated with the blanket brigade, taking care of sponsored races. That way, I would have had the opportunity to deal with the public.

"But Lester said, 'You work for me. I put you in a home and an office near me to handle my business. I want you here, and not running off to the races.'

"I can't very well be at Ellis Park and answer Lester's questions about a farm at the same time. I made this obligation many, many years ago to take care of Mr. Yeager when his health failed. Like all good jockeys, I'll honor my first call."

Roger Kumar explained that although Adkins won't be a mainstay in any of the day day-to-day battles, he won't hesitate to seek her advice. "She'll always be involved," he said. "Whenever and wherever we have problems, she'll be the first to know.

"Lila and I have deep feelings and great respect for her. Ruth's experience is invaluable. She kept Ellis Park afloat during some bleak times. She fought off Churchill Downs and did the best she could with a facility that wasn't the best. She deserves an enormous pat on the back from the management and public she's served so well."

Adkins and her band of loyalists weathered many storms.

Besides the woeful overlap in racing dates with Churchill Downs during 1983-84, there were the normal power failures, jockey and horsemen strikes, streaks of 100-degree days and drought, a horrible barn fire, heavy rain and flooding.

A terrific storm in June, 1983, cost Ellis its only program cancellation in history.

Adkins wore many hats during her race track days that began in 1948.

She started at the bottom, selling programs, selling beer behind concession stands, cleaning the facilities, and doing all the chores.

The number of beer bottles that came whizzing by her — flung by irate gamblers — ended at six. That, in part, sent her to the front office.

The summer of 1984 was her last as ramrod. She takes justifiable pride in colleague Bill Mooney's lengthy spread featuring Ellis Park in an issue of *The Thoroughbred Record Magazine*. Titled "Full of Beans," it won Mooney racing's coveted Eclipse Award for magazine writing.

"I was delighted for Bill and for the track," she emphasized. "It gave the world a true picture of what Ellis Park is all about. There's only one Eclipse Award and I like to think Ellis Park provied him the ammunition to win it."

After high school in Owensboro, Ky., Adkins attended a business college. Her first crack at management came when the gentleman operating as the track's horsemen's bookkeeper showed up for work tipsy. Adkins stepped in and demonstrated her mathematical and office capabilities.

She soon emerged as chief aide to the late Anna M. Fisher, secretary of Dade Park Jockey Club, Inc., which Ellis Park is licensed under by the Kentucky State Racing Commission.

During Adkins' years as chief executive, 10 modern barns were built, along with the Yeager Room in the air-conditioned clubhouse.

State legislators and racing commissioners will attest she didn't hesitate to take off the gloves and fight with bare knuckles for track tax relief for such improvements.

Her character was like a chameleon, changing color depending upon whom she was dealing with. She could be terse, scornful, surly, bull-headed, then kind, obliging, an ally — all in a space of a few minutes.

She was a tough lady in a tough business.

More than once, though, she reached down in her purse for money to give to a down-and-outer and order the recipient to buy himself a pair of shoes, a winter coat or a square meal.

A couple of her best rounds were minutes apart during the summer of 1981.

She was being interviewed by Don Bernhardt, *The Evansville Courier*'s late associate sports editor, when a fellow bulled past the guard into the room.

"What can I do for you sir?" asked Adkins. "It's like this, lady," the gent said. "I've got to bet this horse in the next race but I've blown my bankroll. Here's my Visa card; please give me $100 on it."

"Sir, let me tell you something," she responded. "I don't want your card. But if you're that desperate, I'll lend you the $100 and you can pay me next time you're here."

When 'Hot Horse Harry' left, Bernhardt said: "Ruth, that's the last time you'll ever see that guy."

"No Don," Adkins replied. "A gambler always remembers where his last bet came from and he'll be back to pay up." Two days later, the man settled the debt.

Another man showed up a few minutes later crying over a departed lady love. "I've lost everything. I'm nothing without this woman," he whined.

"Nonsense," exclaimed Adkins. "You've got one thing no one can take from you and that's dignity and pride. Now stand up, straighten yourself up and get back to work."

Adkins called the years at Ellis the best of her life. "This summer will make 63 years for the place and I had more than half of them. I've done my part. At 55, it's time to slow down and enjoy life.

"I'll miss it. But my son, Lester, will be working on the track maintenance crew so I'll still be represented.

What of the future?

First I want to freshen up and get all of Mr. Yeager's business and mine in order. I'm not finished in racing. The Kumars and I have left the door open. I might even get a couple of horses and race them myself.

"The time off will do me good. I didn't want to stagger and fall across the finish line."

She exited like the good horse she is. A bit worse for wear, but in front of the field, drawing off with plenty of run left.

WINNING MEMORIES ON FATHER'S DAY

JUNE, 2000

Hindsight tells me that Charlie was definitely a reflection of Evansville, Ind.

In several ways, he was our fair town at its best. A combination of strength and determination, he worked feverishly, intensely driven by ambitions that reached far beyond his humble roots which sprung out of a shotgun house on an unpaved street in Corydon, Ky.

He wasn't a great athlete. But, like many of that ilk are prone to do, he denied his aches and pains, ultimately working himself to death on June 5, 1990, at age 71.

In other ways, he was Evansville at its worst. Sometimes crude, ruthless, arrogant, manipulative. intolerant and unforgiving.

He wasn't graceful, polished or a smooth operator. But our town isn't Washington, D.C., Rome or Paris.

He was practical, simple, strict, sentimental, big, powerful, generous and tough.

At times during the course of his day, he'd be seen as ridiculous and outrageous or saintly and heroic, depending on whose opinion you accepted.

For example, late one night during the 1968 Ellis Park meeting, he routed a band of would be arsonists by standing in the doorway of his family business and firing off two clips of ammuntion from a .45 caliber pistol — the same one he'd carried during World War II as a sidearm when fighting the Germans and Italians from the turret of a tank in North Africa, Sicily and Italy.

A few days after the incident, he told his only son, then 13, "I don't want to catch you hanging around Ellis Park. You might get hooked on gambling and turn into a bum. Don't let me down."

He always got his point across one way or another. So what followed for several years was the kid fearing for his life, ducking in and out of shadows or hiding in the top row of the track's main grandstand so Charlie's spying friends couldn't blow the whistle.

That all began to change a week after the 1978 Kentucky Derby when the kid looked Charlie in the eye and said, "Fill out this license application. You're going to be half-owner of a horse I bought."

It went over like a lead balloon. But eventually, Charlie fell in love with the horse and immensely enjoyed watching him run. So much, in fact, that until his death, he was a season box holder at Ellis.

Charlie cried very few times in his life. He wept when his parents died; when the beloved Washington Redskins won the 1983 Super Bowl; in 1981 at Ellis when his horse won for the third consecutive time; in 1984 when Swale captured the Kentucky Derby, and about a month before he died in 1990, when Unbridled won the Derby.

That last Derby was strange, because he told the customers to get out of his establishment, then locked the door in order to watch the race on television without interruption. Eyewitnesses said that Charlie broke down and cried like a baby. Not because the son he'd once forbade to attend the races had become a bum, but because the boy had become a decent chart-caller. In fact, he not only charted the 1990 Derby, but he picked Unbridled at 10-1 to win the roses for a national publication of importance.

I know all these stories are true. Because you see, he was my old man.

To some unearthly place, I wish him happy Father's Day and many winners. Even if they're not all in the league of Swale and Unbridled.

ARCHIE TAUGHT US
WHAT MATTERED MOST

DECEMBER, 1998

One of the best and kindest men I ever knew died suddenly Sunday night.

His late parents christened him Arthur Plemon Owen. But, long ago, the world shortened it to "Archie."

He was my idol, my coach, my surrogate father and my truest living friend.

"Kindest" might not be the first word someone who had felt Owen's wrath would use. For in a fit of rage, he could verbally peel the hide off a 300-pound lineman.

But seconds later, he might be offering a soothing message to a quarterback who had thrown an interception that lost a game.

This isn't about Xs and Os or Owen's won-lost record as head football coach at Bosse High School. Or the fact that he was outstanding as a wrestling mentor at North and later Bosse.

Owen wasn't a football coach first. He was a man's man who coached football, using the game as a tool to help young men improve their chances of making it in the world.

Wins and loses can't truly depict a coach. A better measure is the attitude of his former players after they've outgrown the awed hero worship of high school days.

Since his death, an overwhelming number of Owen's former players, assistant coaches, peers and friends have expressed their admiration and affection. At the funeral home from 1 p.m. until 8 p.m. Tuesday, a 60-yard-long line of mourners reviewing his casket seemingly never moved.

Intermingled in that long line were some of the area's top-paid, highest-profiled professionals and a lot of working-class guys in T-Shirts and jeans, too.

It wouldn't have mattered to Owen. He never cared about size, speed, skin color, what side of the tracks a kid came from or how he was dressed. The only thing he demanded was that a person "be on time, be prepared and play like hell."

Perhaps Steve Hughart, an outstanding two-way tackle for Bosse during the mid-1970s, said it best: "I'm here to be close to the memory of a man I loved and revered. I named my second son after coach Owen. I hope my kids grow up to be just like Coach — to be as honest and dedicated as he was. I owe my life to him."

Owen was human, so he wasn't perfect. But he was highly intelligent and organized, persevering and enthusiastic, dedicated, dramatic, apologetic, forgiving, civic-minded and charitable.

His character and integrity were exceptional, his dignity and grace in racial matters exemplary.

Owen had an uncanny ability to understand people on the field and in the classroom as individuals and to select the correct appoach to induce them to perform at maximum capacity. An outstanding teacher, he needed only to be himself to inspire and instill values.

As a high school and college player, Owen described himself as "only a capable journeyman at best." Therefore, it was easy to see why he became a superb motivator, championing those who were too small and a step slow.

He believed great emotion could sometimes overcome superior talent, and he was often right.

In 30 years of friendship, I learned countless lessons from him. But perhaps the most important came in a pre-game pep talk to a young team that was untested in the heat of battle.

The entire squad was huddled around Owen on the sideline after he bellowed that familiar, "Let's team up." A Bosse tradition called for the front-line guys to put their hands on his wonderful bald head for luck.

And he loved it.

So with tears pouring down his cheeks, he yelled: "Men, the true meaning of what happens out here tonight will be lost on the television reports. And it'll be covered up in the newspapers. Those guys only care about the score.

"What matters most is that you don't loaf on your school,

on your teammates, on your parents, on me and most importantly on yourselves."

For Wednesday's funeral service, a huge crowd crammed into Trinity United Methodist Church. Several of the players who'd heard that message were there to pay their final respects.

After the service, the cathedral slowly emptied and behind the limousines followed a two-mile procession of cars to the cemetery.

During the drive, the fact came to mind that all his life, Owen loved to take trips. Whether it be to Europe or Florida with his wife, Louise, for a tennis match; to Tell City or Terre Haute with a busload of players for a game; to Louisville, Ky.'s Churchill Downs for the Kentucky Derby, or maybe just down to Joey's on Franklin Street for lunch, he'd always be ready to go.

Wednesday's five-mile trip to Alexander Memorial Cemetery was his last. Somewhere, Coach Owen was smiling proudly, because many of "his boys" went along.

W. CAL PARTEE, A
GENTLEMAN OF THE FIRST RANK

NOVEMBER, 1999

LOUISVILLE, Ky. — As a horse owner, W. Cal Partee spent more than half of his 89 years trying to win the Kentucky Derby.

And, at age 82 on May 3, 1992, at Churchill Downs, his Lil E. Tee, perfectly ridden by Pat Day, rallied through the long stretch to win the 118th Derby by a length in a considerable upset at 16-1 in the field of 18.

Theoretically, the afternoon was to have been an international one. It was supposed to belong to an over-hyped, ill-prepared colt named Arazi. Favored at 4-5 despite knee surgery, a single prep race in France on turf against a hand-picked bunch of bums and a single three-furlong work at Churchill, Arazi fizzled badly in the Derby.

Instead of going to a French connection, the coveted garland of roses went to Churchill Downs regulars who've raced each season here for about 30 years. And a crowd of 132,543 — the majority Kentuckians — loved it.

Most didn't bet on Lil E. Tee, but they realized the magnitude of the moment when the classy Day, a Hall of Famer who'd spent the previous evening visiting burned and crippled children at Kosair Children's Hospital, stood in the winner's circle and saluted the stands. When he did, fans returned a thunderous ovation to the victors that lasted several minutes. It was extremely emotional.

Partee didn't know what to do. So he did it all.

He whispered, shouted, smiled, cheered, sat down and then jumped for joy.When he reached the infield winner's circle where only Derby winners walk, he reached his trembling hands toward Day, who was still astride the big bay colt. When their hands clasped and their eyes met, their tears flowed freely.

A self-made millionaire who amassed several fortunes in lumber, oil and banking in his hometown of Magnolia, Ark., Partee was a man of few words. And the following morning at trainer Lynn Whiting's barn, Partee's voice quivered and his eyes again became misty as he constructed a few sentences as we chatted. "I don't know how to tell you what's going on inside me. But it's been happening since we won," he said.

This story flashed back to mind when news from the Magnolia hospital explained how Partee died Nov. 12 at age 89 following complications from Parkinson's Disease.

Everyone quoted in his obituary said what a great man Partee was. And they were right. In more than 50 years as an owner, Partee employed four trainers. Whiting, on the job the last 21 years, was more than that. He was also Partee's friend. And by far the best horseman of the bunch.

The obituary described Partee as "quiet, shy and introverted." I never saw him that way. We met for the first time in the spring of 1984 when his At The Threshold won the old Jim Beam Stakes at Turfway Park, then finished third in the Kentucky Derby. And, to one who knew him pleasantly but not intimately, his public manner was a bit reserved only because he was a gentleman of the first rank.

For when something stirred his interest, like a top 2-year-old or Derby prospect, he spoke freely and authoritatively with grace, wit and poise without the least bit of self-consciousness.

Partee certainly spoke freely during the summer before the 1992 Derby when, on the advice of a friend, Partee telephoned Whiting and asked him to go look at a 2-year-old Pennsylvania-bred named Lil E. Tee who had run two corking races at Calder Race Course in south Florida. Whiting liked what he saw and bought Partee the colt for $200,000.

The day he won the Derby, Partee had a doctor friend in tow. The man wagered considerably on Lil E. Tee to win and made a $100 wheel in the exacta with Lil E. Tee on top of every other horse. That means the doc had the exacta 50 times. Each $2 ticket was worth $854.40.

Not to be outdone, Partee went up and made a $200 exacta wheel along with a hefty load on the horse across the board. He cashed out well more than $100,000 after the colt paid $35.60, $12.20 and $7.60.

Mutuel clerks called the money room for more cash in order to pay Partee. He couldn't wait because he was expected at the winner's party in the Derby Museum. He left delighted, agreeing to cash his tickets the following week. The huge score along with the Derby Trophy were the center of attention that evening during the dinner party he hosted at Hasenour's Restaurant.

At Churchill Downs, the day after Partee's death, a filly by Lil E. Tee that he'd bred and owned, one named Little Irene, won the eighth race. That day's third race went to Drayton Hall, a son of Lil E. Tee. Whiting trained them both.

And from somewhere high above looking down, Partee must have smiled his approval. A lot of his old friends in the stands certainly did. It was a fitting tribute and sendoff to a grand gentleman. There's only a few like him still around. Too few.

"MR. COOKE" LEFT A LEGACY OF EXCELLENCE AND CLASS

APRIL, 1997

LEXINGTON, Ky. — Keeneland offers its annual 2-year-old in training sale at 6:30 p.m. Tuesday and Wednesday, when more than 200 well-bred youngsters will face the auctioneer.

The fine print on the sale catalog's cover states: "Including Elmendorf Farm's Horses of Racing Age Dispersal."

There are 14 promising 2-year-olds among Elmendorf's 31 lots. But headlining the venue is Antespend, a 4-year-old daughter of Horse of the Year Spend a Buck, winner of the 1985 Kentucky Derby and earner of $4.2 million.

A multiple Grade I winner of $878,434, Antespend finished fourth in last Thursday's $100,000 Jenny Wiley Stakes for fillies and mares.

She was owned by multi-millionaire Jack Kent Cooke, master of Elmendorf Farm, before Mr. Cooke collapsed and died from a heart attack last Sunday at age 84.

Besides horses and his beloved Washington Redskins, he owned at least six other major sports franchises during his lifetime. So, a lot of history, some of it personal, came to memory.

Immediately, we recall a statement he made before his first heart attack in March, 1973. "You want to live forever. And once I thought I might, you know." With his profound laugh he added, "It would be possible if I could watch a team that I own play 365 days a year."

We refer to him as Mr. Cooke because everyone — from Hall of Fame trainer Ron McAnally who conditions

Antespend, to Hall of Fame coach Joe Gibbs, who directed Mr. Cooke's Redskins to Super Bowl victories in 1983, 1988 and 1992 — addressed him that way.

Before Thursday, Antespend last raced at Keeneland on Oct. 5 in the Grade I Queen Elizabeth II Challenge Cup. She made the pace but weakened to third at the end of nine furlongs. The Redskins were off to a fast start last fall and the following day had a road game with the rival Dallas Cowboys. Mr. Cooke was able to make both events and enjoyed the Keeneland atmosphere and hospitablity a lot more than the reception in Dallas, because Washington lost.

We've talked at least twice annually for several years, including that day. And, although his estimated worth was more than $825 million, he never once failed to return a call if unavailable at the time.

The only thing that rivaled Cooke's pride in winning Super Bowls was the classic challenge of winning the Kentucky Derby. He bought Elmendorf farm with the idea of breeding a Derby winner. But the only horse to carry his yellow and blue colors in the Derby was Flying Continental, 12th in 1989.

Power sometimes creates arrogance accompanied by ego. And it's a fact that Mr. Cooke had plenty of both. But remember, born Oct. 12, 1912 in Hamilton, Ontario, Canada, he rose from humbled surroundings as an encyclopedia salesman to become a media mogul in Canada, then an American billionaire who headed such franchises as the Los Angeles Kings, Los Angeles Lakers and Redskins, along with vast real estate and cable television holdings.

It was no secret that Cooke's personal life consisted of the stuff that keeps supermarket tabloids in business.

But, as Gibbs once explained, "Mr. Cooke is an extremely rare individual. I'd never been a head coach before. He interviewed me personally and actually was very intimidating when telling me about his holdings and great wealth.

"He gave us the job and left us with one expectation: 'Win the right way.' You can't win in the NFL without the right ownership, and he was wonderful. A tough guy who was extremely smart. You find out what people are made of when things aren't going well. When we had problems and weren't winning, that's when Mr. Cooke was at his best."

Last December, on the eve of the final game ever played at Robert F. Kennedy Memorial Stadium, Mr. Cooke was in a cheerful mood. He was an extremely well-read and literate man who loved using an eloquent dialogue, sometimes mixing in a four-letter expletive when speaking of the opposition.

Yet, when asked for his favorite memories of RFK, he teared up and went silent for a couple of minutes to compose himself. Then, after rattling off a list of memorable games and former Redskin greats, he paused and said, "But above all things, I'll remember the fans. We have the bloody best fans in the world. The glorious people who populate RFK are what made it so special."

Construction currently is underway for a new Redskins stadium about six miles from Washingon in Prince County, Md. Mr. Cooke put up his own money for the project. He didn't want to leave RFK, but with a 55,000 capacity, it's been too cramped and minus the luxury boxes of other ballparks for 20 years.

It's a dreadful shame he didn't live long enough to see the new ballpark completed. It's almost as if he chose his own time and place to go. He was world-class in everything he did. In today's era of sports owners, there never will be another like him.

MCCOOL'S FAMILY OUTING
A PERFECT FIT ON DERBY DAY

APRIL, 1999

With only a few exceptions, like during World War II and when it was run after the Preakness in late May as the second leg of the Triple Crown, the Kentucky Derby has been held on the first Saturday in May at Churchill Downs in Louisville, Ky. for 124 years.

And, much like a politician or a classic original oil painting by one of the world's masters, the Derby represents many things to many people.

To children, Derby Day might be a reminder that summer vacation isn't far off.

Clothiers around here and especially in the Derby City will note that race-day marks the official beginning of summer suit season. They'll add that it's also a time of year that men's fashionable straw hats sell briskly.

For owners, trainers and breeders fortunate enough to participate in the great race, it's an opportunity to evaluate their stock against the best competition available while standing in the media's national spotlight.

Police officers and ushers at the track will tell you about the massive headache they have handling the huge crowd. The morning after the Derby, many racegoers will elaborate about the headache they have from tipping too many Mint Juleps.

Yet, for some, like Ralph McCool, Derby Day was the perfect occasion for a family outing at home.

Since Tim Tam, a one-time Calumet Farm second-stringer, came off the bench to dramatically win the 1958

Derby, McCool, along with Harriet, his wife of 50 years, and their family, which increased considerably through the years, hosted a major league backyard barbecue at their home on East Mulberry Street in Evansville.

To Ralph, the Derby was almost a religious experience. He witnessed his first in 1945 as a bachelor in the U.S. Army. He visited Churchill Downs, wagered on Calumet Farm's runner-up Pot O' Luck and immediately was overcome by the annual phenomenon called "Derby Fever."

Anyway, on the big day, it was nothing for 200 of the McCool family's friends and neighbors to mill about the premises, sipping their favorite libations and dining on a main course of hickory smoked ribs accompanied by the trimmings. When it came to the grill, Ralph was a perfectionist. And regardless of the weather, the always exquisitely prepared feast was finished about the time the Derby was made "official" and the mutuel prices posted on the television sets strategically placed around the yard.

Additionally, if somebody had tipped Ralph on a "good thing" to wager on and he'd won big on the Derby or one of the earlier races, the bash would go on until the next morning.

This all came to mind last week when Ralph McCool died in St. Mary's Medical Center. He was 73 and his great heart, which made him an exceptional father of 10 children, a loving husband and devout family man, simply betrayed him and gave out.

Some may remember Ralph as a charter member of Evansville East Side Little League Baseball, where he coached young kids for many, many years. Now grown men with their own families, about a dozen were among the packed house attending their old coach's funeral last Tuesday at Ziemer East.

Others will recall that he retired from Coca-Cola Bottling Works as director of advertising. There was a time when Ralph was one of Ellis Park's best customers. That's why until recently, Coca-Cola was the official soft drink there and also why the Coca-Cola box was the best one in the house, directly on the finish line.

Anyway, at the funeral home, guys like Jim "Tiger" Ritter, Bud Buthod, Jeff Small and a lot of others were spinning tales about the good times they'd had with Ralph. They did so with humor, lest they cry.

There are a thousand to be told about Ralph McCool. But I'll simply remember him as a clever, tough, warm, wonderful, generous, proud, humorous, emotional, sometimes naive, sometimes unpredictable and sometimes stubborn man. He lived life to the fullest and enjoyed every minute of it. A lot of his days were "Derby Days."

The story I'll cherish most happened the morning of the 102nd Kentucky Derby, May 1, 1976.

Daylight had barely broken but Ralph already had the fire in the big pit blazing. All the preparations were in order and it was time to peruse Daily Racing Form, something he revered, before putting the meat on the grill. Remember, the first race went at 9:45 a.m. local time.

We were comparing notes and selections and Ralph mumbled: "You know, working for the *Form* might be something you'd like when you get out of school. You like racing and you'd be good at it. You might think it over and give 'em a call. You never know, maybe they'd even use you at Churchill for the Derby."

I've covered every Derby since 1980 and will provide the *Form*'s official chart for the twelfth consecutive year on May 1. So, for Ralph's advice, I'm eternally grateful.

Being on the road most of the past 10 years, we'd only talk two or three times annually, but a pre-Derby conversation was always a certainty. You see, he liked getting touted and our record together dated back to Derby winners like Bold Forbes 1976, Seattle Slew 1977, Spectacular Bid 1979 (the last two he hated to bet because of the short price), Sunny's Halo 1983 and Swale 1984 to name a few that were solid.

I wish I could've "pushed" him on this year's winner. But instead, I'll toast him after the race is official. He'd prefer lots of ice along with Scotch and water. No twist, please. And if fortunate enough to choose the winner? Ralph, who had a nickname for everyone, would say, "Chief, let's celebrate. We just had the Derby winner. Make it a double!"

"CUTTER" FIGHTING FOR LIFE IN HOSPITAL

FEBRUARY, 1995

FLORENCE, Ky. — "The people and lifestyle of racing have kept me young at heart and on the go all these years."

Those words belong to 85-year-old George Koper. He spoke them in late June of 1991.

On Jan. 30, his wonderful, warm heart threatened to give out and betray him.

"Cutter," as Koper is called by everyone from Churchill Downs President Tom Meeker to hotwalkers because of the old days when he cut and pasted the "cut book" together, suffered a stroke while driving his car.

Of all the places to be traveling, he was headed for his annual medical checkup.

A tough little guy, he nevertheless had the guts and awareness to pull over to the curb and flag down a motorist, who called 911.

Believed to be America's oldest active racing official, Koper worked last fall at Churchill Downs in his familiar position of entry and claims clerk.

When the Downs isn't in session, he accepts entries for Turfway Park and Keeneland, then faxes them to the track that's operational.

He had worked in the Churchill office the morning of his stroke and had planned to visit a funeral home that evening. Koper said of the deceased, "He was a good boy and a friend."

"How old was the boy?" someone asked. "Oh," George responded, "he was only 82."

Koper's condition has improved from critical to stable condition but he's fighting for his life in Room 422 of Saint Anthony Hospital at 1313 St. Anthony Place, Louisville, Ky. 40201.

He's paralyzed on his right side and has lost considerable weight. His spirits are down, and he's a bit frightened after having always taken care of himself.

Understandably, he doesn't want anything to do with a nursing home, and a long, painful rehabilitation lies ahead if he pulls through the initial battle.

It has to be double tough mentally for Koper, too. All his life, the native of Henderson, Ky., has been on the move, working, hanging around and enjoying people, places and most things.

In the old days, Koper, a deeply compassionate and sentimental man, also proclaimed himself "one of Brown-Forman's (a Louisville whiskey distillery) best customers."

He had some real fun when a guy could mix things up without being frowned upon, scolded or arrested.

For 45 years, he manned the police reporter's beat for *The Louisville Courier-Journal*, taking mandatory retirement at age 65 in 1974. He covered everything from the terrible 1937 flood to the late Dr. Martin Luther King's march through downtown Louisville.

Koper originally moonlighted his way into racing as an official at old Miles Park in Louisville and Churchill Downs, beginning there in 1938. He's worked 54 Kentucky Derbys, accommodating the worst and best of horsemen with the same professional etiquette while becoming as much of a 'Downs institution as the famed Twin Spires.

A lot of his summer vacations were spent working as a call-taker for *Daily Racing Form* at Ellis Park. Even last fall at Churchill, Koper compiled entry information for *DRF* for the first two racing days.

We don't wish to be maudlin here, so we'll relate a story to lift the spirits, along with our prayers for this grand little man.

The story revolves around the last race of the afternoon one day many years ago at Ellis Park. A tremendous thunder storm swept through the area. It sent most patrons home and turned the track into a sea of deep slop. Suddenly, though, the sun burst forth and it was beautiful but silent on the grandstand apron.

Koper's voice rang out to one his friends who had a

horse in the race. "Hey," he hollered from the placing judges' stand. "Don't forget to bet something for the boys up here."

The horse won at a nice price and the next morning, all three judges were presented a $2 win ticket. "I was just ribbing you," said Koper, who's prone to do that with the straightest of faces. "But I'll take it and eat well tonight."

George Koper has wept and prayed for a lot of guys. It's time for them to return the favor.

CUTTER'S WAY WITH
PEOPLE EARNED HIM MANY FRIENDS

FEBRUARY, 1995

LOUISVILLE, Ky. — Death last Tuesday morning at age 85 was a release for George Koper, but a sad relief for his friends.

Most of us are unprepared to depart this life, but "Cutter," as his beloved racing industry called him, was waiting.

He was paralyzed, couldn't walk, could barely talk and couldn't work. For a guy who lived his entire life in the big arena of competitive sport and fun, not working is the deadliest thing. And it's no way for a man who became as much of an institution at Churchill Downs as the Twin Spires to live.

His friends and relatives realized that it was ony a question of time after he suffered a stroke on Jan. 30. Now the time has expired. One can only feel that God has shown mercy, because this tough little man was steadfastly against nursing homes or anyone taking care of him but himself.

His friends were many. Included are the racing department and management at Churchill Downs, where Koper labored part- or full-time since 1938; the folks at Turfway Park and Keeneland, where he took entries; people he wrote about during his 45 years as a police reporter in Louisville; the horsemen he dealt with daily; the grooms he slipped extra programs to; the ladies who waited on him at the Blue Boar Cafeteria; those he worked with during his tenures as a *Daily Racing Form* call-taker; his parish priest; and many others whose lives were touched by this wonderful guy with the bad feet, oversized ears and polo cap tipped over one eye.

For each of them, news of his passing had a different impact.

Curiously, two guys were left with the deep loss of a friend who had symbolized an era.

Cutter was a confidante and news source. He never really left the newspaper business because often he tipped young reporters on something eventful about to happen. His death furthered an unyielding despair that the old days are getting older.

Anyway, together, the men silently hoisted top-shelf Glenlivet Scotch and so toasted Koper's memory while telling old yarns. Alone, they probably wept. But, the evening nevertheless brought out some interesting Koper stories.

"I remember when Cutter would spend the evening on the train to Cincinnati," someone said. "He'd have a pint when he got on, buy another at the station, then ride back to Louisville as happy as a lark. He rode for nothing with his press card and had a grand time."

Jerry Forke, *DRF* wire operator, worked many summers with Koper at Ellis Park. One Labor Day, Koper was employed as a placing judge. Forke had several ladies positioned at opposite ends of the plant and was delivering them cocktails between races while laying groundwork for dinner.

Koper reported that another gal had arrived, much to Forke's chagrin. Koper rushed into the press box to warn Forke that trouble was sitting in the last row of the grandstand. "Jerry," Koper said with a straight expression, "you won't believe who's here."

"Oh George, don't lie to me," said Forke.

"Jerry," Koper said, "I'm swearing on my wife, Mary Agenes' grave, that gal is really here."

Forke went down the fire escape to investigate. Much to his relief, he found that Koper was kidding. "George, I can't believe you'd do that to me." Koper broke out laughing and responded: "I just wanted to see if you could get down the fire escape."

A final tale that can't go to the cemetery involved Koper's fondness for Yellowstone Whiskey. This was 30 years ago and his late wife wouldn't tolerate it when the young grandchildren were visiting.

Koper was hiding the stuff in places ranging from his sock drawer to the tank of the toilet. So, being a loving grandfather, he volunteered to take the baby out for a ride in the stroller.

Mrs. Koper didn't know it, but her husband had a route mapped out along Bardstown Road where he could stop, leave the stroller in the doorway of various saloons, and have a nip. He completed his assignment without incident and nobody ever knew.

Seriously, though, it may be trivial to say that the man was about as gracious, charming and solid a person who ever lived. The obits never say this, but nothing else can be said about George Koper that's so true.

He was a loving family man of lofty, glowing principles whose entire existence centered around the pride he held in his family and his friends in racing. We know they miss him lots. So do we.

A THANKFUL REMEMBRANCE FOR THE "TITAN OF THE TURF"

NOVEMBER, 1994

LOUISVILLE, Ky. — Whan Warner L. Jones Jr. died last Feb. 6 at his beloved Hermitage Farm in nearby Goshen, Ky., the obituaries identified the 78-year-old pillar of the turf in several ways.

They remember him as a legendary Eclipse Award winner, breeder of a Kentucky Derby, Oaks and Breeders' Cup winner and the world's highest-priced yearling sold at auction.

In addition, he was one founder of the American Horse Council, past president of the Thoroughbred Breeders' Association of Kentucky and a member of The Jockey Club.

His insight and astute political sense in these arenas helped the industry thrive. He was a humanitarian, giving unselfishly of his time to friends, effort and conviction to his sport, and money to charitable causes.

As Churchill Downs' chairman of the board for 10 years, he applied his deep-rooted will to win. His desire to succeed with all facets of the plant helped improve standards for fans and horsemen alike. He was instrumental in preserving the track at a time when corporate raiders were attempting a stock takeover.

His internal drive and competitiveness brought this storied facility above and beyond standards thought to be impossible. He was instrumental in bringing the Breeders' Cup here on a rotating basis.

He played as hard at gin rummy as he did in attempting to have the leading consignment for a Keeneland sale.

144

At this time of Thanksgiving, fans who enjoyed the Breeders' Cup on Nov. 5, or the races on a regular day during the season, should take time to remember Jones. So should horsemen and riders who compete for Churchill Downs' unbelievable purses.

All of this came to mind recently when an outstanding documentary aired on PBS titled: "Warner L. Jones Jr., Titan of the Turf."

When the Eclipse Awards are selected soon, this 30-minute film that highlights the life and times of this colorful, warm-hearted man whose grandchildren called him "Jonesy" should be the morning line favorite to win.

It's written and produced by Gene Williams, a writer and editor who toils for Churchill's publicity department and Triple Crown Productions. He is retired from a long stint with *The Courier-Journal* in Louisville.

Stan Starks, a press box regular and staff member of WKPC-TV (Channel 15), shot and edited the footage in meticulous fashion.

Narration was handled by John Asher, multiple Eclipse Award-winning correspondent for this city's WHAS-AM and the track's in-house television handicapper.

Asher's work isn't simply a voice-over. He's an authority on the subject and his delivery, spiced with feelings and personal sentiment, wasn't an act.

A wide variety of the sport's hierarchy were interviewed. Included were Mr. Jones' wife, Harriet, Seth Hancock, Arthur Hancock 3rd, trainers Shug Mcgaughey and Charlie Whittingham, Dr. Alex Harthill, track president Tom Meeker and Mrs. A.B. Hancock Jr.

To a person, they offered their praises and humble thanks.

RACING CZAR?
HOW ABOUT JOE GIBBS

MARCH, 1993

FLORENCE, Ky. — A devastating thing happened the morning of March 5, and *Daily Racing Form* wire operator Jerry Forke was first to report the bad news to friends in Turfway Park's pressbox.

"I can't believe what I just heard on the radio coming to work. Coach Gibbs resigned this morning," Forke said.

Phone calls started coming soon afterward. One was from trainer Dale Romans. "Do you have a black armband on yet?" Romans asked the writer. Churchill Downs' Harriet Howard inquired: "Are you going to be okay?"

"Coach Gibbs isn't old. Why would he do this?" asked *DRF* call-taker Tim Holcomb.

Forke didn't have to say Joe Gibbs, head coach of the National Football League's Washington Redskins.

That was taken for granted, because in these quarters, Redskin football and Gibbs' philosophy are part of the environment. Vacations are centered around Redskin playoff games and pork-chop parties.

And, as Forke told some smart aleck who asked why he was wearing a burgundy sweather with a Redskin emblem: "Boy, I was a Redskin fan before you were born."

To say that Gibbs' retirement is a loss to the craft of coaching is an understatement.

Adding further insult on March 5 was what happened in the last race. A horse fell here entering the stretch. Who did the animal race for? None other than Redskins' owner Jack Kent Cooke.

It's time to answer the question of what all this has to do with horse racing, for after all, Gibbs is a NASCAR man.

But the answer is "lots." We'll avoid the impressive statistics, the memorable games, three Super Bowl wins, and all-time great players who made Gibbs' job enjoyable.

Instead, let's focus on Gibbs the man and his values.

What are Gibbs' primary attributes?

Above all, he instilled loyalty, dignity and class in his players.

Gibbs was a master of telling it straight and building for the future. Players loved it, and proved it many times as they would come off the injured list often prematurely to play for him, never dogging it because of their respect and admiration for the man.

"Giving dignity to a man is above all things," Gibbs often stated. "I've always loved football because you can compare it to life. You go through extremely difficult things. You don't like it, but it's there. It can be a job, family or relationship. Anything like that.

"Hard times will always be there. But after overcoming so much, you cherish winning more and learn from everything. Our teams sometimes have been best after coming out of a deep valley."

Gibbs on the sidelines — arms crossed, teeth clenched, eyes piercing — was never a rah-rah type and rarely raised his voice. Instead, he was the orchestrating general, unflappable under fire, always focused two plays ahead of the offense, which he masterminded and called.

Gibbs' basic theories were work hard, know when to take a short break, hire top assistants, delegate authority, set goals, communicate well, be prepared, be flexible.

At a 1992 thoroughbred industry meeting, the idea was again advanced that racing needs a czar, or commissioner, much like the NFL, Major Leage Baseball and the National Basketball Association.

The right man is available now. His name is Joe Gibbs. He would make a tremendous national racing commissioner. And who cares if he's not a thoroughbred man? Nowadays, how many track executives are?

JERRY BURKHART: AN ENTREPRENEUR IN THE ART OF LIFE

NOVEMBER, 1992

LOUISVILLE, Ky. — During the final days of the Keeneland meeting, the plans made with colleague Jim Bolus were to put a party together and head out to Burkhart's Restaurant for dinner, a pleasant evening of storytelling and whatever other tomfoolery could be drummed up.

Burkhart's is a quaint facility on River Road which offers a delightful cuisine mixed with Arabian and American favorites that horsemen and fans on the Churchill Downs-Ellis Park loop have come to admire.

However, death, as the saying goes, intervened. The death of Jerry Burkhart, the facility's owner.

He was only 49 years old when the iceman called through a beastly form of cancer on Wednesday at Humana Hospital-University of Louisville.

Burkhart had put together a popular dining place, which has prospered during a time when many more established operations are teetering.

It wasn't always this way, though, beause we came to know him at least 17 summers ago when he was training horses along with his father, Kenny, for their Attica Farm. And quite successfully, too, as their 2-year-olds were often difficult to defeat during the summer at Ellis Park when a 30-day meeting was the norm.

Jerry Burkhart was a bit of a thowback. He sported a "Wolfman Jack" beard, gold chain or two, along with styled hair that advertisers feature in their photos appealing to men of distinction.

Anyway, about 18 months agbo, Burkhart grew tired of the routine involved with running a stable. Travel and lack of help can do that to a fellow, especially with a young child at home.

So, he invested in a modest structure, remodeled it to his requirements, and turned it into an instant hit.

Had he lived, expansion plans were on the drawing board.

In the end, everyone knew how it was with Jerry. He'd been diagnosed earlier in the year, but never whimpered, asked for sympathy or changed his routine as long as he could keep going.

A visitor to his home in September found him in a reminiscing mood, but displaying no fear from the fate that was guaranteed.

In short, he was a brave man and, like the storied old soldier, fought the good fight despite having the final chapter prewritten. The end came quickly.

Burkhart was a "people person" and few men had more friends on Churchill Downs' backstretch.

That was evident here last Sunday night when a gathering of his most intimate cronies waited until after the last race to enter the celebrated infield winner's circle used only once a year for the Kentucky Derby winner.

Burkhart's body had been cremated with a request that the ashes be spread in that storied horseshoe of flowers.

Comparable to a military honor guard, they lined up. Carla and Don Grego were there. So were Vickie and Greg Foley, and their younger sister, Sharon. Jockey agent Buddy Fife, his rider, Charles Woods Jr., and others also were present.

They play the Derby's anthem, "My Old Kentucky Home," over the public address system following the final race each day here. Soon after its conclusion, Greg Foley, at the request of Burkhart's wife, Teresa, took the urn and spread its contents where only Derby winners walk.

Another of our mutual friends, Don Cooper, who maintains his position as a steward during the Oaklawn Park meeting, served numerous years as racing secretary at Ellis Park. "Ole Coop" normally resided at the same hotel as Burkhart during the Ellis meetings. Many a morning Burkhart would stop by Coop's room to fetch a cup of coffee. "Then," added Cooper, "he'd stop on his way out of the hotel and put in all the sugar he could find, sometimes 10 of those little packets.

"I asked him why he did that, and he'd say, 'That's how I get my energy.' He was a dear friend of mine."

Ours too. And, no pun intended, but Burkhart was a sweet guy who loved life and lived it his way — to the fullest. He'll be missed.

HORSE RACING
WAS IRV SENZELL'S LUST

OCTOBER, 1999

Death last Sunday had to have been a release for Irv Senzell, and a sad relief for his friends.

The end will find the majority of us unprepared. But Senzell, a spare, graying, quiet, easygoing man of 78, must have been waiting. Smitten with a virulent form of cancer, he was also crippled, could barely stand to walk and certainly couldn't work at his family business, Kor-X-All Co. Inc., which he passed on to his youngest son, Mark.

The end probably came sooner because Irv also suffered from a broken heart. You see, he no longer could enjoy his favorite pasttime involving a daily trip to Ellis Park's clubhouse where he held a standing table reservation to lunch, watch and wager on live or simulcast races.

With the exception of Sunday racing, which he disapproved, Irv lived his entire life on two stages. On one, he was a devout family man and adoring father and grandfather. On the other, he relished the competitive atmosphere of race horses, sports betting and bowling.

His final days of uncompromising misery must have seemed like an eternity. Yet, like the good solider he was during World War II, he fought the good fight and never once complained.

It was my good fortune to meet Irv Senzell 30 years ago through friends. If you were one of them, too, you might have known him by his nickname of "Bug Juice."

For the past 25 years during Ellis Park's live meetings, we visited at least once a week, swapped stories, selections and informed one another of the latest local and national racing gossip. His oldest son, Howard (Tiger) Senzell, a former *Courier* and *Daily Racing Form* writer, went on to become successful as a racing manager on the west coast. And Irv was an authority on the subject.

Senzell's obituary in this paper was accurate when it said that "he had a passion for bowling." It was a remarkable skill that this generous and kind little man, elected in 1985 to the Evansville Men's Bowling Hall of Fame, polished from the sport's heyday of the 1950s.

However, if bowling was his passion, then racing was his lust. It was a flame that began buring inside Senzell when he was a kid attending Wheeler Grade School and old Central High School when growing up near downtown Evansville in the early 1930s.

During his youth, Senzell used Ellis Park as a halfway meeting ground and getaway paradise to meet with his life-long buddy, Bernie Witt, who lived in Henderson, Ky. Together, they pooled their money and brains to bet on the races.

Like on Kentucky Derby Day in 1939. They lied about their whereabouts to their parents, hitchhiked to Churchill Downs, snuck in without paying, and thought the game was easy when 3-5 favorite Johnstown romped by eight lengths. They took a wrong turn coming home, were hours late and, almost unbelieveably, never saw another Derby in person.

Since their prep school days, Senzell and Witt meet annually each summer at Ellis Park. Upon retiring, Witt moved to Columbus, Ga. But he came back to town last August to relive the old days while accompanying Senzell to Ellis for the last time. It was a touching scene as Senzell, by then on a walker, was aided by Witt and other friends up the flight of stairs to the clubhouse dining room.

Senzell's love for Ellis Park may have come naturally because he also did business there. Kor-X-All specializes in cleaning and maintenance supplies and was probably the track's oldest service vendor.

Ruth Adkins, Ellis Park's most famous general manager who retired in 1985 after nearly 40 years, always called him "Senzell" whether in person or on the telephone. "I don't recall the year. But it was sometime around 1960 that we started doing business with Senzell," she said. "He was unique because he loved racing, was a huge booster of Ellis Park's, bet his money with us and also gave us unbelievable service.

"People forget how important service is. When you need something, you must have it on time. Senzell understood this like nobody before or after him ever will. When we built the clubhouse, he figured out what kind of cleaner and polish to use on the new tile. He not only was a business associate of mine, but also a loyal, personal friend. A man of his means and knowledge is irreplaceable."

I couldn't agree with her more. Racing in general and Ellis Park in particular will be poorer without him. The dining room, immeasurably poorer.

BUD GEORGE:
BEAR OF A MAN AND COACH

APRIL, 1986

Tell City High School football coach Robert "Bud" George, 51, was a fierce competitor, yet he was a warm-hearted bear of a man who made teaching and coaching his life's work.

The only battle he knew he couldn't win was his last, against cancer.

George died at 2:30 p.m. Wednesday in Perry County Memorial Hospital in Tell City, Ind., after a year's illness.

Not long ago, former Harrison basketball coach Dennis Bays said: "I was two years behind Bud in school at Tell City. He was a man then. In fact, when Bud George was in the fifth grade he was tougher than most high school guys on today's market."

George had a voice that could rise to a decibel level high enough to peel paint from lockerroom walls. Or, remain soft enough to comfort a quarterback after throwing an interception.

When relaxing off the field, he became an easygoing yarn spinner who could poke fun at himself as well as others.

He was the state's 15th all-time winningest football coach with a 172-80 record.

George was a 1953 graduate of Tell City High School, winning 11 varsity letters. He captained both the baseball and football teams. For three seasons, he was the basketball team's most valuable player, won the same honor in football, and was named to the Southern Indiana Athletic Conference honor team three times.

Rarely, if ever, was George better at his business than he was last fall, his eighth season at his alma mater and 26th as a head coach.

He directed his squad to an 8-4 record and a regional appearance. His Tell City teams were 62-25, including five trips to the state playoffs, two Big Eight Conference titles, two sectional crowns and one regional triumph. He was named Region 9 Coach of the Year in 1981, and served as an assistant for the South All-Stars in 1980.

George graduated in 1957 from Evansville College, where he was a quarterback in football and standout in baseball.

He earned four baseball letters and three in football. He was the Indiana Collegiate Conference's most valuable player in football for 1956 and captured the school's William V. Slyker Award for most outstanding athlete in 1957.

His head coaching career started at Richland, Ind., where he remained for two seasons. He then returned to Tell City for three years as an assistant coach.

Later, he became head coach at Huntingburg (1962-63) and North Knox (1964-73), where he guided the Warriors to their only unbeaten seasons at 10-0 in 1969 and 9-0-1 in 1970.

He picked up the reins at Southridge from 1973-1977.

In a conversation before Christmas, he found it difficult to say that the illness, which required surgery last July, had resurfaced. And, that trips to St. Mary's Medical Center were necessary for chemotherapy.

"I'm weak and in constant pain," he said from his hospital bed during the week of the state basketball regionals. "But I'm planning on going back to work. You know, Craig (a junior at Tell City), is putting that shot real well. I think he's going to have a good year."

That was Bud George. Always thinking of a son, a player, a team or a school first. Himself second. Only a few remain like him, too few.

REDSKINS' RIGGINS BOWS OUT GRACEFULLY

DECEMBER, 1985

ST. LOUIS — An unavoidable thing happened in the National Football League last Saturday.

Fans were getting their last look at the warrior wearing No. 44 in the burgundy and gold colors of Washington. It belongs, probably for all-time in Redskins' lore, to running back John Riggins.

Father Time and the bruising game of football have caught up with the noblest Redskin, forcing him to retire at age 36.

"I don't believe I'll be in football next year," Riggins said as he stripped off his pads and yards of tape. "I don't know what I'll be doing. I know I've got one bullet left in the gun if they need me."

That could have been mere wishful thinking on the part of a rugged individualist who is reluctant to call it a job well done.

But there were two seasons when he spent most of each week in the hospital in tractions for an ailing back and hip. He always was there on Sunday, though, cracking enemy lines.

"The main thing about Riggins," said head coach Joe Gibbs, "is that he always wanted to win so fiercely. All the great ones have that."

In his nine seasons with the Redskins — after five with the New York Jets — Riggo became the most feared first-down and shot-yardage runner in the game. His ability to consistently grind out short chunks of high-priced real estate prompted the team to institute the one-back set, a ball-control style particularly suited to him.

His success, plus his durability, was a smash hit with Washington fans. A 2-yard gain would receive a standing ovation in Robert F. Kennedy Memorial Stadium. This led to the formation of "Riggo's Rangers" — paunch-bellied businessmen dressed in camouflage uniforms. They looked ridiculous, but they didn't care as they cheered his every move. He was the general, the leader of two Redskin teams that reached the Super Bowls of 1983 and 1984.

His off-the-field antics were conversation pieces, something to chuckle about and forgive. Like the night at a posh Washington dinner when he told Supreme Court Justice Sandra Day O'Connor to "loosen up, Sandy baby, you're too tight," and then, deep in his cups, quietly passed out under a table in the rear.

In today's society, only a player of Riggins' stature could get by with such indiscretions. He was never vicious, surly or harmful. He simply was having a good time as John Riggins, like Babe Ruth, a big enough man that others overlooked his flaws.

He was stubborn, independent. In 1980, in a contract dispute, he not only threated to hold out unless the club met his figure, he sat out the season when the Redskins didn't.

In all, the 6-foot-3, 240-pounder carried the ball 2,916 times and gained 11,352 yards to rank fourth in NFL history. He scored 104 rushing touchdowns and 12 TD catches. His longest TD bolt was 66 yards. It came against Dallas, the Redskins' arch rival.

Washington special teams coach Wayne Sevier labeled Riggo "the franchise."

"He was a producer and his presence could lift the entire team," said Sevier. "But more than anything, he was a money player. When the cash was down and it counted most, he delivered."

Riggins led the Redskins to their greatest glory in Super Bowl XVII, carrying the ball 38 times for 166 yards in a 27-17 victory over the favored Miami Dolphins.

He made the run that broke Miami's back. Washington, trailing 17-13, had the ball on the Dolphins' 43, fourth-and-1, with 10 minutes remaining.

The Redskins decided to gamble. Every fan in the stadium and every member of both teams knew who would get the ball. The play called was "I left, tight-wing, goal-line, 70-chip" — Riggins on a blast over left tackle.

The play worked to perfection. Riggins busted through the line of scrimmage and rambled all the way to the end zone, shaking off the last defender, Don McNeal.

The play and the image of Riggins stiff-arming McNeal along the way to glory will reside for all time in the memory of the Reskins' faithful. No one in Super Bowl history has carried the ball more often and only one has carried it for more yardage.

Although he didn't play a down in the Redskins' final two games, Riggins was active on the sidelines, offering encouragement to his teammates.

In the locker room, he was alone, a quiet last hurrah for such a tumultous player. He disrobed slowly, seeming to savor each moment of the camaraderie that evolves within a professional sports team.

"Winning the Super Bowl (1983) is nice to look back on, and the ring you get is great. But this is what I'll miss and remember most," he said, gesturing toward the other players and coaches. "It's these guys and the bond between us all that makes the game so special.

"I hope people forget about me as quickly as possible," said Riggins, laughing. "Aw, not really, though. Let's just say I was a guy who had fun. I never cared about stats. And no matter what happened through the week, I was always there on Sunday."

Many of today's well-paid professional athletes get carried away with their own stature, snubbing fans and the media. Not Riggins. Even though he commands a $900,000 annual salary, he remains a free spirit — the guy sipping a beer on the next bar stool who would lend a hand to a pal if a scuffle broke out.

With a handshake and a little wave, he said goodbye. Then came that grin.

Yes, Riggins will miss football and it won't be an easy adjustment. But tough times don't last. Only tough people do. And ole Riggo is one of the toughest.

FRIENDS
REMEMBER KENNY BURKHART

AUGUST, 1996

HENDERSON, Ky. — Death last Sunday probably was a relief for owner-trainer Kenny Burkhart.

It was a melancholy relief for his friends, who remorsefully told humorous old stories involving him, in order not to cry.

The end finds everyone unprepared, but Burkhart was waiting. He was 79 years old, crippled, and in a Louisville, Ky., nursing home. He couldn't walk, couldn't work, and his memory was coming and going. He might have known you one minute but not the next.

For a man who spent most springs of his adult life running horses or entertaining in Churchill Downs' clubhouse, followed by summers at Ellis Park until recently, it had to wear on his mind and soul to be absent. He knew full well that never again would he partake of the life he loved so well.

It seems like only yesterday, but it's been five years since Burkhart's Attica Farm was represented by those familiar white and green silks here.

Through circumstances, Burkhart retired from training and put his time, effort and funds into a restaurant on the outskirts of the Derby City.

His life wasn't always fun. It was marred by tragedies, such as the early death to cancer of his youngest son, Jerry, who also was a trainer, and the loss of Jerry's mother at a young age.

Jerry Burkhart originally opened the restaurant but fell victim to a virulent form of cancer. Upon his wishes, he was cremated and his ashes were spread within Churchill Downs' infield horseshoe of flowers where only Kentucky Derby winners walk.

When his son died, Kenny was thrust into the restaurant business. When his health failed a couple of years ago, so did the eatery.

Legend magnifies the amount that Kenny Burkhart sometimes would wager. But he played heavily at the mutuel windows. And, of all the stories Burkhart liked to tell at dinners — and his routine was as fixed as a stand-up comedian's — perhaps his favorite involved Forrest Kaelin, who was a jockey before he became a trainer.

In the spring of 1958 at Churchill Downs, Kaelin was riding for Burkhart. The trainer entered a gelding named Noble Warrior for a race on May 6. Meetings were short in those days, and opportunities were limited.

So, to be on the safe side, Burkhart entered the horse again for a race on May 7.

Well, Noble Warrior won nicely on May 6 under Kaelin. Seizing the moment, Burkhart gave Kaelin another leg up 24 hours later. The horse won again, and the connections collected two sizeable scores at the windows.

There have been many great memories made beneath those famed Twin Spires. But records show that no horse other than Noble Warrior ever won on consecutive days.

A couple of years ago, I commemorated Noble Warrior's accomplishments with a half-page spread along with winner's circle pictures of both races in *Daily Racing Form*.

The convenience store near Burkhart's restaurant sold DRF. When Burkhart stopped to buy a copy, the clerk asked him to autograph the page.

Always looking for a laugh or center stage, Burkhart roared with laughter and signed every copy of DRF in the store.

Burkhart, you see, greatly admired Kaelin. He's known him since Kaelin was a 10-year-old kid looking for work around the Derby City's stockyards. That was 50 years ago. Burkhart was a buyer for Fischer Packing Company, and employed Kaelin to clean the trucks that hauled the livestock for 10 cents each.

"It was sad the way Kenny went," said Kaelin, whose stable is based here for the summer. "At one time, Kenny had everything. Then things went bad, and so did the health of the restaurant. He was a good guy and a good friend. We'll miss him."

A lof of people feel the same way.

MUSIC, MEMORIES LIVE ON
FOR FRIENDS OF LEO UNDERHILL

DECEMBER, 1995

FLORENCE, Ky. — Memories of Leo Underhill filled the Turfway Park press box last September when the area's foremost broadcasting authority on jazz music and devout horseplayer's bout with cancer was in its final round.

It concluded last Friday, and the mind and heart remain a bit heavy and full of tales.

Before telling a few, it must be reported that Underhill retired in 1984 from WNOP-AM, an all jazz station that once floated on the Ohio River in nearby Newport, Ky. One night before starting one of his shifts after a few friendly belts, he missed a step on the plank that provided access to the station from the shore, and he had to be fished out of the water. It only furthered his legend

He was a whale of a man, looking and acting the part of a classic jazz musician with an ever-present goatee and a deep, raspy, whiskey voice deepened by years of smoking.

Before entering the jazz field, Underhill, 72, was a rhythm and blues man on WCKY-AM. Somewhere along the line, he gave himself the on-air nickname of "Old Undies." The public loved it.

After many missions over Germany with the Army Air Corps as a bombardier-navigator during World War II, Underhill officially went into broadcasting in 1948.

But first, upon his discharge from the service in 1945, Underhill took a whirl in show business, playing the straight man to Jonathan Winters on a radio play in Springfield, Ohio.

It wasn't always a fashionable thing to do, but Underhill loved horses and made certain that race results from Turfway Park (then Latonia where he was a close friend of the late general manager, John Battaglia) and River Downs were part of his shows.

There was a time, too, that he did River Downs' in-house television handicapping. This was long before such endeavors were for personalities wearing nice clothes and makeup.

Underhill normally showed in an old warm-up sweatsuit. And, on a good day, he might comb his hair.

While his on-the-air radio methods were humorous and mischievious, he was completely the opposite with racing. It was serious business, because he reasoned, some poor stiff had bet his hard earned money and was wating by his kitchen table for radio results.

Underhill was a player himself and understood this. So he got to the facts and left the hype alone which brings us to story No. 1.

There used to be a bush league racecaller in this area who also gave results. Underhill was working the station's board and detested it when the fellow would do cute take-offs on horse's names or tell listeners that there was a tight photo-finish and the winner was....with a long, drawn-out pause for suspense, "so-and-so."

Confronting the fellow, Underhill said something like: "You're not only holding up the commercials, but you're just killing people waiting for results. They don't think it's funny because it's their money at stake."

The chap came back at him with: "Leo, you've got a lot to learn about radio."

They rarely spoke afterwards, but Underhill had made his point and the results came out straight thereafter.

Another tale involves Underhill's nature to exaggerate, especially when he attended the races or gambled. His friends knew this and didn't take him too seriously because they knew he wagered "Leo Dollars," often inflating his bets by 1000 percent or more. In short, $2 to win might be $200 to win in "Leo Dollars."

Often, after a race was won by a horse trained by prominent guys like John Hennig or Jim Morgan, Underhill would claim he'd received an early morning telephone call from them, encouraging him to bet on their horse. "I didn't listen. Tried to beat him," Leo would swear.

There were times he'd come rumbling through the press box and crow: "I had that exacta," as he'd good naturedly swat somebody like clocker Richard Bailey on the arm to gain his undivided attention. Then Bailey, after rubbing out the pain, would remind Underhill: "That was a trifecta race, Leo. Wasn't any exacta to play on that race." Underhill would mutter "oh," then toddle on down the hallway.

Once, Underhill came up with a card-playing story. "My nephew called from Nevada and said to 'come on out. There's a game in Lake Tahoe and all the big players were in Las Vegas. And you can beat these guys'. I went out and made $35,000. It was like stealing."

Whether he did isn't known for sure, but it added to his stature as a true character of the turf.

There are a lot more Underhill stories we could tell, but let's end with this one. Jerry Forke, *Daily Racing Form*'s longtime wire operator, used to do a perfect mimic of Underhill's voice. Once, Underhill slipped by unnoticed and heard the imitation. "Jerry," he bellowed with a grin, "you sound more like me than me."

That was Leo Underhill. He loved life and lived it to the fullest. If you learn anything from this, it's probably best to employ Leo's greatest line: "If you don't laugh, you'll cry."

He followed that guidline and laughed about everything — including himself.

We shall miss those jovial tones.

HEARTFELT LETTER CONJURES UP MEMORIES OF DON DELOTELL

FEBRUARY, 1997

FLORENCE, Ky. — This lengthy letter dated Jan. 25, 1997, begins: "I (Rainey DeLotell) am sending this group letter to the many people who sent my father Christmas cards this year and used his previous address of 1275 Cleveland Avenue in Hamilton, Ohio. I don't know if this address was used because you had no awareness of the change in his status or were unsure of his new address.

"Please forgive me if I am providing you with information you already know, but I wanted to ensure that his friends knew of his condition and location."

The letter, in part, read like a weekly injury report from a National Football League team. But it simply was the status of Don DeLotell. His daughter sent it to the Turfway Park mutuel department.

Anyone who has been around awhile knows Don DeLotell. When he was working, he visited the press box daily. He came in for a free cup of coffee and conversation. He always had on a dress hat and was puffing on a Lucky Strike while perusing the day's entries.

DeLotell sold mutuel tickets at River Downs, Latonia and other tracks in the Midwest and Florida for at least 50 years before poor health put him down.

When he had his health, DeLotell often was addressing something of interest to the Kentucky on-track offices of *Daily Racing Form* and other racing figures like Tommy Trotter and Woody Stephens. He corresponded regulary with former NFL great Roger Staubach. They are great friends.

The last letter to *DRF* arrived in 1994 at Ellis Park. The main track was playing to speed early in the meeting, and a story was written about what a field day handicapper Jule Fink would have if he'd have been there to play.

DeLotell read the column and responded, naturally, in wholehearted agreement. Why? Because Fink grew up in Cincinnati. DeLotell knew him well and visited him often during winters in Miami.

As retired clocker Richard Bailey noted: "If you've ever robbed a bank, have a secret or like a horse, don't tell Don. He'll tell everybody in town and won't even know he said a word."

In addition to the tales he told of his World War II exploits in France and Belgium with Gen. George S. Patton Jr.'s famed Third Army, DeLotell enjoyed his Fink stories best.

Sadly, though, DeLotell has been out of action for some time. In January 1995, he suffered an aortic aneurysm that was surgicially repaired. Two months later, he was involved in a head-on auto accident.

On Dec. 31, 1995, he was hospitalized for double pneumonia. His weight dipped below 125 pounds, and he fell and broke a hip in April, 1995. Always on the move, DeLotell hasn't been able to get around since without a walker.

His daughter's letter continues: "This has been very difficult for my dad, and he has lost most of his interest in life. He remains in a depressed state and no longer writes or phones friends and acquaintances. The facility he lives in is nice, but his freedom has been lost and he recognizes that life as he knew it is over.

"While he will not initiate contact with old friends, he's always happy to have visitors, receive phone calls, letters or cards. He appreciated the many friends from whom he heard at the holidays.

"I wanted to make sure you not only know of his condition but also his address and telephone number should you care to communicate with him in the future."

DeLotell's address is The Lodge at St. Charles, Apartment 130, 509 Farrell Drive, Fort Wright, Ky., 41011. The telephone number is 606-341-4157.

By the way, he's a swell guy.

VICTORY IS OVERSHADOWED BY JOCK SHAHEEN'S DEATH

FEBRUARY, 1997

FLORENCE, Ky. — Primistal, a high-priced claiming and allowance mare, overcame trouble nearing the stretch last Saturday to give jockey Donna Barton her 1,000th career victory.

Because the mare is owned by Frank L. Jones Jr., a life-long resident of Louisville, Ky., and trained by another Louisvillian, Jerry Romans, Primistal went off at 4-5 and paid $3.80.

That's to be expected, in part, because Jones is president and CEO of Recreonics Inc, the world's largest aquatics distributor, shipping diving boards, towers and pool accessories around the globe.

He also was last year's president of the Kentucky Thoroughbred Owners and is vice-presidentf the Kentucky division of the Horsemen's Benevolent and Protective Association. In a nutshell, Jones, a self-made businessman, has become a powerful player in Kentucky racing, and his stable averages about 25 victories per year.

Jones watched the race from the Sports Spectrum in Louisville. He loves to handicap and has been know to back his horses seriously when they compete, which he did with Primistal.

Jones and Romans teamed up with their first horse in 1968. They began with cheap claimers, elevating the stock gradually until four years ago when they upgraded enormously after he began buying horses from Allen Paulson and racing a few in partnership with him.

Primistal was Jones' fourth winner of the meeting, placing him in a tie for the lead with W.T. Young's Overbrook Farm.

But Jones wasn't really interested in discussing titles or Primistal. His heart was heavy over the loss of his long-time friend, Mitchell "Jock" Shaheen.

At 84, Shaheen died Jan. 30 at Baptist East Hospital in Louisville. His mind was sharp as a tack, but his great heart quit working.

Jones grew up near the Derby City's Lebanese community and had known Shaheen, one of the most colorful characters the turf ever will produce, long before he entered racing.

"I met Jock in 1960 when I was accepted and invited to all the functions in the Lebanese community," said Jones, 59. "I became a member of that gang, and their primary hobby was going to the races, which also became mine. Jock trained horses back in the 1930s, 1940s and 1950s, and he was a fixture at Churchill Downs. Everybody knew him. He was extremely close to the late Milton and Stanley Rieser.

"I don't think I've ever been to the races without thinking about Jock during some point of the day. He was a daily regular in the horsemen's lounge. I'll miss him greatly, especially when Churchill Downs is open."

Jim Bolus, a 20-year newspaper veteran and author of six books on the Kentucky Derby, also knew Shaheen well.

"I've always said that Jock was one of the guys who missed his calling," Bolus said. "He should have gone to Hollywood and played himself. He never seemed to age. What a grand little character!

"Jock would approach his friends, then talk out of the side of his mouth around an ever-present cigar. He was very quiet and always acted like he was letting you in on a sure thing but didn't want to be overheard by a stranger. He thought there was a cinch or a play in every race.

"Damon Runyon couldn't have created a more colorful character. Jock was always around, whether at Churchill or the Sports Spectrum. He always had an opinion and would share it with you.

"One thing about him, though, most people only know the way to the betting windows. Jock knew everyone and knew his way around the barn area, too.

"Just as there will never be another Joe Hirsch or Ted Bassett, there won't be another Jock Shaheen, either."

Appropriately, Shaheen's family placed a Feb. 2 edition of *Daily Racing Form* in his casket. Jock would have wanted it that way.

It was natural.

TAUZIN HELPED PIONEER
CAJUN WINNING TRADITION

JUNE, 1998

LOUISVILLE, Ky. — Retired jockey Leroy Tauzin, the greatest rider who ever worked regularly at Ellis Park in Henderson, Ky., suffered a massive heart attack while galloping a horse May 4 at Evangeline Downs.

He remains in critical condition at Our Lady of Lords Hospital in Lafayette, La.

Though he's breathing on his own power, Tauzin suffered brain damage and shows no signs of recovery.

From the early 1960s when he came to Kentucky, until 1981, he was a major figure at Ellis Park, old Miles Park and Churchill Downs.

Nobody before or since has dominated meetings at Ellis like Leroy Joseph Tauzin.

He retired from riding the first time in 1981, realized it was too soon and came back to ride again at Ellis in 1985 and 1986. Then he hung it up for good to run several apartment complexes he owns in Metairie, La.

However, the Abbyville, La., native loved being around horses and galloped them daily to stay fit. Tauzin was galloping in company the day he was stricken. His partner said he coughed once and fell from his mount. His heart stopped and he was revived by paramedics.

A lot of stories come to the minds of Ellis regulars when Tauzin's name is mentioned. One in particular happened the afternoon of Sept. 1, 1981, when a strong thunderstorm swept through the Henderson area. Quickly, dense, black clouds blocked all signs of light, and more than two inches of rain was dumped on Ellis Park. The infield soybeans prospered, but the main track — there was no turf course then — resembled a lake.

A cool breeze quickly blew the clouds out, and by the last race, the horizon featured a perfect, crystal-clear blue sky.

That day's finale featured a field of nine nondescript $5,000 claimers going a mile.

Riding a 9-1 shot was Tauzin. As noted during that era, he was to Ellis Park what Pat Day has been and is to Oaklawn Park, Arlington, Keeneland and Churchill Downs.

Anyway, the paddock scene for the aforementioned race was a bit emotional. Tauzin was riding a friend's favorite horse — sort of a family pet, if you will. Tauzin knew the man's sentiments and liked the animal, too. In fact, he was seeking his third straight win aboard the steed.

When being legged up, a half-dozen pairs of goggles overlapped on his helmet to combat the deep slop, he told the owner with a cockeyed grin and Cajun twang: "Baby," — male or female, he always called his immediate associates that — "quit worrying about it. You just get the family together and meet me in the winner's circle."

Running last, 25 lengths behind after the opening half-mile, Tauzin found "the path" as they used to say at Ellis, which was the best part of the track. Tauzin and his mount passed seven horses in a quarter-mile and wore down the final opponent by a neck in a driving finish.

Entering the winner's circle, the only clean points on the horse or rider was the tiny area Tauzin's last pair of goggles covered.

"I told you not to worry," he grinned through a mask of mud.

"Well, you didn't have to cut it that close," the owner fired back through a mixture of tears and laughter. "My family and I thank you, pal. We love you."

As tough and dependable and unemotional as any fellow who ever lived, the jockey had to level with his friends at that instant. He dropped his head and mumbled: "I love you guys, too."

Historical data proves that since the first Kentucky Derby in 1875, small boys — most with no formal education and far under the legal age of manhood — have migrated from Louisiana's backwoods bayous to seek fame and fortune as jockeys.

Riders who immediately come to the local public's mind

are, of course, Craig Perret, Tracy Hebert, Shane Sellers, Kent Desormeaux, Calvin Borel and Robby Albarado. Nearly all of them paid their dues at places like Jefferson Downs, Evangeline Downs, then Fair Grounds, Louisiana Downs, etc. before heading north.

They can thank guys like Clarence Meaux, Eddie Delahoussaye, Glynn Bernis, Weston Soirez and Tauzin for starting the migration.

LEROY TAUZIN WAS AN ELLIS INSTITUTION

AUGUST, 1998

While attention was focused last week on Ellis Park's Gardenia Stakes, the track in particular and racing in general lost a great friend when former jockey Leroy Tauzin died peacefully in his sleep at age 55.

The cause of his death was an infection that arose when his vital organs stopped working. He'd been in a coma since May 4 after suffering a massive heart attack while galloping a horse at Evangeline Downs in Lafayette, La. He fell off and never regained consciousness.

There's so much to write about Tauzin that it was necessary to sit back a couple of days, sort through the memories, pull out the most notable ones and get everything perfect.

A seven-time Ellis riding champion during 1969-71, 1974, 1978-80, Leroy Joseph Tauzin wasn't only a great jockey linked with Ellis Park's glorious past. He also was a loyal friend.

And from the time he won his first Ellis title until he rode his last race, he was a summertime hero to Tri-State racegoers. His name was as synonymous with Ellis Park as the soybeans that formerly graced the infield.

If you think Jon Court was overpowering in the jockey's race this past meeting, you'd have loved Tauzin. Because nobody dominated Ellis Park like he did.

Tauzin officially retired after riding his last race at Ellis Park on Labor Day, 1986.

Bothered by a nagging back injury, he'd retired for the

first time on Labor Day, 1983. But therapy, boredom and a love for competition brought him back for 1985-86.

A wise investor, Tauzin built several apartment complexes in his hometown of Metairie, La., which he oversaw when not with horses.

A native of Abbyville, La., a bayou community that's produced many top riders, Tauzin started his career in 1961 at Jefferson Downs and showed up at Ellis Park for the first time in 1965. He couldn't buy a mount, lasted a week and moved on to Detroit Race Course.

Determined to make it in Kentucky, he polished his skills, came back a year later and entrenched himself with horsemen, fans and management.

There wasn't year-round racing during Tauzin's early years. He never rode more than nine months a year, but still batted home nearly 2,500 winners.

It was 20 years ago this past July at Ellis Park that Tauzin rode eight consecutive winners. He knocked in the last four of a nine-race card and the following day, added the first four.

You can't think of Tauzin without recalling the old chestnut gelding, Don Din. Owned and trained by Steve Duncan of Evansville, Ind., Don Din was Ellis Park's all-time winningest horse. In four years, he recorded 18 Ellis victories, all under Tauzin.

Many think Tauzin was at his best when the weather was at its worst. And history proves that he had countless multiple win days when Ellis' main track resembled a sea of slop.

I'll remember and treasure Tauzin for the effort he gave in the last race on Sept. 1, 1981. After a tremendous thunderstorm, the track was ankle deep slop.

Like a knight in armor, Tauzin had at least six pair of goggles perched atop his helmet when emerging from the jock's room. There was very little conversation when he was boosted into the saddle and no riding instructions were needed.

Finally, Tauzin, with the ever present cockeyed grin and Cajun twang, nodded to me and said: "Baby," he always called his close associates that, "meet me in the winner's circle."

With half of the mile test remaining, Tauzin appeared hopelessly beaten and was last, 22 lengths off the lead. But, in the final quarter-mile, he "found the path" as they used to say and his mount got up to win by a half-length.

A tough, dependable and unemotional little man, he simply said while getting his picture snapped: "Baby, I told you not to worry." Then, when clear of spectators while walking back to the jock's room, he proved he was human and quietly wept for having won for a friend.

Hundreds of riders have passed through Ellis Park. Some had more popular names, loftier statistics and a better gift of gab with the media than Tauzin.

But when it came to the complete package required of a professional, they all were chasing Leroy Joseph Tauzin. He was an institution.

FLUTY'S IMPACT STILL FELT BY LOCAL SPORTS AND PEOPLE

NOVEMBER, 1999

LOUISVILLE, Ky. — Don Bernhardt, a cherished friend, was *The Evansville Courier*'s associate sports editor when he died suddenly on Sept. 29, 1983, while vacationing in Austria.

Two weeks later came the most critically important change in my life.

It happened because a man that I respected but didn't know well enough yet to revere, stopped by the house to visit. His name was Bill Fluty. He was the *Courier*'s sports editor.

We often partied and drank together when my parents, Charlie and Ruth, hosted legendary barbques for the horse set at their summer camp during race meetings at Ellis Park. They also had a box near Ellis' finish line where Bill and his wife, Bridget, often sat.

And for the record, late on countless Friday nights, when I was working part-time for the *Courier*, Fluty gave me great insight after business hours at the old For-Get-Me Not Inn on how to make and enjoy a perfect martini with Beefeater's Gin and jumbo olives. He called them "Hungrys."

But when Fluty visited on that fall afternoon following Bernhardt's death, he wasn't in a partying mood. He was all business. I got him a Coca-Cola and an ashtray. He sat on one side of the large living room. I flopped on the other.

As a conversationalist, his style mirrored his writing. He used as few words as absolutely necessary. Bluntly he said: "I'm going to need somebody that knows racing to cover Ellis Park and the Kentucky Derby. That same guy has to know high school football and basketball, too. You understand the horse business better than anybody I've ever known. And that includes Bernie and Dan Scism. You were with Bernie all those years. A lot of his friends among the coaches are your friends, too. They'll do business with you.

"Think it over for a couple of days and let me know if you want to work for me."

As a matter of principle and respect, I never called Fluty by his nickname of "Flutes" or even "Bill" in public. I used the monicker of "Chief," which to me, still sounded authoritative and a little better than "Coach" or "Boss," although they fit Fluty, too.

With a dual degree in radio/television and speech, I'd never had a day of print journalism. And stunned by his job proposal, I stammered: "Chief, I don't know if I'm good enough. And I sure as hell don't want to let anybody down."

Taking a drag from his cigarette, Fluty calmed the air by replying; "I've already thought about that. Main thing is, you know the races, the overall Evansville sports' beat and the area teams we cover. You don't have many bad habits. I can teach you how to write."

So I said "yes."

Originally, this column was going to be a birthday tribute to another grand friend, Hall of Fame trainer Jimmy Jones, who turned 93. We were discussing Horse of the Year options. Having trained seven champions, he's a qualified authority.

But death, as they say, intervened. Bill Fluty's death. And replaying and reliving those aforementioned moments came as easy as breathing last Wednesday after *Courier & Press* sports editor Eric Crawford reported by telephone the sad news that cancer claimed Fluty at age 72.

For his confidence in hiring me so long ago, his quiet, methodical teachings of how to get the job done, and most of all, for his friendship, I shall be grateful to Bill Fluty all my life.

Few people realize what a fierce competitor he was. He demanded that "his boys" get the story right, and get it first. He explained it this way. "Your job is not only to report the score and get the facts. It's also to take the reader behind the scenes. To the locker rooms, the barn areas and the jockey's rooms. Tell the reader what's going on and what's being said."

It's a formula that works in any era.

His incredibly accurate ear and retentive memory, flaw-less taste, warmth and understanding, his zeal for the game, his laughter and the purity of his words combined to make him one of the great columnists and editors throughout the Midwest. And please understand that guys like Scism, Fluty and Bernhardt were here because they wanted to be. Not because they had to be. Many times, to the good fortune of our subscribers, they turned down bigger newspapers.

A native of Winchester, Ky., Fluty had gone to work for *The Evansville Courier* in 1955. Besides close bonds with local coaches, he developed a strong admiration for Indiana University basketball coach Bob Knight and the values he maintains.

But as a native Kentuckian, Fluty never lost his deep reverence for the Kentucky Derby.

I've covered each once since 1980. But 1984 marked the first time I'd handled one without Bernhardt or Fluty coaching from alongside. Anway, for six months prior to the 1984 renewal, I'd been explaining how an almost black colt named Swale would win it. And he did. Never one to praise, Fluty knew what he jokingly muttered would be impossible when he said: "Nice going. But you know, I'll expect that kind of handicapping every year."

An extremely unemotional man, that's as close to an accolade as he was prone to give. But you knew that inside, he was bursting apart at the seams with pride because one of "his boys" had fared well. It's a group that I'm honored to be a part of.

Charting and covering yesterday's races at Churchill Downs made it impossible to get home for the funeral. Speaking with Mrs. Fluty by telephone, she said that he'd told her often that I'd been his pet project. She said that he would understand my absence "because nothing could ever get in the way of a story."

Fluty retired from the *Courier* in 1989. When people say that during his tenure he did as much or more than any other man personally, and through the people he hired to have a positive effect on the local sports scene, they won't be exaggerating.

After all these years, his influence remains strong.

MCKENZIE COULD
ALWAYS BE COUNTED UPON

FEBRUARY, 1996

FLORENCE, Ky. — During the early portion of the slide, or movie presentation, in the Kentucky Derby Museum's Great Hall, trainer Woody Stephens says the following to his then assistant trainer and exercise rider.

"He looked good Ronnie. And tomorrow, we'll gallop him alongside this big fat rascal right here. That'll do him some good."

This was recorded and filmed in early 1984 when Stephens was preparing Claiborne Farm's ill-fated Swale to win that spring's Florida Derby, Kentucky Derby and Belmont Stakes.

"Ronnie" was Ron McKenzie, a slight Irishman who was an excellent, knowledgeable horsebacker. He was a sharp dresser, articulate and a good old boy who liked to bend an elbow with friends. He worked hard in the mornings and gave equal effort in the evenings.

On Feb. 10, McKenzie made news in *Daily Racing Form*. He sent out Five Star Stable's Bay Street Star against Cigar in the Donn Handicap. The headline over the story read: "McKenzie, Bay Street Star fight battle of their lives."

The piece reported that McKenzie had been diagnosed with lung cancer, that was believed to be curable.

Unfortunately, it wasn't. And on Feb. 16, an obituary from Gulfstream Park read: "Trainer Ron McKenzie, 58, dies."

Speaking from Miami, Stephens recalled McKenzie as "very solid. He grew up in Ireland where the boys rub two horses and gallop two. He knew everything about a horse. You know, finding good help is one of the biggest problems in racing or in any other business.

"Ronnie and I had a lot of great days. Had some bad ones, too. Ronnie had just galloped Swale and had a hold of his bridle when he was getting his bath that morning eight days after winning the 1984 Belmont when he reared up and died."

McKenzie was very thorough with most barn-related tasks, later going out on his own, opening a public stable and enjoying good success. He transformed several claiming types into respected stakes horses. He based his stable in Florida and shipped around the country.

During his days as an assistant and exercise rider, McKenzie's philosophy was simple. He told us: "Pay strict attention to what the trainer wants done and carry out those orders unless some crisis arises while you're out there on your own which forces you to improvise.

"Carrying out those orders will pay off in the afternoons. And remember, you can mess up a year's work with a horse in one minute or less."

For the record, Swale wasn't the only top horse McKenzie ever galloped. During a stint with trainer Leroy Jolley, he was the morning pilot for such standouts as Kentucky Derby winner Genuine Risk, Cure the Blues and General Assembly.

During Stephens' unprecedented run of five straight Belmont Stakes victories in the mid-1980s, McKenzie was the man with Caveat, Swale and Creme Fraiche. Contredance and Miss Oceana were crackerjack fillies he handled, too.

We could go on and on with other notable names. But it's safe to say that stakes horses and well-bred 2-year-olds were commonplace.

It's the opinion of many that a top-flight exercise rider is as important to a trainer prepping a horse for the Kentucky Derby or any other major engagement as the secretary of state is to the President. It's the exercise rider who lets the trainer know how much the horse is responding each morning leading up to race day.

Stephens said that McKenzie had been ill for some time. "He shipped a horse to my barn in New York last year. He had to stop and rest just walking down the shedrow. His passing is a real shame. Not many like him come along in a lifetime."

HERB STEVENS
CALLS IT A DAY AT 79

OCTOBER, 1996

LEXINGTON, Ky. — There was something missing when Keeneland racing secretary Howard Battle's barn list came out last month.

For the first time since Feb. 1, 1946, the name Herb Stevens was absent from the lineup of trainers for the fall meeting.

Jim Bolus, the world's leading authority on the Kentucky Derby and secretary-treasurer of the National Turf Writers, called with the news during the first week of September.

"It's hard to believe, but Herb Stevens is hanging it up," Bolus said. "You know, he's always been a real thorough, all-around horseman. And a gentleman, too. When they coined the phrase 'Kentucky Hardboot' they were talking about Herb."

Actually, Stevens' retirement from training concludes a family training legacy that spanned four generations. For about 120 years, men named Stevens have raced horses in Kentucky.

Herb's late brother, Tommy and their father, James, were highty respected trainers, as was James' father, Thomas H. Stevens, along with his father, John Stevens, to whom the family roots trace.

A nineteenth-century legend has John Stevens and his son, Thomas H., masterminding a foolproof method of winning wagers. They traveled around central Kentucky with a quarter-horse pulling their buggy and another tied to the back.

Nearing their destination, they'd switch horses. When the locals would begin boasting of their horses' speed, John Stevens would remark that he had a buggy horse that could outrun them all. Properly insulted, the townspeople, not realizing the switch, would wager against Stevens' horse. With son Thomas in the saddle, the story is that they were undefeated.

Back to Herb Stevens. Many of his loyal, longtime patrons have left racing, and his stable was down to three horses. On Aug. 30, he took a filly to the track to breeze five furlongs. She was going decently around the turn when suddenly the rider began to pull her up. She staggered into the stretch, collapsed and died.

With the exception of time during World War II as U.S. Army officer in a tank destroyer battalion in Europe, and a couple of years as a University of Kentucky undergraduate, Stevens has worked with horses in some capacity since 1934. So it wasn't his first time for tragedy.

"I've had it all happen to me, good and bad," he said. Nevertheless, the latest incident was the final straw for Stevens.

A big, tough, friendly man who rarely is without a wide-brim Stetson hat, Stevens ranks eighth on Keeneland's all-time training list for victories. At Keeneland, he saddled 137 winners, including champion Rockhill Native in the 1980 Blue Grass Stakes and Jelly Bean Holiday in the 1982 Alcibiades.

He turned his horses and tack over to his assistant, Chris Crowe. And, at age 79, Stevens started a new lease on life.

He's still around and goes to the track each morning. But these days, he's no longer bothered with the problems all trainers face.

"I'm like a volunteer fireman," he said. "If someone needs help or something done, I'll pitch in. I still visit with my friends in the track kitchen every day. I just don't go out as early as I used to. I'm not going to sit down and rot. I've got to keep going.

"Thing is, I can go out to the track now, fool around and walk away whenever I want to. I don't have a routine and no responsibilities. I'm through with those everyday hassles that trainer's have to face in today's game. There's not the kind of loyalty like when I started out, and you can't have nearly the fun. Plus, the help situation is difficult. It's not going to get any better, and it was time for me to go. It was time for a change."

While Stevens enjoys the fall meeting, he reveres the spring, when Keeneland is in full bloom and holds centerstage for Kentucky Derby hopefuls and young horses about to debut.

The Derby has a special place in Stevens' heart, but winning the Blue Grass Stakes remains his ultimate thrill.

"The Blue Grass was the most prestigious race I ever won, and it was here, in front of the home folks," said the Lexington, Ky. native. "Plus, I developed the horse (Rockhill Native) my way, right here at Keeneland."

Stevens wasn't your typical horseman in one sense, because he never really liked to travel. He preferred to ship to Kentucky tracks or River Downs, then return home at night for supper.

He's had his differences with management at times and spoke his piece. But Keeneland was, far and away, and still is, his favorite track. He's a fixture, as they say. And to some, Stevens is one of the reasons the place remains special each spring and fall.

BERNHARDT 'CAP HONORS MEMORABLE MAN

JUNE, 1984

HENDERSON, Ky. — There won't be a band playing "My Old Kentucky Home" when the field goes postward opening day in Ellis Park's inaugural running of the Don Bernhardt Memorial Handicap.

It's a good thing, because Bernhardt, who suffered a fatal heat attack last September, 29 while vacationing with his family in Austria, was a traditionalist. He wouldn't appreciate Stephen Foster's most famous melody being played for his race. That's not because Bernhardt didn't love the song. He merely deemed it proper to hear the theme only for the world's greatest race, the Kentucky Derby, which he covered more than 20 times for *The Evansville Courier.*

At the time of his death at age 51, Bernhardt was associate sports editor of that publication. He was a 31-year veteran of the department, a fixture in the Ellis Park press box and on the Kentucky racing circuit.

Of all the sports he covered, football, golf and horse racing were his favorites. His travels took him to the Derby, Super Bowl, Blue Grass Stakes, Masters Golf Tournament and countless college games involving Indiana University, Purdue University and the University of Evansville.

But it was during the Ellis racing season that Bernhardt enjoyed his profession most. He penned a feature story daily and provided fans with a fine number of winners in his daily selections, "Bernhardt's Best."

He enjoyed his subject immensely and was a stickler for facts. He was rarely a knocker and stressed the importance of accuracy and fairness over knocking. He was scholarly, fatherly, brotherly, but never stuffy or smothering. He wrote as he talked, with wit, down home grace and confidence.

During the Ellis meet, he made Mondays the brightest day of the week with his column on the *Courier*'s sports pages.

"What did Bernhardt write about today?" was a question asked frequently around the community. Not only did his colleagues ask it, but so did the racing people he loved and respected, as well as the novices whose interests were usually far away from the track.

Years before the overlapping of racing dates with Churchill Downs, several of the press box regulars formed Ellis' version of the "Boys of Summer." They were a well-mixed brigade who worked together, socialized together and stuck together when the chips were down.

At the hub of the gang was Bernhardt. If a crisis arose, it was he who would tackle the problem head on. If a favor was needed, he would always extend himself to accomplish it. If management needed its knuckles rapped, he'd do that, too.

It was with the "Boys of Summer" that "Bernie," as they called him, spent his final day of racing, Sept. 2, 1983, closing day of last summer's meeting.

After watching the Monday Night Football telecast, he said, "See you guys down the road," and was gone, leaving for Europe a few days later.

His chief contribution to the world besides his exceptional gift with a typewriter, was his wonderful family and personality. A friendly chap, even to total strangers, Bernie made humor and fun his motto. He would rather tell one of his jokes than bet on a winner, and he loved to tab winners, too.

Track officials decided it only justice that the opening day feature be named for Bernie, for his memory will be held in the highest esteem for as long as they spring the latch at Ellis Park.

In the final analysis, Don Bernhardt left a legacy that won't be forgotten. In the words of one of his friends, "He always gave more than he took."

BERNHARDT ALWAYS STOOD TALL WITH VIRTUES FOR GREATNESS

JULY, 1993

D. Wayne Lukas was glowing with excitement when preparing Marfa during the week leading up to the 1983 Kentucky Derby.

This was back before it was commonplace for horses trained by Lukas to regularly carry the now famed white bridles to victory in major stakes races around the country. Marfa was one of those instrumental in making Lukas a household word.

About the time Marfa was making national headlines, an apprentice writer accompanied Don Bernhardt to Louisville, Ky. for Derby Week.

The apprentice knew Lukas. Earlier that spring, they'd met at Turfway Park for the Jim Beam Stakes, and a friendship was struck.

Derby Week, the younger writer suggested to Bernhardt, then The Evansille Courier's associate sports editor, that a column on Lukas would be appropriate. "Don, Lukas talks your language," he said. "He's a former basketball coach and relates everything he has to say about horse to human athletes."

"Is that so," Bernhardt said. "Well, let's get up early tomorrow and you can introduce me."

Bernhardt and Lukas had a common denominator. Both were on friendly terms with Indiana University basketball coach Bob Knight. When that came out in the interview, Lukas really opened up.

The product of that visit was an award-winning piece

that was titled something like: "Bad Boy Marfa to Try and Bull Derby Foes."

For the record, Bernhardt didn't pick Marfa to win the Derby. Bernhardt was a speed man and opted for Sunny's Halo, who took over and won by two lengths. He was the class of the field that day, and class was something Bernhardt had no trouble recognizing. He saw it every morning in the mirror.

All of this came to mind Thursday at Ellis Park when entries were drawn for today's $50,000 Don Bernhardt Memorial Stakes matching 3-year-olds and up going 6 1/2 furlongs. It will be 10 years this September that Bernhardt died while vacationing with his family in Austria.

Memories of Bernhardt came easily during the past week. It always seems to happen that way.

Jim Kornblum, a mutual friend and Evansville attorney, delivered two boxes of prime cigars on Thursday. Bernhardt would've been inside those boxes faster than the law allows.

It's those little things that keep popping up during one's lifetime that makes you realize how critically important people like Bernhardt are.

Had he lived, he'd be 61 years old. He never believed he was important, although he knew the local sports beat inside and out.

Ellis racing secretary Tim Day has a plaque in his office that says: "A racehorse is the only creature that can take thousands of people along for a ride at the same time."

There are a couple of exceptions to that, one being a racing writer.

A great one is a rarity because you must have unwritten intangibles like personal credibility, knowing the game frontside and backside, knowing how the readers want the news reported, the keen ability to offer praise when justified and the fact-finding ruthlessness to condemn when appropriate.

Being familiar with the sport's participants is vital, too. And without longevity, meeting deadlines day after day and staying the course over an extended period of time, it's all meaningless.

Don Bernhardt stood only 5-foot-8, but he professionally stood much taller and held all those virtues for greatness. He amassed them over 31 years of service at *The Courier*.

When you throw in that he wrote and made selections

daily during Ellis Park meetings, it's safe to say that he took a lot of people along for the ride.

He was superb because he could make a story involving some $1,500 claimer sound as interesting as something he'd written during Derby week.

His success generated from his integrity. When you read his stuff over a period of time, you became aware you were getting an honest, accurate statement.

"The most important things is to get the facts," he said. "If there's time to jazz it up and make it into more creative writing, that's icing on the cake."

The latter set him apart and placed him in a lofty position as one of the best of his time. Yet, he never lost sight of the fact that he was writing for a daily paper whose primary goal was to set the facts in order.

Professionally, there will never be another quite like him. Personally, he was as good a friend as a fellow could have. It was a stroke of good fortune to sit next to him for many years.

Our friendship could have ended only one way, like it did on that terrible Friday nearly 10 years ago when informed by telephone of his death.

So toast him today. He'd prefer it be done with Scotch and water, along with one of Kornblum's cigars.

PEGRAM RECALLS THE
DAY HE BUMPED INTO "BERNIE"

JULY, 1998

In the bar of a Louisville, Ky., restaurant during this year's Kentucky Derby week, friends of the late Don Bernhardt were exchanging stories about him while bantering about who they liked in the big race.

Don would have loved the setting and reveled in the camaraderie of guys like Mike Pegram and Bob Baffert, the owner and trainer of eventual Derby winner Real Quiet, Mike Phipps, president of The Evansville Teachers Federal Credit Union, local attorneys Jim Kornblum and Dennis Brinkmeyer, myself and others.

It seemed like only a short time ago that Bernhardt was around, holding up his end of the chatter.

Bernhardt would've been in total agreement that evening when Phipps ordered a round of Single Malt Knockando Scotch for a nightcap, shook Pegram's hand and sincerely told him: "Man, a lot of us from Southern Indiana are pulling for you and Real Quiet. He's sitting on a win. If I don't see you again before the race, best of luck."

After winning the Derby, Real Quiet also won the Preakness Stakes.

Today's feature at Ellis Park is a $50,000 stakes race named in Bernhardt's memory. If figures matter, it'll be 15 years this September that *The Evansville Courier*'s associate sports editor died from a massive heart attack while vacationing in Austria.

Back to Derby week. Earlier that night in the bar, Pegram, Baffert and Bob Lewis of Silver Charm fame helped out a couple of old friends and had been the featured guests on a live radio show in the restaurant's 250-seat room.

Never forgetting Ellis Park and Bernhardt's race, I asked April Mayberry, Baffert's Kentucky assistant, if she would like to keep Pegram's good sprinter, High Stakes Player in Kentucky for the summer and run him in the Bernhardt event.

April, you see, has deep sentiment for High Stakes Player.

"You know I would," she beamed, "but how are you going to do it?"

I replied: "That's easy. While we're live on the air, I'll bring up a sentimental story about Ellis Park and where Pegram and I grew up. Baffert won't be able to refuse."

Pegram couldn't and Baffert didn't. And today, High Stakes Player will be one of the primary choices in a field of 10 set to start in the Don Bernhardt Memorial Stakes.

When he wasn't reading *The Courier*'s sports pages or a *Daily Racing Form*, Pegram was an excellent basketball forward and baseball pitcher at Princeton High School.

Despite reading Bernhardt for years, he only met him once. And that was by chance. But it was a meeting he never forgot. Here's how it happened.

Member of Pegram's family were daily patrons at Ellis Park. And when Mike became old enough to drive, one of his assignments was to run bets to the track for farmers in Gibson County when they couldn't get away from their work.

One day, Pegram stopped off at a bookie joint and there, playing cards at a table, was Bernhardt.

This was a big deal for a highschool kid like Pegram because he revered Bernhardt, the guy who wrote about Tri-State prep sports the most frequently and eloquently.

"That was a special moment for a kid from a small town like me," recalled Pegram. "To meet the guy who wrote so much about local sports and Ellis Park, my two favorite things, was a thrill. Don laughed and promised not to tell anyone where we met if I didn't. Until now, I never have.

"Bernhardt was the first guy I ever read who wrote about racing," continued Pegram. "He helped me get hooked on it and even wrote a lot about Storm Strike, the first horse I ever owned, when he won at Ellis Park. Now, the only thing that matters is if High Stakes Player wins. It's a way for me to give something back to another era of my life and a guy who helped make it special."

(Editor's note: High Stakes Player won the race by a neck, then returned two weeks later to capture Ellis' Governor's Handicap).

LUKAS LOSES VITAL PLAYER IN DALLAS STEWART

AUGUST, 1997

Annually, on Tuesday night before the Kentucky Derby, the Kentucky Thoroughbred Owners and Breeders' Association holds its awards dinner at the Hyatt Regency in downtown Louisville, Ky.

The program features several trophy presentations, including one to the winning trainer of the previous year's Derby.

In 1996, trainer D. Wayne Lukas sent his "No. 1 man," assistant trainer Dallas Stewart, to accept his award for Thunder Gulch's 1995 Derby victory. It was the same this past spring when Stewart accepted on behalf of Grindstone's spectacular effort in the 1996 classic.

Owned by W.T. Young's Overbrook Farm, Grindstone ran coupled with the farm's Editor's Note.

Young also spoke on the Tuesday night prior to the 1996 Derby. About Stewart he said that evening, "Dallas is so devoted and attached to Editor's Note, he'll probably sleep in the colt's stall the rest of the week. He's so vital to Wayne's operation...."

All of this and a lot more came to mind last Friday when it became official that after 11 memorable seasons, Stewart is leaving "Team Lukas" to form his own public stable.

It was an extremely emotional decision for both men. Stewart has several clients and about 12 horses including several for Willis, Cam, Terry and Leon Horton, lined up to open his stable about Sept. 1.

He'll be based at Churchill Downs "if they'll give me

stalls," Stewart said by telephone from Saratoga. "Wayne (Lukas) is the greatest competitor I've ever known. You know he'll try to beat me every time, just to show I'll always be the pupil and he's the teacher."

The split is amicable, and though they won't be together on a daily basis, they won't be far apart in spirit or philosophy."

"Dallas is like family to me," said Lukas by telephone from Saratoga. "Like with the rest of my assistants who have gone on their own, he has my utmost blessing and he'll do fine, too. Timing wise, I think he might have waited until after the Breeders' Cup. We're going to have a big fall."

Stewart said he "fully expected to continue eating breakfast every morning at 10:30 a.m. during Churchill Downs meetings with Lukas at Wagners Drug Store.

"Wayne has been wonderful to me and my family. It's been a fantastic run. Just look at all those great horses he let me be around. And look at the unbelievable experiences we've had together. All young men should have the opportunity to be around a guy like Wayne. He's like Vince Lombardi (a role model for Lukas) was for the old Packers. Wayne is the greatest role model and motivator in the history of racing. I cherish our times together. I'm the luckiest guy in the world for having the opportunity."

So, you see, for Stewart, being Lukas' right-hand man has not been simply a job in which you go in, say good morning to the boss and serve your time at the office, then forget all the headaches after the last race and go home.

There is a deep personal bond between the men that can only be attained through winning important races in a pressure-packed, closely scrutinized environment.

Like other former Lukas assistants — Mark Hennig, Kiaran McLaughlin, Randy Bradshaw and Todd Pletcher — who passed through during Stewart's tenure and departed to open their own stables, the great trainer took Stewart under his wing. He taught him his system along with the ability to anticipate problems and head them off before they could become major ones.

Without question, Lukas always told the media how valuable Stewart was and gave him considerable credit during the unbelievable string of consecutive Triple Crown victories.

A native of New Orleans, Stewart was 19 when his father died. It's rare when a man finds someone who can take the place of a loved one. But Lukas filled the role. He became teacher, role model, confidant, friend and sometimes surrogate father.

Their relationship started in the spring of 1986. Stewart, then a skinny, freckle-faced, sandy haired 26-year-old kid had asked Bradshaw about employment at the Fair Grounds earlier. Stewart came to Churchill, met Lukas and asked for a job. He'd grown too tall and heavy to be a jockey, but he was exercising horses and working as a valet after learning the ropes at Delta and Jeffeson Downs.

Lukas needed an exercise rider, and Stewart became the regular morning pilot for Winning Colors, their first Derby winner.

A multitude of victories with Horses of the Year Lady's Secret and Criminal Type, and with others like Gulch, Open Mind, Serena's Song, Flanders, Thunder Gulch, Tabasco Cat, Grindstone and a host of other notables make up a scrapbook that gives Stewart emotional chills.

Lukas can't be everywhere at once, but his plan through Stewart was. And many were the days that Stewart held command at the barn from the time he arrived at 4 a.m. until the last one was cooled out following a late race.

At 37, Stewart believed himself to be "at the crossroads. It's like coaching," he said.

"When do you make a move? Do you go when you're 0-for-20 or on top at 20-0? I simply thought that with the opportunity, it was time. Now, though, the pressure is really on me.

"I've been with the best for 11 years. There's an obligation that every one of his assistants has to carry on Wayne's tradition for excellence. All the other guys have excelled. The pressure will be on me to follow suit."

"STORMIN NORMAN" CARTWRIGHT, A PLUCKY RIDER TO THE END

JANUARY, 1985

Jockey agent Bill Berry delivered last Saturday's wake-up call.

It's not out of the ordinary for "Big Bill" to telephone when the horses are running at Ellis Park. But it is during the bitter winter months.

Without thinking, I knew he was about to tell me something I didn't want to hear — the inevitable news that Norman Cartwright had died. It happened late Friday night following a long bout with cancer. "Stormin Norman," as a legion of horseplayers called him, was 52.

Berry booked rides for Cartwright for 29 years at Ellis Park, the track where Norman first threw a leg over a saddle. Cartwright died in Louisville, Ky., and was buried there Monday.

A Morganfield, Ky., native, Cartwright had been ailing since he dismounted for the last time in 1978. Dizzy spells forced his retirement from the jockey ranks.

He was a first-rate rider in his prime. He plied his trade at Miles Park, Latonia, Fair Grounds, Oaklawn Park and Churchill Downs besides Ellis Park.

Included on his list of many victories for the late James C. Ellis was the 1949 Debutante Stakes at Churchill Downs aboard homebred Aunt Jayne Z. Ellis gave Cartwright his riding start and held his contract for several years.

Cartwright concluded his career in the saddle on a Saturday in late August, 1978. He departed the same way he began, as a winner, aboard owner-trainer Junior Montgomery's Important Mission.

Cartwright won the first race he rode in 1948 on Dreamy Betty, a filly saddled by Ray Gates, retired Ellis Park steward and director of racing.

He was one of the more colorful riders to ever leave the jockey's room and Ellis was his favorite track. Somewhere along the line, an Ellis railbird coined the phrase: "Get right with Cartwright." It stuck and he loved it.

After brain surgery to remove a tumor in 1980, Cartwright spent his last years as a jockey's agent, staying around the game and people he loved.

He'd tell you that if he couldn't be around the races, he'd as soon be dead. One of his proudest moments came when his rider, Corey Nielsen, captured the Ellis Park jockey title on Labor Day, 1983.

Cartwright's declining health forced him away from the races last fall but not before he worked the entire Ellis meeting.

The world of sports is loaded with tales of courageous performances. Cartwright's gutsy run from gate-to-wire wouldn't have to enter the back door if there were a hall of fame for heroics.

Most fans never see the morning ritual of agents in the racing secretary's office bargaining and hustling for open mounts, trying to get their riders on something that has a decent shot in the afternoon.

It was amazing to see Cartwright, or "Wheels" as his compadres called him, at the head of the line reminding an entry clerk that his jockey was free for a particular race.

He was so sick last summer that no one knew what kept him going as he hobbled around the backstretch each morning in search of business. He took a pill daily to perk up his appetite. That refrained him from an occasional sip of Kentucky Bourbon and a smoke, both of which he enjoyed immensely.

By this time, radiation treatments had plucked his once-black, full mane of hair wispy thin. His voice had dwindled to a whisper. Yet, he never missed scratch time, a feat which is becoming extremely difficult with today's late night "happy hours."

It's hard to comprehend what a jockey goes through in a career making weight daily. The public tends to overlook the fact that these little men and women flirt with death each afternoon they do business.

Perhaps the profession prepared Cartwright for his final race. He knew he couldn't win. The odds were simply too long. But he gave it a helluva go and crossed the finish line without a whimper.

MEDIA LOSES OUT
WITH GARY ROGG RESIGNING

SEPTEMBER, 1993

FLORENCE, Ky. — Because this is the final Sunday of Turfway Park's 23-day meeting, it's time for the "this and that department" to hold session.

The above thought and others cropped up when word was received that Gary Rogg, the track's media relations coordinator, had dropped off his resignation effective Oct. 14.

How could that be? After all, Rogg, 44, joined the staff here 10 years ago to escape the drab, ho-hum, complacency that his primary job in the private sector brought on.

He's never been strapped for dollars and has fared well as a salesman for a plastics manufacturing firm specializing in grocery store displays.

Rogg is surrendering the title and many responsibilities but is leaving the door open to fill in part time, string for a local paper and perhaps come back Jim Beam Week when national media often require a ton of help while focusing on the nine-furlong Jim Beam Stakes for Kentucky Derby hopefuls.

When inter-track wagering was introduced in Kentucky during September of 1988, his average work week expanded to between 70-80 hours. Rogg has yet to miss a day since hiring on in 1982, and the battles have taken their toll.

Rogg was never among the clique of executives here fortunate enough to travel and have fun at other tracks in the state or country for such premier events as Derby Day, Breeders' Cup Day or Blue Grass Day. He was always one of the good soldiers left behind to mind the fort when he might have been partaking in merriment alongside his peers.

"I'm tired," he flatly admits, "and I'm getting too old to do this every day, week-after-week. I've always loved racing and that makes going to work at the track fun despite the lack of dark days. My private business has suffered some but that was my choice. I'm leaving the door open and will be available to do some specific contract work when they need me at Beam time or something along those lines."

We came to know Rogg while covering the early runnings of the Beam. He was the computer whiz in the press box and handled the agate results and recaps for the papers within a 200-mile radius that used Turfway (then Latonia) as part of their racing page.

By his own admission, he was never the best writer, although he has enough newspaperman in him to know what a story is worth and how it should be played. Nor could he be tagged as the area's premier handicapper or voice-over when doing the ITW package.

However, it is a fact that he is proficient in all those areas and others. And, that he managed his responsibilities in a fashion that would be acceptable at any track in America.

In short, Rogg knows the game and how to play it. He got things done, and has been one of this track's few true constants. He'll be sorely missed. Particuarly by the visiting media.

RAY GATES, A PAL OF EVERYONE AT ELLIS PARK FOR 62 YEARS

JUNE, 1986

"Ray Gates was a pal of yours, wasn't he?"

Mr. Gates was a buddy to most folks who hung around Ellis Park for any length of time. But that's how news of his death came in the dawn hours of Sunday.

He died at Welborn Baptist Hospital about the time he'd have been arriving at his barn while training horses 40 years ago. One of his charges, Aonbarr, set Ellis' 1 1/8-mile record of 1:50 1/5 as a maiden in the Governor's Handicap of 1941.

It lasted until Sweetest Chant lowered it to 1:49 4/5 in 1982. It, too, is ancient history.

At 79, Gates' passing wasn't entirely unexpected. By his own admittance, he'd "been at the top of life's stretch" for some time. Everyone knew how sick he was. And he'd been spending a great amount of time at his Mount Vernon, Ind., home under the oxygen mask.

Still, he had planned to be driven to Ellis Park on Sunday afternoon to inspect the renovations of the place where he'd spent 62 summers, employed in one capacity or another.

Ellis Park veterans sought him out annually to rekindle old memories and exchange pleasantries. Mostly, it was the trainers, jockeys and agents who came up under his presence.

Gates was a splendid little splinter of a man who aided pipe fitters as a water bearer while they put in the track's original plumbing in 1921.

He took some part in in each of the plant's meetings.

His first job in the racing end came in 1929 when he took a fling as an exercise rider, later becoming a jockey. Gates' primary income was as a foreman in various Evansville automobile mechanic shops. However, he took off each summer to answer the call of the thoroughbred.

He rode several years for trainers like Keene Daingerfield, Henry and Joe Forrest, H.H. Temple and Huley Hack.

A close friendship developed between Gates and the late James C. Ellis. It began in 1934. When Ellis died in 1956, Gates remained with the Ellis estate under Ellis' nephew, former track president Lester E. Yeager.

The pair became virtually inseparable. Fair and honest while never a "house man" as a steward, Gates remained at Yeager's call through 1984, retiring following the final year of the Ellis-Yeager regime.

Gates served management in every capacity. From valet to paddock judge, assistant racing secretary and steward. He was in the stand as an association steward from 1965-82. His last two summers were spent as Director of Racing.

"Ellis Park lost one of its original pieces," said former director of operations Ruth Adkins, who was on the job for 37 years with Gates. "Lester Yeager and I have lost a dear friend of unquestionable loyalty and ability. Another piece of the Ellis legacy has departed. There aren't any more like Ray."

Gates was immaculate in a race track sense. His khaki pants, sport shirt and tipped cigar made him blend in whith those he admired and worked next to. His nickname for everyone was "pardner," and with a soft turn of speech, he spun wonderful yarns of the old days for those breaking into the business who thrived on and wanted to know the track's history.

His duties weren't so confining the past two years, allowing him more opportunity to reflect. "I remember when this (racing) was a game for roughnecks," Gates recalled last August on steamy afternoon while holding court on the press box veranda. "There'd be times when you'd have to collect the jock mount in the paddock before letting the post parade go or you wouldn't get it. The starting gate was the greatest invention for horsemen.

"Bookmakers operated freely when I first came around. It's a lot better game today." No doubt, Gates' insight and guidance had a lot to do with that.

I've related this story from Adkins before and will do so again.

During the wee hours of those dog days of August, Ellis is often encompassed in dense fog. Adkins claims that ghosts of Ellis' deceased old guard hold a party on those days within the infield. "It's a select group. Only the real loyalists can attend," she maintains. "And each of them was a tremendous booster of Ellis Park. Let's see, Anna Fisher will be there, my late husband, Clyde, Dan Scism, Mr. Ellis, Don Bernhardt...."

If Adkins' belief is true, the gathering increased by one on Sunday.

Final Calls to Absent Friends

PART 3:

PLACES

Final Calls to Absent Friends

ELLIS PARK:
A HAVEN FOR TEENAGERS

SEPTEMBER, 1999

For the past several months, I've attempted — as well as I know how — to bring you some of the color, interesting subjects and personality of thoroughbred racing.

The bottom line is: Racing is an athletic contest between horses. And if you're fortunate enough to win at the mutuel windows, it leaves a lasting thrill.

It's the opinion of many that people only go to the races to bet. This is probably 80 percent true. But remember, for example, they run steeplechase races at Saratoga and most major tracks. They're the worst betting races on the card, have the smallest mutuel handle but stir up the most excitement as some of the horses fall over the fences, losing their riders, or leave the course to the gasps of the crowd.

To me, though, and many personal friends, aside from racing being big, big business including the source of income for major breeders, race tracks — especially Ellis Park — offer an arena for fun. It's a place people go to escape the daily grind of boring, everyday life.

In short, on Labor Day, the finale of Ellis' 61-day meeting, you won't find introverts. You'll find happy people seeking camaraderie and a good time.

For me, the expiring summer here — like many before it — has been like "The Big Chill" with a racing background.

Ellis meetings annually are stories of reunions and quality time with friends who became compadres because of this grand, 77-year-old facility.

There's a time in life when you're no longer a child but

still too young to be considered an adult. And during their youth, these longstanding pals learned many crucial lessons during the dog days of August at Ellis Park.

For example, as a tyke, Jim Kornblum thought that the guy driving the water truck had the greatest job in the world.

Fortunately, Kornblum had second thoughts and opted to practice law in Evansville. The pay is better and the hours and weather more acceptable, too.

Anyway, after 25 years, this type of fraternalism is certain to happen. We've annually celebrated an unwritten eternal bonding, partied, matched achievements and revived old rivalries between favorite horses, jockeys and trainers from long ago.

More than anything, this group enjoys remembering. Racing and the good times it produces are what jump-start it all.

The theme often turns nostalgic and conversations float back to people from the Evansville sports scene who've passed on.

Since most of my brigade is in its mid-40s or early 50s, we realize our own sense of mortality and deeply appreciate the good times manufactured at Ellis Park. We realize that these are our "good old days."

Dennis Brinkmeyer, another Evansville attorney and longtime boxseat holder, made his first visit to Ellis in 1949. "It's going to be hard topping this meeting for fun," he said. "Didn't have as many winners as I'd have liked. But we've had a lot of fun."

Too many summers have passed to pick a favorite year. But I still can plainly see those Saturday and Labor Day crowds of 12,000 during the 1970s. I can feel the stands rock as those $2,000 claimers scramble to the wire.

Fans then didn't care that the restrooms were disaster areas or the horses cheap. It was racing and the only racing we knew. On Labor Day, you'd have to get there two hours before post time to get a seat. You came early anyway, to smuggle in a pint of Vodka to mix with a homemade fountain beverage called "The Blend" that a lady named Mrs. Morrow sold for 20 cents at the south end of the grandstand.

And there's never been a sweeter aroma than the one wafting through the stands as the popcorn bubbled out of Mrs. Loney's machine alongside those greasy burgers frying on the grill smothered in onions. And don't forget that now extinct, but forever famous, hotdog relish that Owen Wilkerson of Henderson, Ky., used to make.

You didn't even think about the clubhouse. It was sold out a year in advance. And cars would be parked as far away as the cornfields and along U.S. 41.

Ellis Park was a summertime haven for teenagers of the 1970s. It was the August getaway from the pain and punishment of two-a-day football practices that late, great, high school coaches such as Archie Owen, Gene Logel and Don Watson oversaw.

For a few glorious weeks, the track was the one place that was safe from algebra, advanced composition and typing classes, which later came in handy for some.

I hope you'll pardon my reminiscing a bit about the place our fathers and grandfathers referred to as "Dandy Dade."

I hate to see the season end. But hopefully, you've enjoyed this year's meeting. I know my "boys of summer" have.

PLAYERS, FANS
MADE RFK STADIUM
A SPECIAL PLACE FOR FOOTBALL

DECEMBER, 1997

FLORENCE, Ky. — "You're so hard to buy for. What do you want for Christmas?

That's a question most of us have heard at one time or another. So in keeping with the holiday tradition, I'll respond as such: "What I want you can't buy, because I'd like Washington to have home-field advantage throughout the National Football League playoffs."

The Redskins, sadly, are out of the playoffs after having hit a late season skid following a 7-1 start.

To top that off, a melancholy thing will happen Sunday in the nation's capital: The 'Skins will play for the final time in storied Robert F. Kennedy Memorial Stadium.

Football and vacations never will be the same. A recent story in a local paper summed it up: "Next year, the NFL team will christen Redskins Stadium in Prince George County, Md. Despite the weather, more than 1,000 workers are laboring round-the-clock to have the 70,000-plus seat facility ready for the season's opener."

Perhaps it's only fitting that, on Sunday's final day of operation in 55,000-seat Robert F. Kennedy Memorial Stadium, the Redskins, 8-7, will face their archrivals, the 10-5 Dallas Cowboys. Dallas leads the series 40-29-2, but Washington owns an 18-17 home advantage.

But this isn't about Sunday's game: It's about memories of RFK Stadium. So the rivalry — which many believe to be the most intense in sports — must be noted.

Columnist Art Buchwald once succinctly summed up the

rivalry. "It boils down to one thing: Hate. Hate for reasons that nobody understands."

How it all began or why the fire has stayed hot for decades is anyone's guess, but it has been handed down from generation to generation. It reached epic proportions in the 1970s when Washington's late coach, George Allen, and Dallas' Tom Landry literally hissed at each other. Dallas was glamour. Washington was blue-collar, and Allen turned hating the Cowboys into a religion. From it came a 1984 book titled, "The Semi-Official Dallas Cowboy Haters' Handbook."

The venom still flows, too, as Redskins chairman of the board and chief executive Jack Kent Cooke noted recently over the telephone. "It would be wonderful to beat those bloody @#!#@! Cowboys in the final game at RFK," he said. "There have been some magnificient skirmishes there, and this could be another for history."

Sam Huff made the Hall of Fame as a linebacker for the Giants and Redskins. He played in the first game ever at RFK and will broadcast the finale, along with his former teammate and fellow Hall of Famer Sonny Jurgensen.

"Broadcasting the game Sunday will be emotional for Sonny and me," Huff said. "RFK was suitable in the old days because nobody made any money. Now, there's 40,000 additional people wanting to buy season tickets. Like they say, all things must end."

With a mountain of sports ventures, including Elmendorft Farm in Lexington, Ky. — and as one of the world's richest men, Cooke nevertheless holds the Redskins dearest.

"My memories. Oh God, there are so many, many wonderful ones at RFK," Cooke said. "I'm really the wrong guy to ask because there have been so many, and I've been around for most of them, which makes it difficult to point to specific ones."

Cooke chose to remember the people with whom he came in contact.

"It was great when we brought George Allen in before 1971," Cooke said. "He was one of my favorite guys, and he accounted for many thrills at RFK. He took us to our first Super Bowl, and who could forget that NFC Championship game of 1972 when we thrashed the Cowboys.

"It was a similar situation when we hired Joe Gibbs, just a tremendous coach and an even better man. He was very, very good for a long time in this league. Took us to four Super Bowls and won three."

Cooke recalled Joe Theismann's career-ending injury in a game against the New York Giants on Nov. 18, 1985, noting, "we also came back to win."

Quarterback Doug Williams' magical 1988 playoff run was another of Cooke's favorites.

"It was the people who made RFK wonderful," said Cooke. "I had a grand relationship, for example, with Dave Butz. He played 14 years for us and was the epitome of a pro. He was devoted, dedicated and durable. He told me injuries were part of his profession as a defensive lineman and kept on going no matter.

"It's the same with veteran Darrell Green. He is a marvelous person and player along with being a model citizen who does a great deal for the community and charitable services."

How about John Riggins? "You may never find another like him," Cooke said. "He's a different person. But brother, if you were ever in a fight, you wanted him in a foxhole next to you. Riggins and those Hogs he ran behind brought the community together. That's not common in many places."

Cooke explained that RFK, formerly D.C. Stadium, was built for baseball in 1961. "The playing surface is flat," he said. "That proves our fans are the best in the world because they've had to stand for decades in order to see over the people in front of them. All of us had some jolly times there and they never whined."

Personal memories have frigid, sold-out RFK packed with people from all walks of life joining voices repeatedly to sing "Hail to the Redskins." The starting lineups are inaudible over the roar of the crowd.

George Allen is leading cheers or licking his thumb. Joe Gibbs, arms folded, teeth clenched and eyes piercing, is sending in the next play.

Quarterbacks named Billy Kilmer, Theismann or Williams are throwing to Charley Taylor, Art Monk or Gary Clark. Or handing off to Mike Thomas, Riggins or George Rogers — who looks for a seam to run in behind Len Hauss, Russ Grimm or Joe Jacoby.

Defensively, tackles Diron Talbert or Butz is shutting down the opposition's running game. Ends Ron McDole or Dexter Manley are applying pressure to the passer. Neil Olkewicz, Chris Hanburger or Monte Coleman are making a critical stop on third down. Green, Ken Houston or Pat Fischer are picking off a pass near the goal line to stop an enemy drive.

Curt Knight, Mark Moseley or Chip Lohmiller kicks a game winner and the south end zone stands bounce violently under the cheering masses.

It's impossible to think of the holidays without dreaming of those distant afternoons at RFK. There never was a place like it before, and there probably won't be again.

Sunday, Fox-TV announcer Pat Summerall will exclaim in his opening monologue: "RFK Stadium is sold out, packed, as you'd expect it to be when the Dallas Cowboys come calling..."

When the home team scores, he'll bellow for the final time: "Robert F. Kennedy is rocking now."

Sit back, enjoy and remember.

ELLIS REACHES INTO PAST, BRINGS BACK THE SOYBEANS

JUNE, 2000

Early on the morning of June 21, 1972, Mrs. Ruth Adkins, then Ellis Park's general manager and executive vice-president, was at her desk in the track's general office.

She was battling a plethora of problems requiring immediate attention prior to opening day, which was two weeks away.

Suddenly, Adkins was interrupted by a security guard who burst in unannounced. It was serious because NOBODY did that with Ruth. "Call the emergency rescue squad," the man shrieked. "Clyde's collapsed in the soybean field out in front of the clubhouse. We think it's a heart attack."

For those too young to know the storied history of Ellis Park, the infield, at one time, was home to one of the finest soybean crops in Western Kentucky. And Ellis was the only track in North America boasting a cash crop within the infield.

Over a span of time, the track gained a national identity and acclaim from the beans. From Los Angeles to New York to Miami to New Orleans, Ellis was known as "The Pea Patch" when horsemen, jockeys and fans discussed where they raced during the summer.

"Oh sure. I know the place," horsemen would say. "It's the track with soybeans in the infield."

For the record, "Clyde" was Ruth's husband, Clyde E. Adkins, of Henderson, Ky.

Many mornings, Clyde and track president Lester Yeager walked among the soybeans, checking on their progress and noting where the horseweeds and cockleburrs needed to be removed. That was done nightly after the races.

Yeager, a native of Rockport, Ind., and a nephew of James C. Ellis, was a Purdue University graduate with a master's degree in agriculture from Iowa State. Yeager initiated the Ellis soybean crop before World War II. Annually, he took great pride in the crop's height, texture and yield.

At one time, horses walked over for the races on a bridle path cut through the soybeans that was straddled by two, huge pecan trees.

Anyway, back to Clyde. He was dead when medical personnel arrived. Ruth and he had been married only 21 days. Annually, for Western Kentucky's first lady of the turf, June 21 truly is the longest day of the year as she reminisces on her Corydon, Ky. farm.

These stories and a lot of others recently came to mind when Paul Kuerzi, Ellis' current general manager and vice-president, ordered the soybeans replanted for the upcoming race meeting that begins July 12.

The 50-acre infield has been barren since 1990. Former owner Roger Kumar sold the track to Racing Corporation of America in December of 1989. RCA officials thought the soybeans were bush league. They deemed them a disgrace, something hokey, that brought laughter and snide remarks from racing people. They wanted Ellis to be "the Saratoga of the South."

Well, this ain't Saratoga. It's Evansville-Henderson-Owensboro. And were the RCA boys ever wrong! And besides, they had to pay someone to mow the nasty, brown grass that grew where the always green soybeans should have been.

Local racing fans soon realized RCA's snooty thinking and became outraged at the beans' removal. Without them, some patrons even refused to attend the races.

Kuerzi is an opposite chapter. Although a native Louisvillian, he is a throwback — a traditionalist who could easily pass for one of the boys from Western Kentucky or Southern Indiana. In short, he earned his stripes the old fashioned way, by working for them.

It took him all of five minutes to assess that without the soybeans, the track was missing a unique portion of it's identity and history.

Currently, Ellis' soybean plants are eight inches tall. So it's too early to forecast what the crop will be worth when harvested. But Kuerzi has earmarked the track's share of the profit for charity.

That's excellent. Because the soybeans are the very symbol of this great Tri-State.

And personally, I know that somewhere, Ellis Park's deceased old guard like Mr. Ellis, Yeager, Chic Anderson, Don Bernhardt, Charles Morgan Brown, Bill Fluty, Anna M. Fisher, Ray Gates, Clyde Adkins, Gene Smith, Leroy Tauzin, Bill Berry, and many like them, are smiling their approval.

THERE'S NO WALK
QUITE LIKE THIS ONE

MAY, 1999

LOUISVILLE, Ky. — Being responsible the last 12 years for the official chart of the Kentucky Derby used by *Daily Racing Form/Equibase* and about 700 newspapers around the country placed severe restrictions on leaving our fifth floor office located immediately above Churchill Downs' finish line.

It's the best seat in the house. But it's extremely tedious work and you can only dream about enjoying the spectacle that surrounds you. In fact, getting an iced tea from the lunch room or making a final check before the Derby with the stewards was all time ever allowed. That is until last year's Derby when I told my superiors: "Find someone to chart a couple of races before the big one so I can walk over with friends saddling Derby horses. I'll be back up for the race." They said, "Fine."

What followed was an unbelievable thrill, and equally so for the second time Saturday when escorting the Wayne Lukas-trained Cat Thief and Charismatic on the long, solemn trek from Barn 44 to the paddock for their dates with destiny.

Before departing though, Lukas gave his assistants orders like a battlefield commander. At 3:50 p.m. (EDT), he said "vaccum off the horses," then sent a runner to a nearby drink machine for a Diet Mountain Dew.

Was he melancholy? No. "I'm extremely competitive and I get pumped up on days like this," said Lukas, decked out in a navy blue pinstripe Armani suit. "I may get a little sentimental after the Derby's over. Not before."

A few minutes later, he told his aides to put the vet wrap and protective bandages on the horses.

At 4:37 p.m., the public address system echoed: "Attention horsemen, bring your horses to the paddock for the eighth race. Bring them on over for the eighth race. The Kentucky Derby."

We departed at 4:42 p.m. Just getting out of the barn was tough. A crowd of at least 300, several sporting cameras or camcorders, surrounded the opening. Many were stablehands and backstretch visitors. Others were reporters, photographers and well-wishers.

When a path out of the barn was cleared, the assemblage alongside the gate entering the track formed a human gauntlet. It was as if you had to earn your way onto the track by passing this obstacle first.

Once clear of the bottleneck, we joined the rest of the 19-horse field which was assembled in the mile chute. Track officials time it so nobody gets an edge by arriving early or late. The cast headed over in unison, like a wagon train through hostile territory. And it was a bit harrowing. Because as far as you can see on both sides of the track, you're surrounded by a wall of humanity. Unknown faces attempting to get a look at their choices screamed their best wishes, others obscenities. The wall of noise hit like a tidal wave.

About midway around the clubhouse turn, emotions began to soar. And when the adrenalin kicked in, so did cotton mouth accompanied by clammy skin. For a time, it seemed like a trip to the gallows and that nothing mattered. The focus solely was on those two horses. They acted like perfect gentlemen. Everything else was obscured. And while being with friends brought safety in numbers, it certainly wasn't a time to stumble and fall with everyone including a national television audience watching.

Once the procession got started, it was like a river running down hill. "Just keep putting one foot in front of another. We've been there before," said Lukas, who was accompanied by his wife Laura and son Jeff. "Keep your head up and don't look nervous. Hell, there's nothing we can do now. It's up to these horses," reminded Lukas.

Nobody said much after that. Leaving the turn, the noise grew louder and Cat Thief, a typically hot-blooded son of Storm Cat, pranced a bit, then calmed down. The colt's breathing was short and shallow which was normal. Charismatic never blinked an eye. He was all business.

Realizing my own expectations of the outcome, I could

only imagine those of the breeders, owners, trainers and riders involved. It is a combination of hard work, preparation, hope, racing luck and dreams that make the Kentucky Derby such a fantastic, mind-boggling experience.

Riding a bubble of energy while entering the tunnel leading beneath the stands to the paddock, the realization of what this race means took me sweeping back through time to past Derbys and warm memories of absent friends.

The paddock was a mob scene, already jammed by those who didn't make the walk over but merely tiptoed down from the boxseats

Standing there awaiting the paddock judge to call "riders up," I recalled a day not long ago when stating that "no matter how corporate America becomes, or how politically correct people expect you to be, the race itself — not the hype and expensive pleasures it requires for some — remains one of the last pure bastions in sports."

For the race's participants, there are no dress rehearsals. No teleprompters or cue cards (like ABC-TV uses); no margin for error and no second chances. Only once in a 3-year-old's life will they be able to make this walk. Only once can they run for the roses. No horse ever faced such a nervewracking experience before yesterday. And none ever will again. It simply always will boil down to man and beast against one another and the elements for 1 1/4 miles.

Like they say, "if you want to talk the talk, you have to walk the walk." Charismatic and Cat Thief did just that. They finished first and third, a testimony to their trainer's genius. It was a walk I'll treasure always, and hope to make often.

DERBY WEEK AT CHURCHILL OFFERS MAGICAL APPEAL

APRIL, 1999

LOUISVILLE, Ky. — Churchill Downs' 125th spring meeting begins on Saturday. Racing's much anticipated return to this Kentucky town officially marks the beginning of "Derby Week Fever."

It's a period when grown men often become little boys again by betting too much, eating too much, drinking too much, smoking too many cigars and even crying too much when those haunting straings of "My Old Kentucky Home" fill the air as the horses parade to the post for the world famous Kentucky Derby.

The bottom line for lovers of thoroughbred racing is that Derby Week is often a wonderful mixture of happiness, heart break, wackiness, zaniness, frivolity and a flock of memories. It's sort of like a college homecoming. And for solemn Derby veterans who treat the great race like a religious experience, it's New Year's Eve, Christmas, birthdays and every other holiday combined. There simply is nothing quite like it, and never will be.

To horsemen worldwide, the Kentucky Derby has a mystical appeal. And for those making their maiden trips to Churchill Downs, they will find that the magnitude of the first leg of the Triple Crown is difficult to comprehend and impossible to exaggerate.

Of course, opening week is geared to peak next Saturday when a field of the finest 3-year-olds in the land battle for racing's greatest prize over 1 1/4 miles in the $1 million guaranteed Grade I Kentucky Derby. An on-track crowd of 145,000 and a worldwide television audience will be watching.

It's not too shabby on April 30, either, when the best 3-year-old fillies contest the $500,000 Grade I Kentucky Oaks going 1 1/8 miles. Sister-race to the Derby, the Oaks will draw 100,000-plus fans and a field of six or seven fillies.

Many are ducking champion Silverbulletday. Owned by Mike Pegram, a favorite son of Princeton, Ind., and trained by Pegram's longtime friend and winner of the past two Derbys, Bob Baffert, Silverbulletday has maintained her brilliance during training hours and will go off heavily favored in the Oaks.

Pegram also owned last year's Kentucky Derby winner, Real Quiet.

The Derby and Oaks headline 14 stakes races carded this week that offer a total of $3 million in purses. The added money schedule offers something for every age horse— including a Grade I steeplechase on Thursday.

Saturday's traditional opening day feature is the $100,000-added Grade III Derby Trial.

A solid field of nine is scheduled to start in the Trial. Doneraile Court, Yes It's True and Straight Man appear to be the primary choices. They are highly regarded for next month's Preakness Stakes, but nobody in the Trial is under consideration to come back on a week's rest to contest the Kentucky Derby.

With no standouts and many of the prep races requiring photo finishes, a capacity field of 20 is a certainty for the Kentucky Derby. Most owners and trainers of the contenders set up shop under the famed Twin Spires last week in order to fine-tune their horses, acclimate them to the track surface, paddock area and media horde that swarms the barn area, and make final preparations to run for the roses.

As they say, "the Derby is a chance of a lifetime in a lifetime of chance." So in trying to pick the Derby winner, remember, above all, this lone principle for guidance:

Charting the prep-race road to the Derby, nothing matters as much as the destination.

The prep races these 3-year-olds have competed in provide only a small portfolio for potential rather than a true, absolute display of talent.

So during the next week, when arriving at your selections, ask yourself not what these horses have done in preps or workouts, but what they might be capable of doing in the Kentucky Derby.

Having started 33 horses in the Derby since 1981, no trainer has saddled as many as D. Wayne Lukas. Can he win it for the fourth time this year with Cat Thief or Charismatic?

No trainer ever won the Derby three consecutive times. Baffert capture the past two with Silver Charm and Real Quiet. Can he get the job done with Prime Timber? Or with a California-bred gelding called General Challenge? Or with with the filly, Excellent Meeting?

Time, the greatest barometer of all, will answer these questions and a lot more.

REGRETFULLY, DERBY WEEK RUNS ITS COURSE

MAY, 2000

LOUISVILLE, Ky. — It's done.

The most splendid, difficult, memory filled time of the year known as Kentucky Derby week officially ended Saturday.

Reality has returned. Fiction has departed historic Churchill Downs for another 51 weeks.

There isn't enough space to tell all the stories and anecdotes collected and lifelong friendships made during the precious, daily, often pre-dawn visits with Derby horsemen and their associates during the past seven days.

Then what's this all about?

It involves the romance of the backstretch that's rekindled each spring during Kentucky Derby week.

And, for example, like a special, 45-year-old lady who'll never lose her pulchritude, elegance and grace; whose face never will show wrinkles, and who's never far from your heart, the splendor of Derby week never loses its appeal.

Saturday, the Derby turned 126 years old. Despite a constantly changing cast and crew, it remains as fresh as a flower that blooms after a spring rain.

Better people than me have fallen in love with the Derby. And they've said so in mushy, slobbering terms. This most classic race in America can do that to you, reducing the most jaded, hard core people to tears despite the corporate ring around Churchill Downs.

Some of us don't attend the parties or socialize much during Derby week. Working the backstretch takes precedent. When the alarm clock summons you at 5 a.m., you're glad it went off, because in 30 minutes, you'll be on the backstretch, visiting friends and searching for news and a story angle on the Derby.

You always think you won't find anything worthy of the Derby's lofty stature. But once you get started, there are so many things to write about that it's difficult to select the right one.

The barn area is filled with hundreds of reporters from the print and electronic media. Many of them huddle together, because the temperature is cool. Many wouldn't know a top horse from a cavalry mule. They're afraid to ask a question to avoid showing their uncertainty, as they watch steam rise off a Derby colt getting his bath after training.

If you've done this a year or two, or 20, there's a schedule to memorize. Like when Hall of Fame trainer Wayne Lukas, fresh off his stable pony and sporting chaps, jeans, dress shirt and a "10 Crowns" baseball cap, will graze his horses on the patch of grass adjacent to Longfield Avenue.

There's no written script. You simply know.

Or like this year, when trainer Neil Drysdale would hold his daily press conference.

You might run into former National Football League greats like John Unitas or Paul Hornung. They blend into the mob and don't get a fraction of the attention that jockey Pat Day or Jerry Bailey do when dismounting after a colt's workout.

Go to another barn and you may bump into former Governor of Kentucky Brereton C. Jones, former Louisville Mayor Jerry Abramson or others of that ilk. They're lost in the shuffle, too.

At about 9 a.m., you take a break. The smart guys hustle over to the track kitchen for coffee and a biscuit, doing so to avoid the slew of freeloaders who rely on "press notes" and never leave the backstretch press center.

Training hours end at 10 a.m. And sometimes, on a bright, sunny morning, you've got so many thoughts in mind it's difficult remembering where you parked. Or even what day it is. But when shuffling from barn to barn, you can instantly remember that Woody Stephens was always in that barn. And how much you miss him.

Silver Charm came from another barn nearby. And horses trained by the late Charlie Whittingham won two Derbys when stabled in that stall.

Or last year's walk from the barn to the paddock for the Derby with Lukas, Charismatic and Cat Thief. It was the trip of a lifetime.

At the peril of becoming emotional, I'm not ashamed to admit that long ago, I fell in love with the Kentucky Derby's mystique and its participants.

I've realized it before. But yesterday, it struck me again like a blunt club, that the first Saturday in May each year and the week before it are too far apart.

NEW DERBY MUSEUM
PAYS HOMAGE TO RACING'S CHAMPS

MAY, 1985

LOUISVILLE, Ky. — If you like the atmosphere encompassing the Kentucky Derby, you'll love the recently opened Kentucky Derby Museum.

Year-round, it radiates the splendor of Derby Day.

The $7.5 million project, which was three years in the making, is located in the grandstand section of Churchill Downs outside the racing secretary's office. It's the largest museum of its kind in the world.

Louisville's James Graham Brown, late owner of the Brown Hotel and originator of the "hot brown" sandwich, provided a major grant to the non-profit Kentucky Derby Museum Corp.

The exhibit is broken down into four basic parts and takes about three hours to be fully appreciated.

The evolution, breeding and training of the thoroughbred is the first stop.

Next comes the racetrack, its technology and its people. There is a test for handicapping skills, and a shedrow with the working tools of a trainer.

The Derby Gallery is dedicated to the Run for the Roses. A trivia machine will measure your racing IQ — from the tradition of the mint julep to how the famed blanket of roses came about.

Every Derby since moving pictures began can be viewed.

Our old friend, the late Chic Anderson of Evansville, lives on these tapes with his matchless calls. His brilliance was particularly effective in his last Derby — the 1978 duel between Affirmed and Alydar.

They are all there, including golden oldies Whirlaway, Count Fleet and Citation, as described by the gravel voice of Clem McCarthy.

There is a picture display with the pedigrees of every Derby Winner, and portraits of the 11 Triple Crown champions. A gallery donated by some of the world's most accomplished equine artists is alongside.

The most magnificent feature comes when the call to post is sounded in The Great Hall. Get there in a hurry, and you'll find yourself in the center of the stretch with horses thundering past.

Don't fret, you won't be hallucinating. It's the beginning of a breath-taking audio-visual show that presents a beautifully edited view of every part of Churchill Downs on Derby Day. The hall is circular and the 20-minute displays moves rapidly on 96 slide projectors. The acoustics are second to none.

The last two minutes are dedicated to Swale, trainer Woody Stephens and jockey Laffit Pincay Jr. The effects make it seem like Stephens and Pincay are standing next to you.

Before this year's Derby draw, Stephens took in the presentation with several members of the media. The hardboot of 71 years, a man who isn't easily moved, found it difficult to swallow during Swale's 1984 Derby stretch run. If it gets to him, the average fan will find the $2.50 admission the best investment on the grounds.

The museum is a hall of champions. Fittingly, one guards the entrance to the nearby courtyard.

Jack and Katherine Price, who raced the rags-to-riches Carry Back to victory in the 1961 Derby, exhumed their champion from his Florida burial site and put him to rest at Churchill on the Wednesday before Spend a Buck's Derby.

The inscription on the stone reads: Carry Back, 1958-1983. Champion 3-year-old, 1961. "The People's Choice."

The last line also fits his final stop. The museum is a masterpiece.

AT HAGE'S HOUSE OF COMO, THE SPECIALTY IS CUSTOMER SERVICE

JULY, 1995

It's been happening for the past 35 years.

Traditionally in June, near the conclusion of the Churchill Downs meeting, a trainer like Donald Hughes, Forrest Kaelin, Vickie Foley or Bob Holthus will state: "I can't wait to get down to George's place. It's the highlight of the Ellis Park meeting. I can taste the Arabian salad, Kibi and cabbage rolls now."

"George's place" is George Hage's House of Como restaurant. At first glance, it's a plain, white, concrete block establishment about two miles north of Ellis Park on old Highway 41. Upon closer inspection, though, it's a joint you'll never forget.

As a signature calling card, Hage, and daughters Libby and Laura, keep Christmas decorations up year-round inside and out. The jukebox has a long list of holiday tunes, too.

"That theme all started in the beginning with a Santa Claus and reindeer on the roof," Hage noted the other evening. "Christmas is the happiest time of the year, and I want my people happy when they're here."

The walls, though, have strictly a racing theme. And, man, if these walls could talk. In some cases, it's probably best they can't.

There are winner's circle pictures dating back to the early 1950s. Hage loves the races almost as much as he does people. He hustles over to Ellis daily and catches two or three races whether the action is live or during intertrack wagering.

He's a crackerjack handicapper, too. "I stay away from the early junk races. That's why I win most of the time," he said.

The menu says that much of the food is Arabian. Hage grew up in Chicago where his father was an importer. George is first-generation Lebanese, and so is the cuisine.

Delicacies like beef and lamb shishkabobs; Seneya Betinjin (eggplant casserole); Kibi Nea (raw ground lamb or beef mixed with wheat); Yebra Malfoof (cabbage rolls stuffed with meat); Djage (baked chicken with meat, rice and pine nut stuffing) and Arabian bread.

The steaks and chops are the finest available. Hage makes a trip to the produce and meat markets daily. The meat is handcut. You don't have to ask about freshness, because Hage plans for a nightly sellout.

There's also an extensive homemade list of Italian entrees and seafood specialities. There's no question as to the cuisine's excellence. The 70 seats are packed nightly and the bar area is standing room only.

It's one of the few establishments anywhere that reservations aren't taken.

"Tell them not to come in," Hage said to his bartender who fielded a request this particular night. Then Hage explained to a friend, "I don't have anything left in the kitchen to sell and I'm about ready to lock up and go home."

Hage is a dying breed. He is the founder, owner and managing workaholic of a family business. His day begins with his early shopping trips. He comes to work, unloads the wares, then goes home to read *Daily Racing Form* and freshen up. He returns to the restaurant, goes to the races and is back to greet the dinner crowd.

During World War II, he came to this part of the country for basic training at Camp Breckenridge, Ky., shipped to the European Theater as an infantryman, and eventually was captured during the Battle of the Bulge.

When he came home, he is credited with bringing the first carry-out and delivery pizza business to Evansville, Ind.

"It was Como style pizza and that's why I named this place the House of Como — after the pizzas that built it," he noted. And, by the way, he still serves them.

This isn't the first place Hage's done business. Now 76, he owned the old Brown Derby Lounge that burned down prior to the House of Como's invention. He leased the dining room at the Roca Bar many years ago, too.

"A lot of people and especially myself hate change," confirmed Hage. "They said 'don't change the menu and don't change the decorations.' I haven't.

"People are the key to anything. Be it sports, the restaurant business, racing, whatever. You win and lose with people. I don't want my customers to be strangers. I want them to be my friends.

"I have plenty of everything and can retire today if I want to," he said. "But why give all this up?

"If God had told me I could have and do anything I wanted in life, I wouldn't have changed anything because where else could I have made the friends I've got."

Every night there's further proof. You'll find a table full of prominent doctors, attorneys or business people sitting next to group of horsemen. Hage calls them by name while stopping and visiting.

He asks about the food and service and if they need another round of cocktails. They are like his own family and treat him accordingly, asking him to sit and continue.

A lot of people hope it lasts forever.

KEENELAND BRINGS
GRACE TO RACING'S TABLE

APRIL, 2000

LEXINGTON, Ky. — Keeneland's spring meeting annually is among America's finest.

With many of the world's foremost horsemen stabled here, the quality of racing at this internationally acclaimed course — buoyed by a $600,000 per day purse distribution — is second to none.

A multitude of the racing industry's top people have spoken volumes of praise about Keeneland's longstanding dedication to improving the sport and continuing the excellence that's become the track's trademark for racing and the famous sales held four times annually.

Horsemen with leading prospects for the spring classics have long raved about the serene, tranquil ambiance, and the fine patches of bluegrass in the barn area that many of history's greatest runners have grazed and bloomed on.

The accolades didn't fall on deaf ears, because several years ago, the United States government designated Keeneland and Churchill Downs in Louisville, Ky. as national landmarks.

As home of the world-famed Kentucky Derby, Churchill Downs is the most notable track among the public.

However, Keeneland, too, has been the site of many significant feats and achievements by human and equine athletes. Many of those memorable moments happened in the track's Blue Grass Stakes. Centerpiece of the stakes schedule, it matches 3-year-old Kentucky Derby prospects going 1 1/8 miles. It was run Saturday for the 76th time.

Several previous Blue Grass Stakes episodes were dramatic, too. Like in 1987 when eventual Derby winner Alysheba was disqualified from victory for ducking out badly in the final 70 yards and impeding Leo Castelli.

Like over a sloppy track in 1966 when Abe's Hope bested heavily favored Graustark by a nose. Winter Book favorite for that year's Derby, Graustark fractured a bone in a foot during the Blue Grass and never ran again.

In 1995, Wild Syn gave future Hall of Fame jockey Randy Romero his only win of the spring meeting, leading all the way to prevail by 2 1/2 lengths.

There are many others, and the roster of Blue Grass Stakes winners reads like a "Who's Who" in 20th century racing. Like Bull Lea in 1938; Bimelech, 1940; Round Table, 1957; Tomy Lee, 1959; Chateaugay, 1963; Northern Dancer, 1964; Lucky Debonair, 1965; Riva Ridge, 1972; Spectacular Bid, 1979; Summer Squall, 1990; Strike the Gold, 1991; Holy Bull, 1994 and Skip Away, who in 1996 romped by six lengths in stakes record time.

But to this day, 22 years after it happened, when you ask longtime racegoers here their favorite Blue Grass moment, the majority will reply: "Alydar's win in 1978."

It wasn't because of the mutuels. He only paid $2.20 to win. And it wasn't because of the competition. He defeated eight ordinary foes by 13 lengths.

People remember it vividly because of what transpired before the race.

It happened like this. On the way to the post, jockey Jorge Velasquez brought Alydar to the outside rail near the clubhouse lawn. A station wagon had arrived bearing the colt's owners, Admiral and Mrs. Gene Markey of Calumet Farm.

Then in their 80s and confined to wheelchairs, they sat outside the rail while Velasquez positioned Alydar in a saluting position.

The colt stood like a statue for 30 seconds, then, like a circus horse, bowed to the octogenarians as if to say "thank-you for coming."

Even if you didn't like racing, it was a special moment. But come to think of it, Alydar was a special horse.

DERBY MUSEUM, PERFECT
SETTING FOR A LUKAS TALE

NOVEMBER, 1995

LOUISVILLE, Ky. — May 7, 1988, was Kentucky Derby Day. And, as always, the eyes of the world were focused on historic Churchill Downs.

Each Kentucky Derby is special, as several minor components come together at precisely the right instant to make for a wonderful ending.

The 114th running of the 1 1/4-mile classic was no exception. Actually, it had more than its usual appeal and fanfare for several reasons. First, there was no odds-on favorite in the field of 17.

Second, the horses had more of a regional following than normal with the ensuing battle to be over neutral ground.

Third, there was the presence of an outstanding filly. The free-running Winning Colors, owned by the late Gene Klein and trained by the incomparable D. Wayne Lukas, was attempting to become only the third of her sex to capture America's greatest racing prize.

In a week's worth of stories, the eloquent and articulate Lukas is good for a day's copy or more. The uniqueness of a filly trying to defeat males in this setting was a huge plus.

Combine Lukas' grace and poise with the ability of a special filly like Winning Colors, who'd already thrashed the boys in the Santa Anita Derby, and you can imagine the media's daily smorgasbord.

On Derby morning, Lukas visited with Winning Colors' rider, Gary Stevens. The jockey had ridden at Churchill Downs several times, but never had experienced the breathtaking video presentation in the Kentucky Derby Museum. The facility is open every day of the year except Thanksgiving, Christmas, Oaks and Derby Days.

Leave it to an old coach for what transpired that May morning. In an unprecedented, clandestine, motivational move, Lukas requested the museum's director to open the backdoor of the facility at 10 a.m. so he and Stevens could slip in and see the show.

Alone together in the great hall, trainer and rider stood and witnessed the storied history and spectacle of the Derby.

When it was over, Lukas simply told Stevens, "If you want to be among the all-time greats, then you must win the Derby this afternoon."

In a game of inches, you'd have to believe this ploy had something to do with Winning Colors' dramatic neck victory.

Lukas retold the story to several friends Tuesday night when he was honored by the Kentucky Thoroughbred Owners Association as its horseman of the year at a dinner.

It was held in the same area he and Stevens stood that Derby morning, and a record crowd attended the dinner.

"For his Kentucky presence, outstanding successes throughout the last year and by winning the last five Triple Crown races, Wayne Lukas is the prefect choice," proclaimed the organization's president, Frank L. Jones Jr.

The video show has been updated annually and currently concludes with Thunder Gulch, Lukas' second Derby Winner, coming to the wire.

Billy Reed, a mutual friend from the *Lexington Herald-Leader* and *Sports Illustrated*, was selected by KTOA as its guest speaker. His speech went something like this:

"First, some people might say that Wayne Lukas is not a great horseman, but he's a great manager. This is false, because he's handled every one of his Triple Crown and Breeders' Cup horses personally.

"Second, some may think he's a society trainer. That answer to this is never. Sure, he wears a Rolex watch and nice clothes, which some folks might be jealous of or not like. But you'll never find Wayne Lukas on a golf course or in a bar with the boys. His work ethic is unbelievable. A normal day is 3 a.m. to 10 p.m.

"Third, they say he was shocked when Thunder Gulch won the Derby. Not for an instant. He liked his chances and worked just as hard and efficiently with Thunder Gulch as with Timber Country or Serena's Song.

"Fourth, some people believe that Lukas is uncaring about his stock. I've seen his tears of disappointment as well as joy."

Reed explained what a shame it was that the late Warner L. Jones Jr., for whom the horseman of the year award is named, wasn't around to see Lukas receive the honor.

"They have a lot of things in common," Reed said. "Wayne Lukas is the KTOA'S man of the year. He's also the best thing that's ever happened to racing and should be the sport's man of the century."

Before the dinner, the video was played in the museum. By some ironic twist, Lukas, resplendent and dressed to the nines as always, was sporting the same suit — different tie — that he wore when winning this year's Derby.

The end of the presentation was all Thunder Gulch. The emotional moment brought moisture to the great trainer's eye. It's a natural reaction. And for a change, he was among friends.

KENTUCKY FAILS THE
RACING PUBLIC AT FRANKLIN TRACK

SEPTEMBER, 2000

FRANKLIN, Ky. — Quite frankly, the state of Kentucky annually misbehaves itself for seven days by subjecting horsemen and bettors to a backwoods racing retreat known as Kentucky Downs.

Located about two miles from the Kentucky-Tennessee border off Interstate 65 in Franklin, Ky., this facility formerly was called Dueling Grounds.

It might have been suitable during the late 1800s for gentlemen dueling with cap and ball pistols over state's rights and fair, southern belles. But as a racing venue, it's not as good as some county fairs for several obvious reasons.

When the place originated several years ago, officials bellowed that business would prosper because of the untapped market in nearby Nashville, tenn. But crowds average only 300-500 fans who bet pitifully small amounts on site.

Bottom line: The live race meeting is conducted in order to meet state laws required for year-round whole card simulcasting, where purse money for the seven-day meeting is acrued. Live racing generates very little business and even less enthusiasm.

What does go over big is year-round bingo and $1 pull tabs. Droves of bingo players pile into the place when the races conclude.

All races at Kentucky Downs are conducted over a 1 3/8th-mile turf course that runs uphill-downhill like a roller coaster. The footing is hard (six furlongs in 1:09) when it's dry and a bog (six furlongs in 1:18) when it's raining. And there aren't poles on the course to designate every point of call.

Worst thing, though, is that the track is located in Simpson County, which is "dry."

Equally important, there's no totalizator board or timing system. Odds are calculated at Turfway Park and shown on television. The races are hand timed, which is suspiciously dangerous.

The videotape replays are akin to shooting a home movie with a hand-held camcorder while standing in a row boat and are totally worthless.

Various tote companies rent infield totalizator boards that are perched on the backs of flatbed trailers. At the very least, the Kentucky Racing Commission should insist that one be in place for 2001.

A horse race begins when the gates clang open and the flag drops. It's over when the horses pass the finish line. In between, there's not one ounce of mechanization. It's simply riders and their mounts, same as it was 100 years ago. If you enjoy racing in its purest sense, then next September, check out Kentucky Downs. Things are likely to change. Racing there is ample proof that some will bet on any thing, any place, anytime.

And if you go, don't forget, B.Y.O.B.

AT JOEY'S PLACE, THE
GOOD TIMES ALWAYS ON A ROLL

MARCH, 1996

FLORENCE, Ky. — The James B. Beam Distilling Co. celebrated its 200th anniversary in 1995.

To enhance its public image, the Clermont, Ky.-based company has sponsored the $600,000 Jim Beam Stakes at Turfway Park for the past several years.

It does so again for the 15th time on March 30 when 3-year-old go 11/8 miles in this important Triple Crown prep.

On that day, for the first time in Evansville, Ind., Joey's, a neighborhood tavern, will host its inaugural Jim Beam Stakes Party.

One of the distilling company's foremost proclamations goes like this: "Over the past 200 years, there are two things the Beam family has never considered: leaving Kentucky and changing the recipe of our bourbon."

Some of those principles also apply to Joey Pelaski, founder and owner of Joey's. A native of Union County, Ky. in western Kentucky, he's never considered leaving the tavern business. Since those days long ago when he worked as a cleanup and cameraman at Ellis Park's, he's held Kentucky racing — the Derby in particular — in the deepest regard.

Located just off the Lloyd Expressway near the downtown business district on West Franklin Street, Joey's is the type of saloon where everyone feels comfortable.

The clientele varies from judges, attorneys and bankers to construction and coal company owners, secretaries and retired coaches.

236

Those folks were present last Wednesday. Because of a winter storm, racing was canceled at Turfway Park and the city of Evansville was paralyzed by a foot of snow. Schools, malls and county and federal courts were closed.

But Joey's was hopping. Pelaski had whipped up two kinds of soup and filets were the luncheon special. "Everybody else is closed," somebody told him. "Weather never bothered me," replied Pelaski. "I've always remembered a sign I saw on the jail in Shawneetown, Ill. It read, 'We may doze, but we never close.' That's the way I am."

Joey's Jim Beam Party will offer authentic decor, too. Pelaski will hang the same signs and banners on his walls that you'll see on ESPN-TV's telecast from Turfway.

Pelaski, himself a horse owner, noted that he would create a massive batch of "Golden Beams," the official drink of the race. It will consist of Jim Beam bourbon whiskey, of course, orange juice, pina colada mix and syrup. Shaken well, it's then poured over ice and topped off with a dash of amaretto.

"That's a pretty significant switch from our regular Saturday special of $1 Sterling Light Beer," laughed Pelaski. "We'll have mounds of our famous Buffalo Wings as always."

To accommodate a large turnout, Pelaski will have his entire staff on duty. Johnnie Maveety, the day manager, doesn't work Saturdays. But he'll be in to oversee the kitchen.

The place figures to be packed and reservations are suggested to gain a television vantage point.

It's also worth noting that advance wagers on the Jim Beam will be taken Friday on track and at Ellis Park, the intertrack wagering facility near Evansville. Several shuttles from Joey's to Ellis will be available on race day.

For the record, here's how Joey's production came about. National Wine and Spirits of Indianapolis, has the Jim Beam consignment for southern Indiana.

The Evansville salsman, Ken Brashier, was looking for a place with roots that rocks and rolls on Saturdays. In short, he needed a place like Joey's to bring in his party favors.

"Kenny has us lined up with plenty of the same horseshoe-shaped shot glasses they give away at Turfway," said Pelaski. "We'll also have plenty of Jim Beam T-shirts."

The owner will be sporting a white Jim Beam jacket a friend gave him after last year's running. To give the day a bit more charm and meaning, he disclosed a private early morning breakfast he'll host for some of his personal friends.

"This is going to be something like the governor of Kentucky has on Derby Day," said Pelaski. "I'll have some of my boys down early for country ham, hog jowl, eggs and biscuits and gravy.

"They'll help me get opened up and ready for what should be quite a day. I'd love to go to Turfway but can't get away. Bringing the Jim Beam day atmosphere to my joint is the next best thing to being there."

Post time at Joey's is 11 a.m. (CST) and noon (EST) at Turfway. Best advice for both locations — get there early.

JOEY'S CROWD IS HIGH
ON DERBY HOPEFUL ALYDEED

MARCH, 1992

FLORENCE, Ky. — An informal luncheon is held each Monday in Evansville, Ind., at Joey's, a near downtown pub that caters to the racing crowd year-round.

Discussion at the Round Table ranges from girl friends to sports cars. And, while the proprietor, Joey Pelaski, a horse owner himself, puts out a fine cuisine, the primary brunt of the conversation is always horses. The kind that run in the eighth race on the first Saturday in May at Churchill Downs.

This has been especially true the past month as trainers around the country have been unleashing their hopefuls in prep races for the upcoming Triple Crown.

A sigh of relief was breathed by several diners last week when trainer Roger Attfield, that multiple Sovereign Award winning trainer from Canada, announced he would send Kinghaven Farms' Alydeed to Turfway Park for next Saturday's 11th running of the Grade II Jim Beam Stakes at 11/8 miles.

With a purse of $500,000 guaranteed, the winner will earn $300,000 and take a sizeable leap in reaching the starting gate on May 2 in the 118th Kentucky Derby in Louisville, Ky.

Anyway, news of Attfield's plan for the well-bred Alydeed was greeted with delight. Several astute fans at Joey's knew of the colt's ability which carried him to victory at first asking last June in the Victoria Stakes at Woodbine in his native Canada going five furlongs.

Then, there was Alydeed's near 10-length romp over non-winners of two on March 1 at Gulfstream Park. He was there the right way in both outings. And, while light on seasoning, Alydeed has the credentials, pedigree and handler to be a very good one. Solid enough, in fact, to be favored for the Queen's Plate, Canada's premier race for 3-year-olds.

The gist of the matter is that several took a flyer on Alydeed some time back at 70-1 in the Kentucky Derby Future Book wagering. A victory in the Jim Beam would confirm his credentials and advance him substantially toward greater fame in the Run for the Roses.

Alydeed is the apple of his trainer's eye, and has wintered well in Florida at Payson Park. He was a possible starter in last weekend's Swale Stakes at Gulfstream Park going seven furlongs. But Attfield knows his horse and has opted for the Jim Beam.

A native of Newbury, England, Attfield is a man worth listening to. Achievements by the former jump and amateur steeplechase rider include a flock of awards in Canada while building Kinghaven Farm into a perennial power, back-to-back sweeps of the Canadian Triple Crown with With Approval in 1989 and Izvestia in 1990, and numerous wins in the Queen's Plate with the likes of of Norcliffe, Market Control and the aforementioned duo.

Attfield is a man who hits what he aims for and his horses finish in the top three more than 50 percent of the time no matter where they compete.

Alydeed raced but once at 2, then underwent arthroscopic surgery for removal of a chip in an ankle. The bay colt recuperated during the fall and spent the winter in Florida. He has worked extremely well of late at Payson Park. Tactical speed, that sought after ability to race off the pace and accelerate when called upon, appears to be his forte.

Attfield put Alydeed on a van Saturday and the colt was scheduled to arrive Sunday at Keeneland.

"Our plans call for vanning from Keeneland to Turfway and working on Wednesday or Thursday," said Attfield by telephone from Florida. "I understand the weather there can be quite unpredictable, so you can't say for certain."

Attfield would love to win the Jim Beam. But, the colt doesn't have to. The trainer is looking for "advancement."

"We want him to go forward at this point. But, we're not going to rush him to make the Kentucky Derby. If he's going to the Derby, he'll let us know by his performance and that's what the decision will be based on. There are many, many races for him ahead."

The trainer liked the colt from the beginning. He spoke of his exceptional appearance, strong conformation and combined them with the fact that he breezed like a top horse at first asking — all desired traits in young horses.

How about going around two turns for the first time?

"I'm sure he can handle it well," said Attfield. "Naturally, one has to see it done, but I believe he will. His pedigree suggests he'll run long. We have Craig Perret to ride him and that's a plus, too."

Looking down the road, and knocking on wood that all goes well, Alydeed will likely be seen at Keeneland in either the Blue Grass or Lexington Stakes.

The progress Alydeed displays in the next few weeks will make for some interesting conversations by racing men in Canada and wherever else talk of the Kentucky Derby pops up.

Especially on Mondays at Joey's for lunch.

FAVORITE SON
BACK FOR PEGRAM DAY

JULY, 1998

Sunday's theme at Ellis Park features an open "Mike" — as in Mike Pegram, owner of Kentucky Derby and Preakness winner Real Quiet.

The day is billed as "Mike Pegram Day." The feature race is named the Arches of Gold for one of his fillies who won a stakes race here several years ago. And Pegram, accompanied by a large entourage of his boyhool friends, will present a blanket to the winner, spin tales to the public and give the facility a Sunday afternoon like it's never seen before.

For the record, there have been only two other days in the track's 76-year history named for racing people, and both are Hall of Famers. The first was for the late Eddie Arcaro in the early 1960s. Woody Stephens was the second in July, 1986.

Ellis Park vice-president and general manager Richard Schnaars is leaving nothing to chance for this occasion. His staff has interviews and autograph sessions planned, and everything else imaginable that accompanies the arrival of a guy who sells racing as if he's got the market cornered.

And what does Pegram charge for all this?

"Just a good time," he joked. "That's all I want. A good time for my friends and me. And we're real low maintenance. A few beers and maybe a barbeque. Nothing fancy, please."

Although the native of nearby Princeton, Ind., was here to watch one of his horses run opening day, June 29, Sunday is the "official" celebration of one of southern Indiana's favorite sons.

It was here, 40 summers and a thousand years ago, that Mike Pegram accompanied his late father, "Big Jim" Pegram, and his brother, "Little Jim," to the races for the first time. It was an era of infield soybeans, Sterling Draft Beer, Ellis' once-famous slaw on the hot dogs and $1,500 claimers.

Mike Pegram came back as often as he could. And, during his youth, that was daily, as he learned the lessons of life — how to judge people and read *Daily Racing Form.*

With his tears flowing freely in Churchill Downs' press box an hour after Real Quiet's Kentucky Derby victory, Pegram hugged a fellow Hoosier and said: "Guys like us, from where we come from, aren't supposed to make it. But boys like Larry Bird, Don Mattingly and Scott Studwell did. I think we're in that league now."

How true. And from a charismatic standpoint, you can search up and down racing's history and count the owners like Pegram on one hand.

Sure, he's the owner of 22 McDonald's franchises in Washington state. However, he's still a man of the people, a fellow who'd rather swap sweat and stories with the $2 players on a track's grandstand apron in blazing heat than schmooze in the air-conditioned sky boxes with celebrities.

By his demeanor and sometimes appearance, you wouldn't know he had the price of a track program to his name. That is until he says: "Come with us. We ain't got a schedule or a budget. It's time to run a race and that means a party."

It was here that his father's dream of owning top-flight horses began and ended. And it was here that Mike Pegram owned and raced his first horse in the mid-1970s, a wonderful colt named Storm Strike, who was the ideal rags-to-riches runner. Storm Strike started in the claiming ranks and moved right up the ladder to win stakes when trained by another Princeton, Ind., native, Jim McGarrah.

"That was more than 20 years ago," Pegram said, "and Ellis Park is the place that got me hooked on racing for life. I love the place because you can mix with your friends, wear shorts and a T-shirt, drink cold beer and not be bothered with anything more than picking a winner and an occasional sweat bee. It's home to me, and I'm glad I can give something back to the track that I started at."

So Sunday, if you want Pegram's autograph, don't be

bashful, just ask. From the cleanup crew to the track's CEO, he treats everyone the same.

Why?

"Because dignity," as Pegram says, "is the most important thing a person can have. And no matter if you win or lose a race, the people you meet are what make the game so special. Racing needs people. I like people — no matter what they do."

AT THE YMI,
48 FRUSTRATING
YEARS ARE FORGOTTEN

MARCH, 1985

HUNTINGBURG, Ind. — Southridge's 72-54 victory over L&M in the championship game of the Indiana High School Athletic Association's Boys' Evansville Semistate last Saturday ended nearly half a centry of frustration for local fans.

Not since 1937, when Huntingburg's Happy Hunters bowed to Anderson, 33-23 in the championship game, have they had the opportunity to follow their team to the Final Four.

"I was 9-years-old then," said Russ Kendall, "and I've been waiting for this for 48 years."

At 11:30 a.m. CST Saturday in Indianapolis, the Raiders (23-4) will meet top-ranked Marion (27-0) at Market Square Arena. Richmond (21-6) plays East Chicago Washington (24-1) in the 10 a.m. opener.

Monday afternoon, a dozen of Southridge's fans were mulling over the team's accomplishments at the Young Men's Institute, a private club founded in 1897 which stands two blocks from the town's gym.

The YMI wasn't as lively as it was Saturday night, when a standing-room-only crowd danced in the aisles, watched a video tape replay of the L&M game again and again, and hit long and hard at the bar until the birds began a morning chant.

But the subject of conversation remained the same — Southridge basketball and a Final Four appearance.

Don Breoeker has been a season ticket holder since he graduated from Huntingburg High School in 1959. He is among a group which reserved 25 rooms at an Indianapolis motel where the fans hope to stage yet another victory celebration.

Broeker said the team has been the talk of the town since it won the sectional.

"It's a wonderful thrill going to the Final Four," said Broeker. "We had rooms last weekend in Evansville but decided to come home to the YMI to party after we won it. We're staying in Indianapolis no matter the outcome. it may be a once-in-a-lifetime adventure."

The emplyoee of Kimball Corp. said the surprisingly lopsided win over L&M made up for some other bitter disappointments.

"One game stands out," he recalled. "We got beat in 1959 on a last-second shot by Odon in the regional. Alan Nass, who's the father of our center, Andy, was on that team. That was a heartbreaker, but getting by L&M made up for it.

"Who knows if we can put another game together like we did against L&M? We'll take our chances and play the good defense and let the chips fall. The main thing is being there."

Greg Zink, a carrier for The Evansville Courier who also works at Styline, Inc., for Larry Patberg, father of starting guards Ron and Rick, said the team has pulled the communities of Huntingburg and Holland together more than "even a great catastrophe could."

He said the difference in the tournament has been Southridge's defense and the effort of coach Gary Duncan.

"Those are the two main things and Duncan is the key," said the 1973 Southridge grad. "Gary doesn't get a lot of ink but he ranks with the best around."

Zink, also a season ticket holder, added that the only things needed were more tickets. "That's our biggest gripe," he said. "The world will have to end for me to miss it. But some of our people might not get in."

Ken Morgan, who played for Hunters in 1957, said this team was representing a lot of former players who never made it to Indiapolis. "We'll be as proud of this team in years to come as we would have been of ourselves," he said.

Morgan said high school basketball was the center of the town's social life.

"Being at the YMI and rehashing the game is the hub of it," he said. "I can't say enough about these players. They have class, they've all been on the honor roll and they're close-knit. It got to me when they won the semistate. I can't describe the feeling. I was nearly overcome with tears."

IN THE PALACE, PRINCETON HIGH SCHOOL'S BASKETBALL TIGERS ARE KINGS

MARCH, 1985

PRINCETON, Ind. — The only event that rivals the Princeton Tigers basketball team at high school tournament time around the downtown square here is at Christmas, when lights and decorations adorn the stores and shops.

Now, with Hoosier Hysteria building, windows of businesses and the courthouse are painted with pictures and slogans: "Go Big Red; Take Us To State On A Silver Plate; We Love You Tigers; Fight Tigers Fight," and of course, "We're No. 1."

One establishment outwardly calm and unmarked by graffitti is The Palace Pool Room on State Street. But that appearance is deceiving.

The 50-year-old den is home for three billiard tables, four pin-ball machines and is one of the town's leading meccas for sports enthusiasts.

Its walls are filled with pictures of racehorses, 45 years of Princeton High School basketball, football and American Legion baseball memorabilia. Within arms reach of customers is a file of *Daily Racing Forms* and newspapers spread open to the sports sections.

In the front part of this ancient, high ceiling building, is an Indiana University poster along with a large bracket containing all of the state's 64 sectional winners and where they will travel this weekend for regional play.

The Palace is a landmark in southwestern Indiana history. A sporting emporium straight out of the pages of Damon Runyan or the Hollywood blockbuster film, "The Sting."

Naturally, Palace talk, as well as that everywhere around town, is of the beloved Tigers, unbeaten and ranked fifth in the final *Associate Press* regular season poll.

The Tigers will carry a 22-0 record against Vincennes Lincoln (16-6) in the nightcap of Friday's Evansville Regional at Roberts Stadium. The return engagement follows another rematch between Heritage Hills and Bosse.

Jack Todd, former Princeton Legion baseball coach, was behind the counter on Tuesday afternoon. Todd Cundiff, one of Princeton's starting forwards, and reserve Dave Turpin played Legion ball for him.

"I can't believe these guys have grown up and and are seniors," said Todd. "They grew up by my house and here they are on a 22-0 team and ranked fifth in the state. It's a great thing for this community and I'm proud of them."

Todd noted that the Tigers' faithful show up in any kind of weather.

"Our people will consider this a great season no matter how far they go in the tourney. They've been fired up about this team all season. We have excellent season ticket sales. We have the type of fans who aren't with you win or tie. It's win or lose and that's rare. The only thing people are worried about is getting a ticket for certain."

Another in attendance was 60-year-old George Hedrick, proclaimed by the rest of the Palace regulars as the Tigers' No. 1 fan.

Hedrick will be highly visible Friday night. He'll be the guy wearing the red and white helmet with miniature backboards and basketball goals on each side, a Princeton T-shirt and red pants.

He's followed the Tigers since 1948 and is famous for sometimes dancing a jig in stadium aisles to salute a Princeton victory.

The former carrier for *The Evansville Courier* and currently the *Princeton Clarion* just picked up the latest line from another place down the street. "At Evansville, Bosse is a four-point favorite over Heritage Hills and Princeton is 5 1/2 over Vincennes," he reported. "Washington Catholic is 4 1/2 over Southridge in the Washington Regional."

Hedrick, who claims his favorite players are center Brian Fichter and guard Joel Warren, said the Tigers play at the level of their competition. "That's why the two games in the secitonal were close," he said. "But we're going to win the regional. Heritage Hills will beat Bosse, we'll beat Vincennes, then win on Saturday night."

Jim Coomer, assistant manager at neighboring J.C. Penney, stopped by for a cup of coffee and the latest scoop on the team. The 1963 Princeton graduate, who witnessed the Tigers' state final appearances in 1965 and 1983, explained that the Princeton cheerleaders were responsible for most of the window art work.

Coomer said the game he will always remember was the Tigers' four-overtime hand-wringer in the 1983 regional over Bosse. "I was in the second row of seats and hoarse for three days afterward," he said. "It ranks as one of the all-time great games. History around here says you're not going anywhere unless you beat Vincennes and Bosse. They both have something to prove since we beat them earlier in the season. I'm hoping we got the bad games out of our system in the sectional."

Balance is the word which best describes the Tigers, according to Coomer. "I think this team is more unselfish than the one in 1983," he said. "We've got five guys capable of scoring and pretty good depth."

Coomer agreed with Todd on the team's accomplishments.

"Sure, it would be disappointing if they lose. But we'll still celebrate and be as proud as champs. You can't buy what the team has done for this town."

PART 4:

OTHER FAVORITES

Final Calls to Absent Friends

THE WILL TO WIN
DETERMINES A CHAMPION

NOVEMBER, 1994

LOUISVILLE, Ky. — Trainer D. Wayne Lukas is on the threshold of winning another Eclipse Award for his expertise this year.

He's virtually locked up the race for purse money won. Timber Country and Flanders are champions.

It's hasn't happened by trial and error, but through preparation and conviction to a regimented system and an all encompassing philosophy.

From the beginning, Lukas always has underlined a horse's mental aspect. The mental outlook of horses wearing those traditional white bridles might have gone overlooked during the course of last Saturday's Breeders' Cup battles at Churchill Downs.

But, at a second glance, they never were more apparent. The difference in championship events rarely boils to a physical indifference. The fine line of separation is the will to win.

Last Saturday's Breedeer' Cup day was for the people. No matter where men and women have gathered to compete, their performances have been swayed by those who come to watch.

The scenario remained unchanged Saturday. Long before the 70,000-pus arrived beneath the Twin Spires, Lukas surrounded himself with many old friends, most of them former athletes or coaches who understood the trainer's task and responsibility.

Their light conversation and sturdy outlooks had a calming effect.

One guest took a personal interest in Overbrook Farm's Flanders, gallant winner of the B.C. Juvenile Fillies. The man's name is Billy Kilmer. Now in his late 50s, his former profession was quarterback in the National Football League, most notably as the heroic leader of coach George Allen's "Over the Hill Gang," know better to some as the Washington Redskins of the early 1970s.

Nobody wanted to win more than Kilmer. A first-round draft choice in 1961 out of UCLA by the San Francisco Forty Niners, he suffered a near-fatal auto accident soon after. Doctors said his football days were over. But they weren't.

He became a well-traveled journeyman. And in 1971, Kilmer was traded by the dreadful New Orleans Saints to Washington, lasting until 1978. His final pass was complete for a touchdown, as he went out a winner.

The old Redskin grew up in the shadow of Santa Anita, had owned several solid horses of his own, and was optimistic about his friend Lukas' chances, reaffirming that Flanders was something special.

"You can't improve on an undefeated horse," Kilmer said. "Plus, it's always tough on a guy when he's got horses in the same race for other owners like Wayne had. It's like any other sport, there's a first and second team. There's got to be a winner and somebody's likely to be unhappy."

His assessments were nearly perfect, but nobody could've been unhappy after the Juvenile Fillies.

Here was Flanders, the odds-on favorite, so swift, game and dependable, locked in a battle royale with her outstanding stablemate, Serena's Song.

The video tapes of the race prove that the favorite looked beaten. But, soon after that frame of tape, something divine kicked in. It was willpower, that immeasurable, sometimes insurmountable intangible.

This was a race for history. And for Kilmer, it was like the NFC Championship game of Dec. 31, 1972. Like Churchill Downs, RFK Stadium in Washington was jammed to the rafters. Fans stood the entire game as Kilmer masterfully carved the heart out of the Dallas Cowboys, 26-3.

That day was for the people, too, and the old quarterback departed both arenas smiling broadly.

A REUNION WITH OLD TEACHERS

JANUARY, 2000

Have you ever found and lost a great coach, boss, teacher or friend?

You don't get many opportunities, because patience, loyalty, devotion and love are severely tested when great people take you in as a raw, unskilled recruit and polish you with enough wisdom to carry the torch after they've passed on.

But if you're fortunate enough to discover such role models and lose them, stay calm. You'll always find your way back to them. It may only be in your mind, as it's recently been with me. But they're there, and they'll show up again when the game's on the line.

For example, one of this winter's projects was to research the 78-year history of Ellis Park. The *Evansville Courier & Press'* library of microfilm — dating back to *The Evansville Journal* days — is the primary place to pick out the notable tidbits of news required to produce a media guide.

Imagine a facility like E.P. that's touched so many generation of lives in the Tri-State alone not having a definitive historical work.

Paul Kuerzi, the track's general manager, and Jeff Smith, president of Churchill Downs Inc., Ellis' parent company, couldn't believe there wasn't one and thought it appalling. They suggested producing a media guide that will improve the track's growing credibility nationwide.

By entertaining the project, I've happily rediscovered

Dan Scism, Don Bernhardt and Bill Fluty, three of the wisest teachers, coaches and bosses that any one person could ever have.

Their tenures in sports at this paper comprised nearly 125 years, making them authorites on most issues dealing with fun and games, especially racing. They commanded respect on all fronts. And, with an aura of E.F. Hutton, people listened intensely when they wrote or spoke. I spend most mornings perusing their daily reports and witty columns from Ellis Park meetings of the late 1920s through 1989. They're as wonderful today as when they were printed.

A comparison of their work reveals that their temperaments and styles varied greatly. They weren't "house men," but their love for the local racing establishment was unquestioned.

While representing the best interests of John Q. Public, they weren't afraid to bash Ellis Park in print on occasions when duty required. For example, Fluty was chiefly responsible for a long overdue electronic timer.

Nevertheless, they promoted the place 24 hours a day, seven days a week, 365 days a year. In short, when in their presence, other writers at Keeneland or Churchill Downs during Derby week knew better than to fire a cheap shot at Ellis Park or its staff.

It was known as Dade Park when their careers began. And it's accurate to state that today's Ellis Park owes Scism, Bernhardt and Fluty a huge debt of gratitude for their positive approach and insight. I know I do. And hopefully, producing this media guide will go a long way toward settling the obligation.

When Scism died in January of 1982, Bernhardt wrote a farewell column titled: "Dan Scism the legend." The last line read: "The legend left more than he took with him." That sentence fits all three men. Proof of that is on microfilm. And hopefully, if I don't mess it up, in a media guide this spring.

"GALLANT ALICES" LOST, BUT THEY DIDN'T GO OUT LOSERS

MARCH, 1984

INDIANAPOLIS — It's a shame there had to be a loser in Saturday night's gut-wrenching state championship bout between Vincennes and Warsaw.

No one in the crowd of 17,490 can deny they received the price of admission by the effort given on the court many times over. It was typical of what longtime observers expect during an Indiana High School boys' basketball championship.

The teams were on their emergency fuel tanks when the horn sounded after 32 relentless minutes. But, alas, a winner and loser is why they keep score.

The gallant Alices, forced to play from behind nearly the entire way, were on the ropes several times but refused to yield. Character was this team's byword until the end came, 59-56.

The Alices forte was defense. They grabbed the game by the nape of the neck and reurned it to a simpler era — a time when togetherness and hard work could overcome pure talent. There was no big gunner who would shoot 25 times a game. This club won and lost as a team, and, even in defeat, never lost its poise.

They had their opportunities early in the second quarter. Ahead 17-16, Warsaw committed three turnovers on consecutive trips down the floor. Unlike the regional and semistate, Vincennes failed to make a run and assume command.

Who can say what would have transpired if Warsaw

would have had to play from behind at Vincennes' pace. Perhaps the Tigers' long-range shooters would have cracked in the heat.

Paul Hendrixson, one of two Alices' sophomores who play like veterans, shoved Vincennes ahead for the final time at 38-37 with a 10-foot bank shot with 2:48 left in the third period.

The Alices controlled a Tiger miss and Tim Swan fired from 15 feet at 1:57. He was hammered on the attempt which barely creased the lip of the rim. No foul was called, which brought Vincennes' coach Gene Miiller off his seat, clutching his wrist, pleading for a holding call.

None came, but a technical foul on Miiller did. Referee Roger DeYoung tooted the whistle. It was Miiller's first technical in five years and his first at Vincennes.

Warsaw's Jeff Grose canned both foul shots, shoving the Tigers into the lead, 39-38. The contest would be tied three more times, but Vincennes would never lead.

With 1:02 left in the third period, Vincennes' Randy Hobson was assessed a technical foul for not giving the allotted three feet to a Warsaw player trying to inbound the ball and knocking it out of his hands. Grose again drilled the free throw.

After all the bad bounces, Vincennes still had a chance.

Trailing 51-45 with 5:00 left, sophomore Charlie Waggoner drilled two free throws. Dean Tolbert, Vincennes' floor general who made the all-tourney team, drove the lane for a short jumper at 4:25. Moments later, he knocked in both ends of a one-and-bonus to square things at 51.

Hobson tied it for the final time at 56 with one of two free throws at 1:05.

Grose failed from 17 feet with 50 seconds left and Hendrixson grabbed the rebound. As he turned to pass, Warsaw's Marty Lehmann swept in from the blind side to force a jump ball.

Tolbert fouled Scott Long at :36. Long sank the first, making it 57-56 Warsaw, but his second shot rattled out and Hobson rebounded.

Vincennes held on for a final shot to win. Hendrixson's 10-foot-baseline jumper at :04 missed hitting nothing but string by two inches. It was a good shot. Another pass and the clock may have been out.

Warsaw's Steve Hollar rebounded Hendrixson's miss and was fouled. He drilled both free throws at :03 to end the Alices title hopes.

A gathering of 2,500 Alices' faithful turned out Sunday in brisk weather under gray skies to welcome their heroes home.

The team bus was met by fire trucks and police units. After boarding a fire engine, the players and coaches traveled across town to Adams Coliseum for a 90-minute pep session.

Said a tearful Miiller, "It's hard to get beat like we did. These wonderful kids are why it's so hard to take. The coach gets a lot of credit in this game but the credit should go to the players. They're the ones who paid the price and did all the work.

"It's been fun taking the tournament ride with this bunch. If you're going to measure heart, no team has more than this one."

The school received a holiday Monday, befitting of a near championship team.

PRINCETON BOWED OUT WITH CLASS

MARCH, 1985

In recording the school's only unbeaten regular season, Princeton's Tigers won 20 straight games with courtesy, dignity and class.

They added three more wins in the tournament before Bosse eliminated them 81-63 in Saturday's Evansville Regional final.

Princeton coach Jim Jones offered no alibis or cheap excuses. Neither did his team.

"We didn't play well enough to win and they played extremely well," said Jones. "Bosse's shooting was outstanding and we were impatient with ours. They controlled the boards and that was the whole story.

"It has been a great season. We thought we had a legitimate shot to win the regional in 1983 when we upset Bosse in the four-overtime game (82-77). They were unbeaten and champs then. We treated their players with the utmost respect. Tonight, they returned the favor. That's a tribute to both of our programs."

Losing in the tournament is inevitable for all but one of nearly 400 contestants. As Jones said earlier in the week, "I compare tourney play to the gladiators of ancient Rome. A lot of them go in but only one comes out. There is no tomorrow."

The Tigers didn't die easily and could have gotten themselves in a position just before halftime to make a run. Three turnovers denied that.

Princeton's Brian Fichter, hampered with a muscle rupture in his back, and point guard Larry Arnold, combined to hit 12 straight attempts from the field in the second half. Fichter finished with 20 points on 10 of 11 shooting. Arnold, who drilled 28 in Friday night's win over Vincennes, scored 18 on 9 of 12 floor shots.

They, along with their mates, accepted the final sentence but found it difficult to swallow. All true competitors are like that. And no coach wants guys who don't hurt inside.

Someone obviously not familiar with what goes through a young man's mind after such a defeat, asked Jones what he would tell his team. Jones merely shook his head and smiled. Later he would explain, "You don't have to say anything to tough competitors. They figure it out for themselves at times like these."

It's hard to decipher what this Princeton team meant, and accomplished for the town. Having been around tournament play for two decades, I have my impressions.

The Tigers were the only game in town. Their loyal following, which performed at a high vocal pitch throughout the season, was proof of that. When the Tigers played, businesses closed, entire families and townspeople traveled in a caravan throughout Southern Indiana to root on their schoolboy heroes.

Twenty years from now, the outcome of individual games will be forgotten. But the perfect regular season will always be rekindled. It's what high school basketball is all about.

"SHOE" BUCKS THE ODDS
IN THIS YOUNG MAN'S GAME

MAY, 1986

LOUISVILLE, Ky. — Ferdinand's legs and Bill Shoemaker's brains were too much for 15 other contenders and pretenders in Saturday's 112th Kentucky Derby at Churchill Downs.

Ferdinand, a royally bred colt by Nijinsky II, rallied from last, nearly 20 lengths back after a half-mile, to prevail by 2 1/4 lengths under the Shoe's left-handed whip.

English-bred Bold Arrangement finished three-quarters of a length prior to third place Broad Brush, who edged Rampage by a neck.

Early fractions of 22 1/5 seconds for the first quarter-mile, 45 1/5 for the half and 1:37 for eight furlongs were respetable.

But not much running went on after the first six furlongs in 1:10 1/5. The winner negotiated the 1 1/4 miles over a lightning fast surface in 2:02 4/5, the slowest clocking since Cannonade required 2:04 in 1974.

Ferdinand was shuffled far back early. It was a task for Shoemaker to keep from being jammed through the inner rail.

Second choice Badger Land experienced similar difficulty at the break.

He left in a tangle, as a horse on his immediate outside came in and nailed him. Badger Land's jockey Jorge Velasquez nearly was unseated and forced widest of all through the initial stretch run into the first turn while last.

The rangy Codex colt reached contention turning for

home but the early problems took their toll on energy. He tired to fifth.

"We were eliminated at the start," said Wayne Lukas, who trains Badger Land. "I still believe we ran the best horse. But like I told you earlier in the week, I can only control two things: How the horse comes into a race and who will ride him. I can't control racing luck, and we didn't have any."

Favored Snow Chief had no excuse. His lack of pedigree told the story. He stopped to a walk and finished 11th.

Whether anyone will admit it, Ferdinand, with his powerful lineage, left the post at 17-1 because most of the 123,189 in attendance forgot that "It's the horse, not the rider," who does the running.

Ferdinand, who carries the pink and blue colors of Mrs. Elizabeth Keck, was a member of *The Evansville Courier's* Top 10 all spring. But he was eliminated when Shoemaker became his regular rider.

Why? Because the Derby weighs heavily on tradition. And no jockey past his 42nd year ever won it until Saturday. Shoemaker is 54.

Ask any tariner. They'll tell you the rider is only about 10 percent of the performance. It makes the chestnut colt's stretch run evern more commendable.

The comparison of Shoemaker's fourth Derby win to Jack Nicklaus in The Masters at Augusta, Ga., isn't a good one. Nicklaus doesn't face death if he misjudges the distance of a hole — only embarrassment and monetary loss.

Shoemaker and his fellow craftsmen face the loss of life each afternoon they work.

Shoemaker follows a daily exercise routine of pushup, pullup, stretching and situps to keep his body, scarred by 37 years in the saddle, in shape. Even with all that, he admits, his legs aren't what whey once were.

No matter, his brain never was better as he guided Ferdinand thorugh heavy traffic like a can opener biting aluminum.

The decision Shoemaker made to stay on the rail and save ground instead of going around a wall of horses in the stretch was the difference.

"I had a choice of going to the outside or trying to get through along the rail," he said. "I took the chance of getting through and that was it. I had about three seconds to make the call."

It had been 26 years since trainer Charlie Whittingham

had saddled a Derby starter. He vowed then never to re-turn without a contender.

"I didn't come this year with a case of the shorts (short horse)," Whittingham said. "This is a great race to win but it's not going to make me live any longer. I've always been one to run a horse where he belongs and I haven't had one I thought could win here.

"You guys (reporters) are what make this race so spe-cial to the public because of the coverage. "

Whittingham said he didn't measure Shoemaker's abil-ity in years. "You do it in wins," he said. "Heck, I had confi-dence in Bill. I didn't get excited until the eighth pole. I quit doing that years ago. I knew last year and told Bill that we might have some fun in Louisville with this colt."

Just after first light last Tuesday morning, Whittingham was entertaining newsmen at barn No. 41 on Churchill Downs' backstretch.

Alongside the tall, 73-year-old member of racing's Hall of Fame, was William Lee Shoemaker.

The world's winningest rider was adorned in red wind-breaker and helmet. He fielded questions like a kid riding in his first classic.

It was Shoemaker's 24th trip postward to the strains of "My Old Kentucky Home," increasing his own record. The Derby marked the 8,537th victory, including his fourth in the Run for the Roses.

He was there the last time with Lucky Debonair in 1965, following stops with Tomy Lee, 1959 and Swaps, 1955.

"This is the best one of all because it was with Charlie," said Shoemaker. "I had tears for the first time. I know I'm in the twilight but I try not to think about it. Riding is a day-to-day thing with me. I tried to retire 15 years ago but couldn't make myself do it.

"Winning this one made me glad I didn't."

So experience paid great dividends in this year's Derby. "'Shoe" wouldn't admit it that way in the room with his fellow riders, softly saying: "These are all good riders, highly professional. They all knew what to do. All I had was luck and the horse under me."

Those commodities, and the intellect to find the best way home, proved that Shoemaker can still get the job done against the best when it counts the most.

BRERETON JONES
GIVES UP POLITICS FOR
HIS TRUE LOVE — RACING

APRIL, 1996

LEXINGTON, Ky. — He wasn't a prisoner of war. Nor was he serving jail time. But there were probably many days before he left office last December when former Kentucky Governor Brereton C. Jones felt like an inmate.

Oh, not in a punishing sense, but like today, when a man's heart yearns to go to the races at Keeneland as an unscrutinized private citizen and his soul straddles the black fences of his family's Airdrie Stud in Midway, Ky., a political career is sometimes a harrowing experience. A sort of sacrifice, if you will.

For the record, Jones is not a career politician. He's a career horseman who stepped away from Airdrie's 2,000 acres to become lieutenant governor and governor.

We met for the first time nearly 10 years ago. Regardless of his position, whether it was booking a mare, discussing one of 125 foals born annually at the farm, going over pedigrees of Kentucky Derby horses or even a construction project, Jones always has talked in the plural.

He included his wife, Libby, and their children in all arenas. He believes and relies on a "team theme," something he probably picked up during his days as a University of Virginia gridder.

"We gave up a great deal during the past eight years," he said. "There were many, many times I wanted to be in the foaling barn or at the races and couldn't. But sacrifices had to be made.

"I'd like to think it was all worth it and considerable

265

good came about for others. But now it's back to the real world. And the thoroughbred world in Kentucky is greater than it's ever been."

Successful endeavors begin at the top. And during Jones' governorship, the Commonwealth of Kentucky made strides in a number of areas.

For example, his team reduced welfare by 22 percent or 50,000 people; more than 200,000 more people were employed when he left office than when he entered; he reduced the number of government jobs by 2,000 and did all this by cutting taxes.

"We couldn't balance the state budget and were $400 million short when we started," Jones said. "We left with the biggest surplus in state history. If you can't pay your bills, you can't do anything, and that includes health care, education and roads.

"I think we did well for the state by taking politics out of many areas and going with the best possible people to get the job done," he said. "This was the way we found to be most successful, including the racing commission."

During Jones' era, wagering at Kentucky facilities has risen from $464 million to nearly $700 million.

It takes a horseman to know a horseman, and Jones realized it was vitally important to have the industry represented by knowledgeable horse people. He combined the thoroughbred and standardbred commissions, and tabbed a thorough, thoughtful chairman in Wayne Lyster, whose insight and leadership were blessings.

Jones was 100 percent accurate when deeming it a necessity to have a working trainer like Carl Bowman on the commission, along with owners like Glen Bromagen and Betsy Lavin, who also are members of the breeding industry.

The commission lineup was altered recently when new Gov. Paul Patton made some switches.

"Things were never better than under Gov. Jones' commission," Turfway Park chairman Jerry L. Carroll said during Jim Beam week. "We got things accomplished in a fairly harmonious manner. And it all started with the man from Midway (Jones)."

Jones recently attended the inaugural running of the $4 million Dubai World Cup. He had a rooting interest and enjoyed a great thrill when Soul of the Matter pushed the great Cigar to his limit.

We say rooting interest because Jones will stand Soul of

the Matter at Airdrie when the colt is finished racing, along-side his former stablemate, Afternoon Deelites. Burt Bacharach raced them both.

"We acquired the rights to Afternoon Deelites at 3 and Soul of the Matter at 4," Jones said. "Talk about a great thrill. Soul of the Matter ran an outstanding race and did so in front of the entire world. His effort gave him an international identity with the Japanese, English, French and Arabs. They know him now and that'll be good for business."

Does he miss the political arena? Not really. "You do miss the people though. The friendships and relationships you develop are an important part of life. You know the people who got things done.

"I did what I wanted to do. Be lieutenant governor, learn the system, then be governor. Now, I'm still doing what I want to do. Airdrie is my favorite place in the world.

"Our founding fathers never envisioned professional politicians. They envisioned people who would serve when duty called, then go back to their professions when it was time. That's what I did. I'm a farmer who's come home."

So if you run into Jones some morning in the Keeneland barn area or during the afternoon in the grandstand or paddock, don't ask him about some governmental project or federal funding.

It's springtime in Kentucky. He'd rather discuss a colt who was foaled last week or the upcoming Kentucky Derby. As he'll tell you, the manure in the barn area often smells better than the manure in the state capital.

And about those Derby horses? Be prepared. He knows his stuff.

LISTEN UP:
THERE'S A LESSON TO LEARN

NOVEMBER, 1997

LOUISVILLE, Ky. — There are a million ways to lose when wagering on a horse race.

So the following excuse for missing out on a good thing may sound like fiction. But it actually happened to a man Sunday on Churchill Downs' opening-day program.

The name of the unfortunate soul, of course, has been changed to protect the innocent from too much hazing from his friends.

Let's call the guy "Sonny Ray." It all began Saturday night during an informal dinner party at a local restaurant.

Sitting at the table was the mistaken-ridden Sonny Ray. He was formally introduced to the others seated — owners Willis and Cam Horton, and their trainer Dallas Stewart, who was accompanied by his wife, Yvette.

Naturally, the conversation turned to the Horton's promising 2-year-old Squall Valley. The bay son of Summer Squall was making his third career start in Sunday's fourth race and seeking his second straight victory.

Someone asked Stewart why he was running the colt on lasix after he'd just won a maiden race at Keeneland without it. "Oh, he trickled just a drop of blood when he worked the other day. So we might as well take every edge."

Stewart didn't go out on a limb and guarantee that Squall Valley would win. But he did state: "I like him a lot. He'll really run big Sunday. And you know his sire, Summer Squall, was a top horse on an off track like we're going to run on tomorrow."

A few other items were covered, and the party broke up with Sonny Ray noting: "Boy, those are fine people. And that's one winner I'll have tomorrow."

Unfortunately, for Sonny Ray, it wasn't to be. Sometime during the night, his memory failed. He forgot the name of the horse, owners and trainer.

Sonny Ray even went to the paddock to see the fourth-race field being saddled. But evidently, he also forgot what the people looked like.

His case of mistaken identity cost some of his friends, too. Before the race, Sonny Ray told his pal, Blinky (another alias): "I've got this buddy who introduced me to the people who own and train a 2-year-old in this race. He's the No. 4 horse, I think."

"What do you mean, you think?" asked Blinky.

"Well, that's what I think. I can't remember their names. I met them last night. I think their name is Davenport and someone by that name owns the No. 4 horse. So that's who I'm betting on."

The No. 4 horse was a thoroughbred named Pine Harbor, owned by William and Dee Davenport.

You know the rest of the story. Under Pat Day, Squall Valley splashed through the slop along the inside to win by two lengths and paid $13.20. The trifecta was sizeable, too.

Sonny Ray had brought his daughter to the track. And when the mistake was discovered, she consoled her father by saying: "That's all right dad. It's no big deal. Everyone makes mistakes." He responded by saying, "That's fine for you to say. I'm not only embarrassed, but it cost me about $600."

If that wasn't enough, Sonny Ray's misery was compounded when he returned to his vehicle in the parking lot following the last race. For the record, it was a rainy, foggy, dreary day that made headlights a requirement when driving to the track.

Sonny Ray was driving his wife's car and had failed to turn off the lights, which go off automatically on his. The battery was dead, and he had to be jump-started by Churchill Downs' parking lot trouble shooters.

As the saying goes, when it rains it pours. And it proves that a good memory is sometimes vital for success at the windows — and to get home on time for dinner.

For Sonny Ray, it was that kind of opening day.

BUSE BORN TOO SOON,
BUT MADE MOST OF NBA TIME

AUGUST, 1997

Donald R. — or plain old Don Buse, was born 20 years too soon on Aug. 10, 1950 in Huntingburg, Ind.

This is purely speculation, but had his arrival date been Aug. 10, 1970, he naturally wouldn't yet be 30 years old. And financially speaking, he'd be a whole lot better off.

Why? Because when Buse was in his prime, he was one of the most tenacious, ball-hawking defensive wizards not only in the storied history of Evansville College (now University of Evansville), but the National Basketball Association.

He also maintained a high assist ratio and possessed a steady, all-around, team-oriented floor game that all contending teams must have.

As an unselfish big guard, Buse would be in great demand around today's NBA.

And, with the league's television money blasting salaries into another galaxy, the rangy, 6-foot-4 Buse would be assigned to defend guys like Michael Jordan, Penny Hardaway and Steve Smith. And make a ton of money doing it.

"I was around when Michael Jordan just came out of college. He's the greatest player I ever saw or played against, and he learned how to play the pro game better than anyone," said Buse, who still has the walk, body language and physique of a big-time athlete. "I always had more problems handling those small, quick guys like Nate Archibald than I did with Jordan or Magic Johnson."

So you see, if he'd been born in 1970, Buse would have more cash, fame, glory and nice thoroughbreds than he, or anyone who ever saw him play during his high school days at tiny Holland, Ind., or during a stellar, All-American career at UE, or through 13 professional seasons, could imagine.

But Buse, who dabbles in two modest horses each summer at Ellis Park, graduated from UE in 1972. And the most he ever made for a season in the pros was $160,000.

"My old coach, Bobby "Slick" Leonard, said I'd be making a minimum of $2.5 or $3 million a year if I were still playing," said Buse. "He's still around the game and knows what salaries are. Life would certainly be a lot different with that kind of money. And I'd have a couple of top horses, too."

Drafted by Virginia of the old American Basketball Association, Buse promptly was sold to the Indiana Pacers and Leonard when they were still in the ABA.

He entered the NBA with the Pacers when they were absorbed into the league in 1976. Stops followed at Phoenix from 1977-1980, Indiana again for the 1981-1982 seasons, Portland for 1983 and Kansas City in 1984-1985.

He also was an assistant coach for two seasons at San Antonio and one at Sacramento.

Buse was named to the NBA's all-defensive first team four consecutive times from 1977-1980. He led the league in assists and steals in '77.

He also was a two-time member of the ABA's all-defensive team and has a ring from the Pacers' 1973 ABA championship.

As a collegian, he led UE, then EC, to the 1971 Division II title and was named the tournament's most valuable player.

"I never even dreamed of playing professionally until my senior year at Evansville," said Buse. "As a kid growing up in a small, southern Indiana town, you live, eat, sleep and breathe the game. I came from a poor family, and there's no way I'd ever have gone to college without a basketball scholarship. You might say I owe everything I have to the game. Especially a lot of very good friends."

Sometimes, there is a fear among those who dream of being a professional athlete. Slowly, they realize the finality and frightening unknowns that the end of a career brings.

When their playing days are over, they realize that they've spent a lifetime playing a youthful sport. And at about age 36, the youth and games are all but finished.

Buse never looked at it in the manner that the typical warrior class of athlete does. He knew it wouldn't last forever. And the bottom line is, the "Dutchman" never wanted to leave his roots, and the cornfields of Holland, Ind., anyway.

He noted that he's "half-assed retired," but helps out during winters coaching the local high school team at Southridge, spending summer afternoons at Ellis Park with guys like coach Leonard, Larry Bird and other friends.

Now, added Buse, "if we could just win a race...."

Like the man who said it, that statement fits any era.

RACING'S FUN, WIN OR LOSE, FOR IRISHMAN MCCLARNEY

AUGUST, 1997

Pureblooded Irishmen descend from a strong line of tradition and fiction.

Stories tell us that, hypothetically, a real Irishman is a merry, carefree lad. At times, he can be hot-tempered, volatile, troublesome and irresponsible.

A mood swing may find him poetic, gallant, nostalgic, humble and maudlin.

Legend says that God made Irishmen for several reasons. And that, through the centuries, their battles and wars are fillied with merriment, joy and happiness. But nevertheless, the songs they compose about them afterwards normally are sad.

The best modern-day illustration might be the world-famous institution of Notre Dame football. The Fighting Irish— especially the fans and alumni — always seem happiest on Saturdays each fall when their heroes are battling against teams from the University of Michigan or University of Southern California.

And it's also fact that their fight song sometimes can be haunting to the opposition.

Owner-trainer Jerry McClarney, a longtime Ellis regular, isn't a Notre Dame man. He's a graduate of Murray State University with a master's degree and a devout fan of Indiana University.

But, through his great-grandfather, James McClarney, his roots do trace to the gaels of Tipperary. And the 62-year-old Jerry McClarney, youngest of eight siblings, definitely brings an Irish illustration to the track.

At first meeting, you'll find him to be a quiet, reserved fellow who is slightly above average height, stoutly built with a closely cropped and finely manicured silver beard. "I grew a beard a long time ago when I got out of the military," said McClarney, a former United States Army colonel who became a high school teacher and insurance man. "I ran into my old high school grammar teacher once. She'd just returned from Ireland and said, 'Jerry, you look more Irish than they do in Ireland.'"

To further authenticate his heritage, he runs his horses under the banner of Shamrock Stable. His silks, rather than being green with white four-leaf clovers, are red with white horseshoes and white bars on the sleeves.

Oh well: nobody's perfect.

And the huge crowd of friends, associates and business partners who packed Ellis Park's winner's circle on Aug. 10 didn't care about the red colors worn by jockey Terry Thompson, who piloted Shamrock Stable's Happy Legionaire.

The 4-year-old gelding by French Legionaire had just won his second race of the meeting. He defeated a field of nine $10,000 claimers by 1 1/4 lengths in a six furlong sprint and paid $13.

The winner's circle celebrants — many of them 21 or younger — exchanged high-fives, whooped it up and celebrated well into the evening at the barn when McClarney's been known to keep a libation or two. "That's for medicinal purposes only," he noted.

"We do have a good time, win or lose, don't we?" beamed McClarney. "That's what racing is all about. It's a family affair to us. Take for example, my friend, and legal counsel, Dennis Brinkmeyer. He's an Ellis Park boxholder. And when we run a horse, he comes out with his wife and all their kids. Their kids bring their friends, too.

"When we won the other day, there was half of the Memorial High School football team in the win picture. We've got to have that kind of thing to develop new fans for the sport to continue.

"Ever since I was a kid, I've always wanted to train a nice horse. I started trying to fulfill that dream with a couple of old broodmares and started training one horse in 1983. Sooner or later, we'll get a good one."

McClarney's parents migrated from western Kentucky to the outskirts of Evansville, Ind., in the late 1930s. Jerry and his wife, Gayle, own an equestrian riding school at their home on Shutte Road.

Gayle gives lessons and Jerry uses the paddocks and indoor-outdoor arena to freshen his horses and get them ready after layoffs.

If McClarney has a favorite among his horses, he didn't mention it. But suspicion says he has a special affection for Hopeitsnows, a filly who nearly died in a terrible van accident several years ago at the Georgetown, Ind., exit along Interstate 64.

She had run at Churchill Downs that day. The trailer turned over and she suffered multiple wounds and extreme blood loss, requiring 2,000 stitches.

But McClarney babied her and nursed her back to fighting trim. She came back less than a year after the accident to win an allowance race at Ellis.

She's retired now, and McClarney is anticipating the foal's arrival. Maybe it will be the colt he's been waiting for.

ACCURACY, SPEED
MADE SCARAVILLI A
FIRST-RATE CHART-CALLER

JULY, 1985

Trainer Steve Duncan asked a question which enters the minds of thousands of racing fans each afternoon. Exactly how does the *Daily Racing Form* (*Equibase* beginning in 1998) compile its data for past performances during the running of each race?

When informed that at Ellis Park, one man calls the race and one woman scribbles down the call, Duncan shook his head in disbelief. "It's impossible for one guy to call every horse at the assigned points of call, much less anyone taking it down so fast," he insisted.

Duncan recently found out differently. He took up an invitation and visited the Ellis Park press box to eavesdrop on the *Form*'s trackman, Charles "Chuck" Scaravilli, and calltaker Barbara Borden.

"Well, you're right," Duncan said. "One guy calls the whole thing. And man, is he good."

"Good" might be an understatement. Scaravilli, who started three years at free safety for the football team before graduating with a psychology degree from Ohio Wesleyan Unversity, is outstanding.

It's a good thing, too. Ellis Park's video department isn't versed in the unexact science of putting a chart together, and doesn't have a monitor showing the head-on view of a race in the press box.

"The head-on view is extremely important because it gives me another perspective of any jostling or tight quraters a horse may wind up in after breaking," Scaravilli said. "We have a pan shot monitor but something important could be occurring at an angle we can't see.

"Luckily, the stewards have a head-on monitor. So I can go over to their office and watch a problem I might see or any inquiries or foul claims."

Scaravilli, his wife Jean and three children, reside near Latonia in Edgewood, Ky. He works the Kentucky circuit, calling the Kentucky Derby and Kentucky Oaks at Churchill Downs, the Blue Grass Stakes and other major races at Keeneland and the Jim Beam Stakes at Latonia. He also writes two columns weekly at Keeneland and Churchill.

While many chart-callers call numbers, Scaravilli's retentive memory allows him to call the names of the horses.

If you think it's easy, try memorizing the names of the contestants in a small field of six and watch them switch positions like a Rubik's Cube going down the backstretch. If that's not tough enough, increase it to 12, then 20 horses, which has been the norm in three of the last four Kentucky Derbys.

"It usually takes me about a minute and a half to get the colors the riders are wearing in mind during the post parade," said Scaravilli. "You do that by associating names with colors instead of numbers.

"Then I put the glasses down. I won't look at the field again until there's about one minute to post time. If a couple of the colors look alike, I check out various equipment like blinkers and shadow rolls."

Scaravilli became acquainted with racing through his father, Chuck. The elder Scaravilli is a trainer-turned-trackman. He covers Thistledown in Cleveland and other tracks on the Ohio circuit.

The younger Scaravilli began in the publicity department at Thistledown in 1971. He was publicity director at Commodore Downs in Erie, Pa., in 1973-73 before going to work for the Form. He broke in as they all do, taking the call.

"I was going to college and filling in during summers for guys on vacation at Thistledown, so I knew the ropes. I started calling charts fulltime five years ago and came to Churchill Downs in 1982 to fill in and didn't want to leave. The opportunity came up to take the Kentucky circuit and I jumped at it."

Scaravilli never wavered when asked the toughest race to call.

"The Kentucky Derby, for several reasons," he said.

"First, it's the most important one. We use two callers for the Derby because the field is usually a big one and the world is waiting for a chart. Jack Wilson has come to Louisville the last couple years. He calls from the front and I call from the back to the front."

"The pressure of not making a mistake is intense with this race and the noise from the crowd's roar makes it nearly impossible to hear. Plus, there might be 500 writers in the press box waiting on the chart, and 450 of them are inexperienced and don't cover three races a year. They're the ones who gripe — but they're counting on a copy of the chart to make their deadlines."

It's up to the individual to use the past performances and chart footnotes to calculate their choices in a race. Whether the selection reports on time is entirely another matter.

But with Scaravilli's accurate charts, at least you've got a fighting chance.

WIN OR LOSE, DAY CARRIES
HIMSELF WITH GRACE, HONOR

JUNE, 1996

LOUISVILLE, Ky. — Feather Box, 12th and last in the Preakness Stakes, barely had crossed the finish line when the following happened.

Someone in the Churchill Downs press box holding a winning ticket on Louis Quatorze pointed to the program where it said "Pat Day" and exclaimed: "He's the best distance rider in American racing, especially on a free-running horse."

Shortly after that, the man added with a laugh, "come to think of it, he's the best bull rider among jockeys, too."

Bull rider? That's right. Born Oct. 13, 1953, in Brush, Colo., Day grew up on the family farm in Eagle, Colo. His father wanted him to be a rodeo rider. So Day spend two years on the rodeo circuit before going to the races.

He's quick to tell you, too, that staying on a 1,000-pound beast who is bucking, jumping and trying to gore you is a tough proposition.

"I have the utmost respect for people in the rodeo business," Day said. "Each one of those events is a tough proposition. They certainly earn their money."

Day left riding bucking broncos and rode his first thoroughbred winner in July, 1973, at Prescott Downs. He migrated to Turf Paradise and then to the Midwest, where he achieved instant stardom at Sportsman's Park and Hawthorne.

Venturing to New York in 1976, he disliked the place and returned to the Midwest. It was in 1982 that Day first found the national spotlight when he outfinished Angel Cordero Jr. by two winners for the national riding title on New Year's Eve.

The beam of light has shone brightly on Day ever since, and may glow even brighter after Saturday's Belmont Stakes.

No one ever has dominated the Midwest like Day, and no one ever will. Fans normally send his mounts off beneath a fair price. That's respect, but also pressure. Churchill Downs' all-time leading jockey and producer of nearly 50 riding titles during a glorious and still aspiring career, his lists of achievements for races, stakes and money won could fill this page.

They include a magic Derby day here in 1992 when he brought Lil E. Tee to the winner's circle; the 1984 Breeders' Cup Classic with Wild Again; five Preakness triumphs and two Belmonts; the 1994 Arlington Million; a flock of other B.C. races.

Enshrined in racing's Hall of Fame in 1991, Day became the seventh rider to win 6,000 races in 1994. He once won with eight of nine mounts on one card at Arlington; was the Eclipse Award winner as the nation's top rider in 1984, 1986, 1987 and 1991, and handled Horse of the Year Lady's Secret.

The Olympic torch symbolizes pure desire for victory by people of class and substance competing on a fair playing field. It's little wonder that the Atlanta Committee on Olympic games selected Day to carry the Olympic torch down Central Avenue, into the paddock and through the runway onto this storied track.

Through all his travels, Day has been a man of dignity.

Give most famous coaches or athletes an office and they can't resist putting a slogan or motto on the wall. For example, when the late Billy Martin managed the New York Yankees, he put his rules-to-live by on his wall. Rule One said: "The manager is always right. Rule Two: "See Rule One."

You won't find these around Day's locker in the jockey's room here. Why? Because it's no secret that Day puts his faith in the Lord. We've known Day a long time, and while he has justifiable pride, he has no ego. But if he did, something that symbolizes him would state: "To give dignity to a man is above all things."

Even when he doesn't win, no rider looks better or does a better job of preserving his dignity or that of the sport. When Day was taken off Prince of Thieves for the Preakness, he didn't whine or moan. He had been on both ends before.

Instead, he tightened his chinstrap and rode a brilliant race on Louis Quatorze to illustrate once again his magnificent ability under fire.

You must be focused and psychologically astute to use honesty as a motivational strategy and make it work like Day does. Few things are tricker than telling the truth without doing harm.

That's always been Day's forte. As to his chances on Saturday, Day put it like this: "I haven't been in constant contact with Nick (Zito, who trains Louis Quatorze) and he'll tell me how he wants things done in the paddock.

"From what I can tell, Louis Quatorze doesn't have to be on the lead, either. He's got a lot of versatility, and you know Nick will have him well-prepared. We'll see how the race unfolds and take it from there."

From eight seconds on a bull's back to about 2:29 or so in the Belmont Stakes, Day has made the trip with dignity above all things.

ABOUT THE AUTHOR

Since 1980, Cliff Guilliams has covered for newspapers and magazines every Kentucky Derby and six editions of the Breeders' Cup's day of champions.

His experiences have been extremely unique, because not only has he entertained readers in southern Indiana and Kentucky with his prose, he's also one of the country's premier chart callers for *Equibase Co. LLC.* He's charted or co-authored the official chart of the Derby's past 13 runnings, as well as the B.C.

Thus the title for this book: *Final Calls to Absent Friends.*

Born, raised and educated in Evansville, Ind., Guilliams covered his first race in 1977 at his home track, Ellis Park, in Henderson, Ky., for *The Evansville Courier & Press.* Since then, he's missed only one day at Ellis in 1998 to attend the funeral of his friend, Hall of Fame trainer Woody Stephens.

In the late 1970s and early 1980s, Guilliams bred, owned and raced several thoroughbreds. But his love affair with racing began in 1960 when his father took him to Ellis Park for the first time.

Besides his assignment with *Equibase*, Guilliams is a sportswriter and turf columnist for *The Evansville Courier & Press.* It's his second tour of duty with the paper. The first was from 1977-1986. While racing is his sporting passion, southern Indiana high school basketball and football aren't far behind. When the Indiana High School boys' basketball tournament was played in a single class system, he ranked it only behind the Kentucky Derby for spirit, emotion, and everlasting importance.

From 1986-1998, he covered Kentucky tracks for *Daily Racing Form*. Additionally, since 1996, he's been the co-host of "The Kentucky Winner's Circle," a weekly radio show devoted to thoroughbred racing on 790 AM, WWKY, in Louisville, Ky.

His stories and columns also have appeared in The official *Kentucky Derby Souvenir Magazine*, The *Blood-Horse Magazine*, The *Backstretch Magazine* and *Southern Gaming And Destination*.

Besides *Final Calls to Absent Friends*, he researched and wrote the first media guide in Ellis Park's 80-year history.

Printed in the USA
CPSIA information can be obtained
at www.ICGtesting.com
JSHW022213140824
68134JS00018B/1032